Introducing Historical Orthograp

Historical orthography – the study of how writing systems have changed over time – is a rapidly growing area of historical linguistics. This book provides the first comprehensive introduction to this exciting focus of research. Written in an engaging and accessible way, it surveys the purposes and methods of this field and how it has developed as a discipline over time. The volume also discusses the various levels of analysis that historical orthography can carry out, as well as key historical orthographic processes such as standardisation and language change. It covers a range of non-western and western languages, including English, in order to discuss the breadth of typological issues that can arise in the documentation of writing systems. The book also establishes links between orthography and a range of other related disciplines, a quality which makes it an essential resource for advanced students of orthography, writing systems and historical linguistics.

MARCO CONDORELLI has written *Standardising English Spelling* (Cambridge University Press), edited *Advances in Historical Orthography, c. 1500–1800* (Cambridge University Press) and co-edited *The Cambridge Handbook of Historical Orthography* (Cambridge University Press, with Rutkowska). He has also written articles for research journals, including *English Language and Linguistics*, *English Studies* and *Neuphilologische Mitteilungen*.

Introducing Historical Orthography

Marco Condorelli

University of Central Lancashire, Preston

CAMBRIDGE
UNIVERSITY PRESS

CAMBRIDGE
UNIVERSITY PRESS

University Printing House, Cambridge CB2 8BS, United Kingdom

One Liberty Plaza, 20th Floor, New York, NY 10006, USA

477 Williamstown Road, Port Melbourne, VIC 3207, Australia

314–321, 3rd Floor, Plot 3, Splendor Forum, Jasola District Centre,
New Delhi – 110025, India

103 Penang Road, #05–06/07, Visioncrest Commercial, Singapore 238467

Cambridge University Press is part of the University of Cambridge.

It furthers the University's mission by disseminating knowledge in the pursuit of
education, learning, and research at the highest international levels of excellence.

www.cambridge.org
Information on this title: www.cambridge.org/9781009100731
DOI: 10.1017/9781009122009

© Marco Condorelli 2022

First published 2022

A catalogue record for this publication is available from the British Library.

Library of Congress Cataloging-in-Publication Data
Names: Condorelli, Marco, 1990– author.
Title: Introducing historical orthography / Marco Condorelli.
Description: Cambridge, United Kingdom ; New York, NY : Cambridge
University Press, 2023. | Includes index.
Identifiers: LCCN 2022022834 (print) | LCCN 2022022835 (ebook) | ISBN
9781009100731 (hardback) | ISBN 9781009114172 (paperback) | ISBN
9781009122009 (ebook)
Subjects: LCSH: Language and languages – Orthography and spelling. | Historical
linguistics.
Classification: LCC P240.2 .C66 2023 (print) | LCC P240.2 (ebook) |
DDC 411–dc23/eng/20220520
LC record available at https://lccn.loc.gov/2022022834
LC ebook record available at https://lccn.loc.gov/2022022835

ISBN 978-1-009-10073-1 Hardback
ISBN 978-1-009-11417-2 Paperback

Contents

Contents   vii

Figures

1   Introduction

1.1   What Is Historical Orthography?

Anyone with an interest in historical linguistics will be aware of a few fundamental truths about studying the historical development of language – all of which are inevitable products of the limitations intrinsic to what linguists commonly call *evidence*. First of all, we only know historical languages from what we have evidence for to the present day, whether direct or indirect. Secondly, there is only so much evidence available to us, depending on the moment in history and the specific historical language that we are interested in; this means that the linguistic material that we work with today may not only be partial but perhaps even unfairly distorted. The third and last point embraces the two points established above: most of the evidence that we have about any aspect of historical languages, whether it is about how they were taught, structured or even pronounced, comes from writing. This last point about writing as a paramount form of evidence in historical linguistics is central and yet sometimes forgotten or, perhaps worse, taken for granted. Writing constitutes the first-order witness of the more distant linguistic past and, as such, it is of fundamental importance to anyone with an interest in any aspect of the history of language. Despite the importance and relevance of writing in historical linguistics, only recently has this area of academic endeavour outgrown its traditional status of a subsidiary or even illegitimate area of linguistic discussion. A useful quote that can be used for the purposes of illustrating the stigmatic approach of the early fathers of modern linguistics is that from Fred Householder. The well-known American linguist and professor of classics and linguistics at Indiana University once affirmed that among "the propositions intuitively felt to be basic by friend and enemy alike", in the American Structuralist School of Linguistics, was that "language is basically speech, and writing is of no theoretical interest" (Householder, 1969: 886). Other relevant names that are often associated with and identified as precursors of the same opinion to the one expressed above are those of Ferdinand de Saussure, Edward Sapir and Leonard Bloomfield – the last one being the main point of reference for Householder when making his statement about writing.

The superlicious attitude that originated from the fathers of modern linguistics has fostered a long-lived tradition of neglect for writing as a subject of rigorous, scientific endeavour, in favour of a prescriptive approach aimed to lay down rules for how to minimise errors in writing. Embarking on a review of most of the prescriptive efforts aimed specifically to perfect the art of writing goes beyond the remits of the present book, but there is one quick example that is particularly telling and worthy of mention here. Ironically, my example stems from writing itself: think about the word *orthography*, which is indeed a key word in the title to this book. A search for this word in the *Oxford English Dictionary* gives something quite revealing about the traditional approach to writing that we have all inherited from the past. The word *orthography* comes from Hellenistic Greek ὀρθογραφία, 'orthographia', which is a compound form made of ὀρθο-, 'ortho', which means 'correct' and -γραφία, 'grafia', which means 'writing' or even 'spelling'. As evident from this brief etymological overview, the very word *orthography* carries in its own 'genetic' material, its etymology, the inescapable idea of correctness, intended as a set of rules that should be followed in order to ensure systematicity and predictability in writing. Interestingly, the word *orthography* found its way into English from Anglo-Norman and Middle French *ortografie*. The French have a long prescriptivist tradition in linguistics, which eventually culminated in the establishment of the Académie Française, the French Academy, in the early seventeenth century. While the English never had an institution which formally regulated the English language, the French Academy was, and still is, a pre-eminent authority on the usages, vocabulary and grammar of the French language.

While some of the key words that we have inherited for writing provide food for thought about how much the past may have influenced our view of orthography, a lot has changed since the American Structuralist School of Linguistics cast a shadow on orthography as an unworthy element of study in higher education. One might say that much of the change has been encouraged by the pressures exerted by modern society on 'correct' writing, that is to say, the way in which a writing system is expected to be used and the rules by which it should abide. Because of the long-recognised complexities arising from orthography, and the fact that these were never fully resolved in present-day systems, there is a tendency, today, to view correct spelling "as an index of intelligence, moral fibre and general trustworthiness" (Horobin, 2013: 15). The social value of spelling correctly has led to a paradoxical scenario, where, Horobin continues, "[p]eople who can't spell properly are considered to be ignorant and slovenly, and certainly shouldn't be trusted with running the free world". In addition to the social value of writing correctly, orthography also holds the power of bridging a successful intellectual relationship between teachers and students, as reflected, for example, by the fact that most of our university assessments in the arts and humanities are conducted in the form of essays and other written assignments. If using correct spelling is so important in our society, then why is orthography still not a core subject for most courses in linguistics? And if orthography is in its turn so important within the context of the historical study of languages, then why is historical orthography not yet an area of teaching and research with its own publicly and widely acknowledged place under the sun? Why is it perhaps not even co-habiting the evergreen tangled forest that is historical linguistics? I am sure that there will be many more answers to these questions besides the fact that the subject is essentially comparable to a child, that is looking to find their own steps in the complex world of adulthood.

Rather than indulging in any more suppositions and metaphors, therefore, this book will focus on potential solutions in order to give historical orthography more relevance in the academic scenario. I am indeed confident that there is enough material, to date, in order to justify a book like this, where concepts and ideas inherent to historical orthography finally find their home in a hopefully coherent whole. In order to get started, thus, let us address what is perhaps the most important question in this book: what is historical orthography? Providing a definition of *historical orthography* is important, given the fact that it is a relatively new name and has been used in the past in ways that could mislead some unexpert readers and confuse more seasoned others. Potential ambiguity might arise as a result of the combined use of the terms *historical* and *orthography*, which does not give sufficient information about whether the perspective is that of individual philologies or that of historical linguistics as a comparative umbrella. For example, one may say that they are reading a book about the historical orthography of French, which could be taken to mean that they are learning about the history of the French writing system. The term historical orthography, however, by analogy with other subfields of historical linguistics such as historical phonology and historical morphology, can also refer to something broader, I argue, than that applicable to individual philologies. In this book, historical orthography is intended as an international field of theoretical and empirical inquiry, mainly centred around four components – a linguistic core, which is the primary subject, and also general history, palaeography and bibliography, which work as ancillary, informing disciplines.

Historical orthography is, therefore, the scientific study of writing in history. The field focuses on the description and study of orthographies, their development over time, as well as the forces and the processes which shaped and directed modifications in historical writing features, from the creation of the first writing systems to our contemporary era. With this definition, writing systems are intended as a hyponym to orthography, since a set of conventions for writing a language may in principle stem from the overlap of multiple writing systems. That said, there are of course also conceptual and practical overlaps between writing and orthography, one being broadly intended as the act or art of forming visible letters or characters specifically, and the other being more specifically understood as the conventional set of rules underlying writing. While I am, to my knowledge, the first person to write a definition of historical orthography and one of the first contributors responsible for actively defending the identity of historical orthography as a subdiscipline of international academic inquiry, orthography in historical linguistics rests on a solid, albeit relatively recent, scholarly tradition. The study of orthography in history has followed a variety of venues and was shaped by different approaches and methods, according to various geographical areas and periods of time. Areas of discussion and investigation have ranged from the question of biscriptality, the topics of codification and nation-building, to spelling reform, and the role of the introduction of printing technology in orthographic developments and standardisation. The variation related to the study of historical orthography around the world should not surprise us, if we consider the obvious differences across languages in Europe alone on different linguistic levels (including orthographic, phonological and syntactic) and the different political decisions made in the administration of educational curricula, especially at university level. The natural divergence of interests in orthography may also be owed to profound historical, cultural and political differences in every corner of Europe – all of which undoubtedly represent an element of richness and diversity which should be valued and fostered in the future for the sake of progress in the field. As a result of the great diversity in the field, the relevance of historical orthography as a branch of scholarly inquiry is not defined only in the constraints of a community of those who are interested in orthography per se, but rather it is applicable to a much broader audience of scholars, not least those interested in phonology, etymology, lexicography, sociolinguistics, corpus linguistics, philology, literature, social history, art history, history of writing, palaeography and bibliography.

The lack of homogeneity existing in historical orthography is also owed to historically grounded approaches to philology more generally. In Europe especially, philologies had and still have a strong national orientation. This holds true with respect to the research structures as well as to the nationally limited thematic contexts which characterise the historical study of a given language. From a historical perspective, these patterns could be explained by the fact that philologies are the product of the national age, i.e. the formative period of the European nation-states. The dichotomy between generalised perspectives and individual philologies has been discussed extensively in Condorelli and Voeste (2020), and I do not intend to repeat here the argument presented in previous work. There is, however, one important point that needs to be made at this stage about the relationship between orthography as a synergic branch of historical linguistics *and* as a topic of interest within the context of individual philologies. The attention to historical orthography within the histories of individual languages has been and continues to be strong, and has provided a solid foundation for historical orthography more broadly. It is also thanks to the growth of individual philologies that the renewed interest in orthography has redeemed the subject from its traditional status of a subsidiary or illegitimate area of linguistic discussion (see de Saussure, [1915] 1993: 41; Sapir, [1921] 1949: 20; Bloomfield, 1933: 21) and encouraged the growth of a large amount of scholarship aimed especially at language-specific orthographies.

For English, there are several broad as well as detailed accounts of historical orthographic developments, see especially Scragg (1974), Carney (1994), Upward and Davidson (2011), Crystal (2012) and Horobin (2013). Other relevant monograph-long titles for other languages include Osipov (1992), Baddeley (1993), Elmentaler (2003, 2018), Rössler (2005), Voeste (2008), Bunčić et al. (2016), Franklin (2019) and Schaeken (2019). There are also volumes and shorter contributions which focus on the interrelation between orthography and cognate areas of investigation like palaeography, typography and transmission from manuscript to print, e.g. Dumville (1993), Traxel (2004), Janečková (2009), Kaverina (2010), Hellinga (2014), Shute (2017) and Condorelli (2020b, 2020c, 2022). The knowledge available from these and many other titles omitted here for the sake of brevity provides present-day scholars with a set of guidelines and material for research in orthography, but also a vision of spelling that is, generally, focused on individual languages or specific geographical areas. If we are to adopt a cross-linguistic perspective that encompasses the diversity of scholarly efforts in historical orthography, we must strive, I believe, to get language-specific publications to work also as individual components of a bigger picture. The knowledge available from all of the language-specific titles existing to date provides present-day scholars with information that is undoubtedly useful to those interested in diachronic orthography more broadly – as long as the national perspective of each reference material is not made historically absolute in retrospect.

Despite the differences existing today in how historical orthography is approached across different corners of the world, some common threads are identifiable in our attempt, as human beings and as researchers, to understand writing across languages and cultures of the past. Spelling evidence can be and has been widely employed by historical phonologists and dialectologists as a primary source for uncovering distinctive features of phonological and morphological systems of languages and dialects in history. Spelling evidence has been used for these purposes both from a synchronic perspective, at a given point in time, and diachronically, at different chronological lengths. For a few decades, orthographic evidence has also been used by historical sociolinguists in their search for correlations between socio-historical and socio-cultural factors and linguistic features. The end of the twentieth century and the beginning of the twenty-first century in particular have marked the beginning of a change in the field of historical orthography, thanks to the advent of historical sociolinguistics. For approximately two decades now, historical orthography has enjoyed a worldwide renaissance, which has fostered enthusiasm not only in various sociolinguistic aspects of writing systems but also in orthography as a much more complex linguistic universe than has even been portrayed in the past.

As briefly mentioned above, there is to date sufficient seminal work which provides some useful background information for an informed introductory volume to historical orthography. *The Handbook of Orthography and Literacy* (Joshi & Aaron, 2014), *Writing Systems* (Coulmas, 2012) and *The Nature of Writing* (Meletis, 2020), for example, are some of the most relevant titles which provide an informative basis for key elements in orthography from a present-day perspective. Unfortunately, a great deal of the theoretical system that we have to date derives directly from discussions applied to present-day orthographies, so much of the work done for this volume with respect to theory has been that of synthesising and evaluating what was relevant for historical writing systems and what had to be discarded. From a historical point of view, recent years have seen an upsurge of useful collecting contributions, such as *The Cambridge Handbook of Historical Orthography* (Condorelli & Rutkowska, forthcoming). This volume, in particular, is a collection of more than thirty chapters. It represents the most extensive platform where linguistic issues related to historical orthography are discussed at length, and, as such, it provided a solid basis for informing chapters in this volume.

Key chapter contributions that were paraphrased and followed more or less closely for making sections of the present volume, besides my own, are those written by Per Ambrosiani and Elena Llamas-Pombo (Chapter 6, section 6.2), Javier Calle-Martín and Juan Lorente-Sánchez (Chapter 4, subsection 4.2.3), Stefan Hartmann and Renata Szczepaniak (Chapter 4, section 4.2), Amalia E. Gnanadesikan (Chapter 4, section 4.1), Gijsbert Rutten et al. (Chapter 9, sections 9.2, 9.3 and 9.4), Annina Seiler and Christine Wallis (Chapter 6, subsection 6.1.1), Aurelija Tamošiūnaitė (Chapter 7, especially paragraphs in sections 7.1 and 7.2) and Anja Voeste (Chapter 6, subsection 6.1.2). Many of the references and linguistic examples which inform the chapters in my book directly reflect the material made available in these contributions, thus inevitably leaning towards some languages and topics more than others. Some of my chapters often contain simplified, student-friendly syntheses of the handbook contributions above (or, rarely, rephrased versions of salient chapters). Thus, readers who would like to follow up on most of the topics touched upon in this book are encouraged to get hold of those chapters for more complex, richer perspectives. In addition to the handbook, there are a number of recently edited collections of research-oriented contributions, which have a focus on language-specific aspects of orthography in historical linguistics, and which have also informed this book. Among the most relevant, *Advances in Historical Orthography, c. 1500–1800* (Condorelli, 2020d), *The Historical Sociolinguistics of Spelling* (Villa & Vosters, 2015) and *Orthographies in Early Modern Europe* (Baddeley & Voeste, 2012b) are key flagship titles. Other relevant focus-specific titles include single-authored contributions on the history of writing (e.g. Christin, 2002; Fischer, 2003; Gnanadesikan, 2009; Robinson, 2009), palaeography (e.g. Sperry, 1998; Žagar, 2019) and bibliography (e.g. Gaskell, 1972; Bland, 2010).

There is, at this point, one important message that needs to be conveyed about the nature of this book, in relation to historical orthography and its current limitations. This is a very ambitious project: it sets out to articulate a field that is definitely not as fully or clearly codified as other branches of historical linguistics might be, for example historical syntax or historical phonology. The book is envisioned mainly as a pedagogical resource used in the classroom, but given the current gaps in the field it may also serve as a scholarly point of reference, and it is hoped that it will be applicable to and up to the standards of as many readers as possible. Because of the relatively early stage of development in which historical orthography is placed, one cannot compare the present volume to some of the hugely monumental introductions existing, for example, in historical linguistics (e.g. Campbell's *Historical Linguistics: An Introduction* (2021), a 500-plus-page volume). Rather, my book-length contribution aims to work as a compendium of some of the most important pieces of information that stem from what we know so far about diachronic orthography. In other words, the book does not attempt to propose or frame anything more than what is already out there in the existing material – however incomplete and frustratingly one-sided it may sometimes be. Inevitably, this conservative approach means that there might be gaps and limitations (but hopefully no glaring oversights). These are a natural product of the relatively young state of the field itself and may be used by future writers as points of departure to extend our knowledge in historical orthography, on the basis of more substantial empirical evidence.

The reason for remaining a conservative reporter – or selective synthesiser, even – of what is known today within the field is that there are many areas of discussion that are simply impossible to contribute to without a consensus from the scholarly community. One of the most relevant examples here is that of a definition of historical orthography as a field and as an object of inquiry. The two spheres – a field and an object of inquiry – are clearly not always the same thing, but even in more mature fields like historical phonology and historical syntax there is still, to date, a tendency to blend together objects of inquiry and the overall field profile. In order to set out or even outline parameters across languages and across the scholarly community that belongs to historical linguistics, one would need to work towards a shared apparatus, including common protocols of academic practice to be generally accepted by researchers in the field. This shared apparatus can be achieved only by improving scholarly communication, and overcoming some of the conceptual boundaries which stem directly from scholarly disunity, egoistical competitiveness and individualism. Unless some common ground is built, it can be difficult, if not impossible, to overcome the differences existing in the approaches and policies used to study individual orthographies, which are largely owed to the very history of each individual language.

While I had to take every step to retain a serious approach to writing the book, careful definition and negotiation of terms and concepts within historical orthography is a key objective in any volume of the kind proposed here. Since general agreements on *orthography, writing system* and *script* are not always a given, I take in the book the following functional definitions. The definition of *script* is that of a set of graphic signs for writing languages, that of *writing system* a set of graphic features working together to write a given language and that of *orthography* a standardised way of writing the graphic signs that make up a particular writing system. Script is therefore the actual physical symbols of the writing system, for instance Roman or Cyrillic alphabets; orthography, on the other hand, is the rules for using a script in a particular writing system, that is to say, how the symbols spell out words, etc. In less precise usage, the terms *writing system* and *script* may be used synonymously, focusing on the sets of signs and their basic typological relationship to linguistic units rather than the specifics of a given language's spelling rules. In such usage, for instance, the Roman alphabet could be referred to as either a script or a writing system. Philip Baker makes a particularly neat distinction between *writing system* and *orthography*, instead, and, where possible, I employ the same distinction as follows. A writing system refers to "any means of representing graphically any language or group of languages", while "orthography is employed more narrowly to mean a writing system specifically intended for a particular language and which is either already in regular use among a significant proportion of that language's native speakers, or which is or was proposed for such use" (Baker, 1997: 93; cf. Sebba, 2007: 10).[1] That said, the three terms are inevitably overlapping from many angles, and it is possible that slips in the uses of the three may be found in the volume, especially where context may ambiguously allow for more than one of the three words.

These explanations are simple but sufficient for the purpose of serving my own narrative and my own book, rather than presumptuously prescribing a set

---

[1] However, these terms vary considerably in meaning between writers. Sproat (2000: 25), for example, uses the terms *orthography* and *writing system* interchangeably.

of rules for the field as a whole. In addition to the elements outlined above, there are some more fine-grained distinctions that had to be made in the book in an attempt to engage with current theories of writing. While individual letters may be intuitively graspable units of analysis, terms like *graphematics*, *grapheme* and *graphemic inventory* refer to categories and units of analysis that are applied on the basis of a particular theoretic model, that of graphematics. These terms are briefly discussed in Chapter 4 and Chapter 6, but I remain fully aware that the present contribution cannot provide an extensive account of theoretical definitions and frameworks existing to date in graphematics. Readers are therefore encouraged to make use of the suggested reading lists provided at the end of the two chapters mentioned above in order to become more familiar with more theoretical background. In Germany, some important contributions to theory formation and methodology have already been made since the 1960s (by Fleischer, 1966; Mihm, 2007; and others). The same applies for French (Völker, 2003) and Italian (Videsott, 2009), and there is therefore plenty to read for the curious mind.

Given the extensiveness of information available, I realise that my intention to focus on the most important pieces of information in orthography, as expressed above, may not be a sufficiently convincing statement for the most cynical reader. How can one judge what is really important for such a broad audience as the one envisaged for the present book? In this case, there might in fact at times be no need to make a conscious judgement at all. One important way in which the book naturally becomes manageable within the languages, time and length constraints existing is by occasionally allowing for a relatively specialised focus. While an effort is made to make a mention of all important elements relevant in the field, the discussion occasionally focuses in greater detail on alphabetic orthographies, defining basic units and elements in histor-ical writing systems that can work as individual foci of analysis or can combine together for a broader empirical perspective. Such a restriction in scope, and especially the focus on predominantly European orthographic traditions, some of which derive specifically from the early modern era (1500–1700), presents a rather limited and narrow view of orthographies; however, it reflects the focus that has prevailed so far in orthographic research, both generally and in my own personal experience.

When a multilayered distinction across different elements of orthographic analysis is not necessary in order to discuss a given topic, preference is given to spelling over, say, capitalisation or punctuation, as a tool for making relevant examples. Even then, the book does not aim to address all characteristics and nuances related to spelling, but rather it makes selective references with a view of following the narrative outlined in the table of contents. The justification for an occasionally selective and focused approach is, besides that of my personal expertise, the practical need to provide a functioning, relatively succinct narrative. Rather than acting as an articulation of the field of historical orthography by and large, therefore, the book departs from a smaller and more humble objective: that of providing those interested in historical orthography with a first, beginning-level point of reference. If readers will then want to see the present volume as anything more comprehensive than that, this would of course be entirely welcome.

Where appropriate, topics are treated in this book in enough detail to provide definitions and explanations, while avoiding overloading the narrative with too many references. Sometimes, however, leaving out issues related to detailed developments across time, and across social and linguistic contexts is inevitable, and readers are reminded of the importance of understanding these issues in publication material that goes beyond the present book in every chapter, at the cost of sounding repetitive. The reference material provided in this book is not to be taken as a fully exhaustive bibliography of the relevant publications for a given topic, but rather it is aimed to give readers across a range of languages and a number of academic disciplines suggestions for books that they can use as a point of departure. Overall, the present volume aims to build a compendium of knowledge stemming from and summarising some of the patterns and definitions built so far more implicitly in previous work. For this reason, the purpose of my book is subsidiary to – and not in competition with – all other efforts currently being made in the field. The enthusiasm from the academic community for topics related to historical orthography, the extraordinary breadth and diversity of topics in the field, as well as the increased awareness of the relevance of orthography as a subject underlying most areas in historical linguistics, are all convincing indicators of the field's growing maturity and justify an introductory volume entirely devoted to the subject. In this spirit, the present book aims to offer material of crucial importance to all those interested in the subject and should hopefully become a useful addition to the library of a student of orthography.

1.2   Contents of the Book

This book aims to equip the reader with the necessary skills to trace the historical development of orthography, discussing the components of historical writing and providing some key knowledge tools for those interested in understanding and exploring orthographic variation and standardisation. The volume proposes an understanding of *orthography* which encompasses strictly regulated writing systems with fixed word writing, as we know them from modern standard languages; this linguistic understanding of orthography thus includes the character units which make up a word (normally referred to as *spelling*), as well as additional layers of information, like accents, diacritics, punctuation and capitalisation (Condorelli, 2020c: 5). In addition to these elements, my definition also embraces design features such as alignment, page layout, abbreviations and aspects of visualisation (e.g. calligraphy) – all of which are not necessarily commonly regarded as constitutive components of orthographies. The concept of orthography proposed above is deliberately very broad and may in fact deviate from that of a few linguists, who see the term as embracing issues about language more strictly and less about materiality. The singularity of my choice is not a sufficient reason to exclude these important topics from my definition of orthography, however. Given the importance of all elements outlined above in the dynamic and multifaceted diachronic development of orthography, I believe that the extended definition proposed above is entirely relevant.

The book focuses on both theoretical aspects of orthography, for example definitions and classifications, and practical elements of analysis, for instance issues related to the relationship between orthography and phonology. For some of the elements belonging to the more extended category of orthographic components, the same theoretical, methodological and practical considerations that relate to spelling are not required. The mixed, flexible format of the volume aims to embrace current knowledge in the field, as well as providing readers with an overview of historical orthography as a field where theoretical endeavour and investigative practice co-exist and inform each other. The focus of some of the chapters rests slightly more markedly on English orthography, for two practical reasons. First of all, using English as a baseline for discussion naturally guarantees as broad an audience as possible; and secondly, an explicit agreement on English as a working language avoids unwanted conceptual pitfalls. Anyone who seeks to achieve anything monumental like covering as many languages worldwide as possible would probably set themselves up for failure, as no single writer can cover every corner of the world satisfactorily and in fair proportions for every language group.

This is not to say, however, that the focus of the book is on English only: extensive examples from a wide range of language families are supplemented in the book, including those belonging to the Germanic, Romance and Slavic groups, but also older languages like Ancient Greek and Ancient Egyptian, and various extra-European languages. The reasons why other languages are brought in when a topic could be covered more easily than just using English is that the overall focus of the book is on principles of diachronic orthography (thus answering the question of 'how does orthography work?') rather than on the orthographies of specific languages ('how does orthography in a given language work?'). A nonetheless still important reason why English is sometimes used as a convenient point of reference for discussion is that of focus. Addressing historical orthography from the point of view of any possible historical language in the world inevitably raises questions that are impossible to address all in one book. With the different writing systems in the world, how do we conceive of *orthography* as a concept? Is it perhaps not even relevant for some languages? If there are unique orthographic conventions in particular languages or language families, how can these be covered?

Clearly, a narrower linguistic focus also means that there will be issues in orthography that might never come up in relation to the languages discussed in this volume. In other words, my own linguistic choices have inevitably, in one way or another, guided my approach to outlining and defining historical orthography, but I cannot see this as anything other than an inevitable short-coming in a project like the present one. This potential weakness is all the more outbalanced by greater focus. Needless to say, further work will be needed to see how the conceptualisation provided in my book will fit other languages and language groups, from a typological and a universal perspective. While there are inevitable practical issues, my decision to adopt a more focused approach than one might perhaps hope for did not have an effect on the breadth of reference material that I used for informing the present piece of work.

In terms of structure, my book has been divided into ten different chapters – if we also include this introductory chapter. These ten chapters are designed, in principle, to enable the reader to begin at page one and march through to the last page. While front-to-back reading may perhaps be the most preferred method for most readers, each of the topics in the chapters contained in this book were developed in a way that each chapter – and indeed each section in every chapter – can be accessed as an independent, stand-alone entity, according to the interests and needs of those who may want to use the present volume as a scholarly resource. The chapters of the book are organised in four parts: the first part of the book is entitled ORIGINS AND SOURCES, the second part ELEMENTS OF ORTHOGRAPHY, the third part ANALYSING ORTHOGRAPHY and the fourth part UNDERSTANDING ORTHOGRAPHY. The two chapters in Part I focus on the history of writing and on the sources available to us, which give a testimony of the development of writing. The chapters in Part II overview theoretical aspects of the field, providing readers with a number of orthographic definitions and classifications. The two chapters in Part III focus on more practical aspects, particularly orthographic analysis and interpretation. The two chapters in Part IV cover issues related to orthographic developments, especially in relation to standardisation and language change.

In terms of chapter contents for each of the four parts, Chapter 2 offers a short history of writing; Chapter 3 describes some of the primary materials which contain evidence of and were used for writing; Chapter 4 outlines fundamental elements in writing systems; and Chapter 5 focuses on some of the most frequent ways in which orthographic elements are structured and presented. Chapter 6 introduces a number of key methods for studying histor-ical writing systems; Chapter 7 discusses the issue of orthographic convention-ality and its connection with writing system analysis; Chapter 8 engages with the relationship between orthography and standardisation; while Chapter 9 discusses the intersection between orthography and language change. Chapters 8 and 9 are relatively denser with reference material, and this is because they summarise selected research work as a way to engage with the elected topics. In order to assist non-expert readers, my use of phonetic symbols across all of the chapters above corresponds to standard International Phonetic Alphabet conventions; the rules concerning ortho-graphic notation, instead, generally reflect the flexibility and nuances intended for each individual language and follow the conventions established in Condorelli (2020), and reiterated in Condorelli and Rutkowska (forthcoming), for handling orthographies across different language groups. In general, angle brackets enclose graphemes, vertical lines graphs, slashes phonemes and square brackets allophones. Italics, instead, are used to indicate words as more general entities. Italics are also used to refer to foreign words or letters of the alphabet, free from the linguistic assumptions that stem from the grapheme and the phoneme.

In terms of a more detailed summary of the individual contents of each chapter, the contents are generally structured as follows. Chapter 2 provides a concise history of writing, from ancient times to the present day. The chapter departs from proto-writing and then the first writing systems, which arose independently in different corners of the world. The discussion shows evidence of the earliest roots of writing from the Egyptian and Mesopotamian areas, as well as in China and Mesoamerica. The chapter then covers cuneiform writing, drawing on examples from the Middle East, like Ancient Sumerian. Other early writing systems discussed include Egyptian hieroglyphics and the first alpha-bets, like the Phoenician one, from which came the Aramaic script, followed by the Greek and Latin alphabets. Following an overview of writing in the Middle Ages, the focus shifts to the invention of the printing press by Johannes Gutenberg. Insights from European developments are integrated with some references to the influence of East and South Asian writing. The chapter also discusses the changes in writing brought about by a series of modern events and inventions, from the Industrial Revolution to the Internet.

Chapter 3 focuses on some of the most frequently found historical materials and writing instruments which were used for writing. The chapter begins with a discussion of some of the most ancient materials, including stone and metal, as well as some other perishable materials which were in use among the first civilisations around the world. The discussion then moves on to describe papyrus, parchment, vellum, how they were made and what they were gener-ally used for. The chapter also provides an overview of paper as a source of primary evidence, focusing on some of the key steps in the history of paper-making which can provide useful pieces of information for a student of orthography. Moving on, the narrative focuses on a short history of typographic styles, while also providing an overview of how to describe and classify type. The sections on paper and typography are informed by some extensive information already existing in the field of bibliography, while also including elements from palaeography.

Chapter 4 describes the fundamental components of historical writing systems, in order to provide a first compendium of definitions immediately relevant to historical orthography. The chapter departs from an overview of different types of writing systems, covering similarities and differences between pictograms, ideograms, syllabaries and alphabets. The discussion then focuses in greater detail on alphabetic orthographies, defining basic elements in historical writing systems that can work as individual foci of analysis or can combine together for a broader empirical perspective. These elements are defined in my chapter under the following categories: *graphemes* and *allographs* (4.2.1), *letters*, *graphs*, *characters* and *glyphs* (4.2.2), *punctuation* (4.2.3) and *capitalisation* (4.2.4). Within these general categories, my discussion also covers definitions and examples for terms like *graphemic inventories* and *word division* as concepts conceptually related to the elements above. The graphemic inventory of a writing system consists in the full collection of graphemes used in a specific language where the writing system is used. The expression *word division* indicates the ways in which words in historical texts usually appear, i.e. joined, hyphenated or separated.

Chapter 5 focuses on the most frequent ways in which the orthographic elements established in the previous chapter are organised, following segmental, suprasegmental and morphological structures. Examples include the interrelation between graphemes and other orthographic units, like tildes and accents; the recurrence of graphemes in frequently recurring clusters and the use of ligatures across orthographic units. A short section on the importance of direction (left-to-right, right-to-left, top-to-bottom, etc.) in historical orthography is also provided. The chapter also focuses on the overlap between orthographic structure and the visual aspect of a document, namely the ways in which writing participates to the *mise-en-page*. This section argues for the importance of a full, physical document as a considerable part of the overall communicative event that is orthography. The visual programme in a given text, namely its layout, decoration and illustration, usually acts as a cohesive and structural tool alongside written marks, such as chapter headings or metatextual commentary. Lastly, spacing, justification and abbreviation are also discussed in the chapter.

Chapter 6 introduces a number of key methods and frameworks of analytical inquiry for approaching historical writing systems, including traditional approaches and more recently developed perspectives which lean towards a comparative approach. The first focus area explored in the chapter is that of philology: the chapter discusses how far philological approaches pertain to the study of orthography. The discussion also focuses on facsimiles and transcribed material for empirical analysis, while also pointing to the limitations stemming from digitally driven methods of research inquiry. The chapter discusses in particular the intratextual, intertextual and cross textual analytical approaches, each of which has inherent advantages and disadvantages. The discussion then focuses on an overview of recently developed empirical frameworks of inquiry in historical orthography for a synergic perspective. Relevant topics in this section include, but are not limited to, comparative graphematics, which refers especially to the comparative analysis of individual orthographic units (e.g. punctuation features); and biscriptality, which includes bigraphism, biorthographism and bygliphism.

Chapter 7 indicates some of the possible ways in which those working in historical orthography can recognise patterns in how writing systems function. The first half of the chapter in particular seeks to illuminate some of the formal aspects of writing that more directly inform principles in orthography. In alphabetic writing systems, the set of rules, conventions, regularities, patterns or preferences that govern spelling practices and/or their interpretation can be differentiated in two individual groups: phonemic and morphological. The chapter also focuses in great detail on the relationship between orthography and sounds, together with some of the complexities underlying the interpretation of phonemes as a result of diachronic developments. The complexities inherent to analysing historical writing systems lead to the issue of deciphering lost or enigmatic scripts, intended as one of the end results of the challenges related to interpreting historical writing. In most cases, I argue, the task is complicated by the paucity of evidence, its state of preservation and its typology. This topic constitutes the second half of the chapter.

Chapter 8 introduces readers to the concept of spelling standardisation, offering an overview of the *ways* in which spelling standardisation occurred, the *agents* behind the modern-like developments in historical spelling and the *chronology* of the process of development. For practical purposes, the discussion of this particular chapter focuses exclusively on historical English. The chapter departs from the idea that historical spelling represents one of the most complex facets of linguistic standardisation, and one where disagreements exist about its overall process of development. The chapter moves on to discuss the idea that standardisation in English spelling was, for some scholars, an intralinguistic, spontaneous process of self-organisation, and for others, a process involving many parties, including authors, readers, the printing press and linguistic commentators of the time. The final section of the chapter summarises findings from recent work that focuses on large-scale developments in printed orthography over the sixteenth and the seventeenth centuries, and overviews the role and relevance of theoreticians, schoolmasters, authors, patrons and readers in the Early Modern English book market.

Chapter 9 discusses the relationship between transmission, diffusion and orthography. While diffusion may be seen as a more dominant driver of orthographic change, changes induced by transmission are also possible in some historical scenarios, for example through formal instruction or via closely knit social networks. Drawing on a number of examples from previous studies, the chapter also engages with supralocalisation, intended as an antecedent to standardisation, as local and regional orthographic conventions in the pre-standardisation era give way to more supraregional writing traditions. Thus, instances of geographical diffusion across communities frequently provide essential groundwork for later standardisation initiatives. The chapter ends with a reference to the importance of including pluricentricity in our understanding of standardisation. It is by studying regional writing traditions that one can trace the formation of a standard not as an exclusive national form, but rather as a pluricentric scenario. In the development of many European pluricentric orthographies, not least German and French, some writing traditions eventually became part of the overall profile of the regional influence through diffusion, while still not becoming a uniform fixed set of shibboleths for the whole geographical area.

Overall, this book makes a case for a more serious study of orthography as a core element in historical linguistics, and it does do so following a number of steps aimed to introduce linguists to the field, offering material for those who are relatively new to the subject. By relatively new, I do not intend absolutely first-year linguistics students, but those who have had enough knowledge of linguistics to be able to attend a historical linguistics class. The audience that this book will hopefully speak to, thus, includes those who have had some exposure to subjects like phonology, morphology, syntax and semantics. In addition to historical linguistics students, it is hoped that the book will also be of interest to more specialised readers with an interest in different branches of linguistics; this category also includes academic teachers and research students who want to explore specific research questions directly or indirectly related to historical orthography. Current work in present-day orthography frequently makes reference to historical data, and, as a result, the present book should also appeal to those who do not necessarily conceive of themselves as diachronicians and have an interest in present-day orthography. The potential tangential relevance of the present book as a scholarly resource is owed primarily to the fact that there is, to date, no authoritative guide on historical orthography as a field, despite the rising interest in topics related to orthography coming from different academic angles. It is hoped that the present volume will act as a first bold step in this direction.

Part I

Origins and Sources

2 A Short History of Writing

2.1 Origins of Writing

The first form of writing that eventually led to the appearance of well-defined writing systems in human civilisations is generally called proto-writing and consists in a range of systems of ideographic or early mnemonic symbols. For a long time, proto-writing was deemed to have arisen from one group of people and a single civilisation – a thought which formed the basis of a now controversial theory called *monogenesis*. According to this theory, writing was the product of the ancient Sumer in Mesopotamia and expanded across other human civilisations via a process of cultural diffusion. The monogenesis theory suggests the basic idea that language was represented using written symbols, and as a matter of course, the mechanism instrinsic to this system found its way through to other civilisations thanks to the work of traders and merchants, who moved to different parts of the world. Today, a more commonly accepted theory for the origins of writing is one based on the evidence of scripts from ancient Mesoamerica, far away from Middle Eastern sources, which suggest that writing may in fact have appeared spontaneously more than once in different corners of the world. A *script* is to be intended here as a most general orthographic category to indicate a set of letters used for writing a language. Any language-specific writing system encompasses a script, that is, a set of actual graphic symbols with prototypical forms and prototypical linguistic functions and language-specific writing or spelling conventions that systematically relate graphic units to linguistic units.

With regard to the geographical origins of writing, the most widely spread hypothesis among scholars is that writing may have developed independently in four different ancient civilisations: China, Mesoamerica, Mesopotamia and Egypt. Ancient Chinese writing is very unlikely connected to that of Mesopotamia, because there exist to date no traces of a historical and linguistic link of any nature between ancient China and the civilisations of the Near East. The most ancient find for the Chinese script consists in the collection of inscriptions on oracle bones and bronze from the late Shang dynasty, dating as far back as *c.* 1200 BC. In truth, there are also tortoiseshell carvings, which date back to *c.* 6000 BC, such as the Jiahu script and the Banpo script, but it remains unclear whether these pieces of evidence represent a complex enough system to qualify as a form of writing. Other potentially relevant finds are those from Damaidi, in the Ningxia Hui region, consisting of 3,172 cliff carvings which are probably 7,000–8,000 years old. These carvings feature 8,453 symbols, including celestial bodies, divinities and scenes of hunting or grazing. If these finds provide enough evidence to argue for the existence of a self-standing written language, rather than some kind of proto-writing, then it is possible that China was in fact the earliest area of the world where writing appeared.

The Mesoamerican writing systems, which include the Olmec and Mayan, are also commonly thought to have arisen independently from the other strains identified above. In Mesoamerica, a stone slab with 3,000-year-old writing, the Cascajal Block, found in Veracruz, is the oldest-surviving script in the American continents and predates one of the oldest Zapotec examples of writing dating back to *c.* 500 BC. The Zapotec civilisation, which came before the Mayan, also left some inscriptions dating from about the second century BC. Of the few pre-Columbian examples found in Mesoamerica, the script that seems to have reached the highest level of systematicity and complexity, and has been fully deciphered, is that of the Mayan civilisation. The earliest Mayan inscriptions are from the third century BC and the script was in use at least until the arrival of the Spanish conquistadores in the sixteenth century AD. While the Maya definitely made a great use of writing, they were not the first to invent writing in America. It was in fact the Olmecs who were the first people in Mesoamerica to create a calendar, where writing of some kind was fundamental. The first Mayan stele surviving to the present day with a reasonably precise date is that from Tikal, AD 292. The Mayan script was chiefly hieroglyphic but also had some phonetic traits. Mayan writing has a long history of scholarly interpretation that goes as far back as the sixteenth century, and the script has been almost completely deciphered today (more about this in Chapter 7).

From all this research, it seems that Mayan writing was used for two reasons: drawing calculations in relation to the calendar and astronomy, and drawing a list of the kings, their families and their achievements. For the Mayan civilisation, writing was therefore very much the business of religious and palace official people, while the majority of the population had no access to literacy. With regard to the Indus script of the Bronze Age Indus Valley civilisation, the Rongorongo script of Easter Island and the Vinča symbols from *c.* 5,500 BC, matters are not as clear. These scripts have not yet been deciphered, and it remains a matter of contention whether they should be classified as writing systems or as examples of proto-writing, or indeed anything else.

With respect to the chronology and the modality of the development of writing, matters are slightly clearer than for the geography of early writing. During the third millennium BC, cuneiform, a script made of wedge-shaped lines impressed on stone and other archaeological finds, made its first appearance in the region of fertile land that covers the Nile, up into the territory known as the Fertile Crescent. This name refers to the inverted U-shape of land that stretches up the east Mediterranean coast and then turns east through northern Syria and down the Persian Gulf. The earliest instance of writing comes from the lower ends of the two greatest rivers in the Fertile Crescent, the Nile and the Tigris. The Egyptian and the Sumerian civilisations in particular were the cradle of the first organised forms of writing. The Sumerian pre-cuneiform writing and Egyptian hieroglyphs derived from older proto-literate symbol systems from 3400 to 3100 BC, with the earliest coherent texts from *c.* 2600 BC. The Sumerian script in particular is thought to have appeared first in *c.* 3100 BC, while the Egyptian script goes back to *c.* 3000 BC (but these dates have been a matter of contention). Quite recently, Günter Dreyer, a German archaeologist, found in Egypt small bone and ivory tablets recording, in early hieroglyphic form, the items delivered to a temple – mainly linen and oil. These finds date back to 3300–3200 BC. The dating of the earliest cuneiform tablets from Sumeria has in its turn also been revised to around 3200 BC due to new findings being made.

Beyond chronology, there are some common features identifiable among the first writing systems. The Sumerian pre-cuneiform writing system consisted in clay tokens used to record material goods; by the end of the fourth millennium BC, this system had become a systematic way of keeping accounts and consisted in using a round-shaped stylus to press soft clay at different angles in order to record numbers. Over time, this system was integrated with pictographic writing, an improvement achieved by means of a sharp stylus to indicate the object of counting. In general, most early writing systems consisted in a series of icons and forms used to indicate things – quite often, material, everyday objects or animals. When the icons and forms represented something by illustration in early writing, these are generally referred to as *pictograms*, and when writing systems used symbols to indicate words or morphemes, they are generally called *logograms* (further discussed in Chapter 4). Pictograms and logograms were not foolproof: some physical objects are not easy to represent as an image; and human speech often refers to concepts detached from material objects. In order to address these difficulties, early writing went through different routes: for example, pictures started to be combined in order to depict more complex concepts; sometimes puns were used to express more sophisticated scenarios, so that an image of an object was interpreted by analogy to indicate a different object with a homophonous name.

As an example of both developments, consider a simple symbol representing a roof – something that looks somewhat like an inverted V, to indicate 'house'. If one draws something that even vaguely resembles a woman under this roof, the new combined symbol could indicate something that comes close to 'home' or 'family'. This example occurs in Chinese to indicate 'peace' and is an instance of a conceptual character. If one had to turn this symbol into a pun, one might draw a sloping symbol to indicate the bank of a river under the roof symbol. The resulting character would in this case represent a financial institution – the type of 'house' that is a 'bank'. Going back to Sumerian writing, logograms were integrated with phonetic components by the twenty-ninth century BC. By around 2700–2500 BC, a wedge-shaped stylus – which is what the word *cuneiform* refers to – eventually supplanted the round-stylus and sharp-stylus writing. From *c.* 2600 BC, cuneiform was used to indicate syllables of the Sumerian language, but also logograms and numbers. Gradually, this script was adapted to the Akkadian language, and from there to other languages like Hurrian and Hittite. Other examples of largely comparable scripts (in terms of outlook and structure) are those for Ugaritic and Old Persian. By this time, in the region that we now call Asia, the Middle Bronze Age Indus script had already made an appearance. The Indus script is known from thousands of seals, carved in steatite or soapstone. In general, the core part of each seal features a realistic representation of an animal, as well as a short string of formal symbols on top of the animal representation (see Figure 2.1). The fact that only small fragments of writing were found probably indicates that the Indus script was used only for trading and for keeping counts – the seals may have indicated numbers and ownership of material goods. This script dates back to the early Harappan phase of *c.* 3000 BC in the region that is now called Pakistan, and has not yet been deciphered. Perhaps because of the mystery revolving around this script, scholars are still unsure today whether to consider the Indus script as a form of proto-writing or a specimen of logographic-syllabic writing of the Bronze Age family.

A writing system that we know a great deal more about, instead, is that of Ancient Egypt, which may have come shortly after Sumerian writing. A hypothetical statement is used here with reference to chronology for a specific reason. During the 1990s, some glyphs were discovered in tomb U-J at Abydos, written on ivory as labels for some items found in the grave. The findings made at Abydos were dated to between 3400 and 3200 BC, which means that there is evidence to argue, potentially, that the Egyptian system predates the Mesopotamian one. Admittedly, however, the evidence uncovered for Egyptian writing at that time is only a one-off instance, while on the contrary Mesopotamia has an evolutionary history of early writing which can be traced all the way back to *c.* 8000 BC. The Egyptian characters are much more directly pictorial in kind than the Sumerian, but the system of indicating

Figure 2.1   Steatite seal, from the Indus Valley (Source: DI DEA /G.
NIMATALLAH/Contributor/Getty Images)

objects and concepts is quite comparable. The Egyptian characters were later
dubbed as *hieroglyphs* by the Greeks, because by 500 BC, this form of writing
was used exclusively for holy texts (*hieros* = 'sacred' and *glypho* = 'engrave' in
Greek). Owing to the role that hieroglyphic inscriptions had in temples and
tombs, hieroglyphs were often considered by Ancient Egyptians to be
a prestigious piece of art that deserved devout attention from professional
painters, sculptors and craftsmen modelling in plaster. When papyrus began
to be used for writing, scribes became more commonly responsible for writing
Egyptian hieroglyphs. Scribes were a restricted caste in Ancient Egypt and
often wrote using a fine reed pen and a papyrus scroll. With the introduction of
a different way of writing, hieroglyphs acquired a more fluid appearance than
the traditional sharp and edgy forms carved and painted in stone.

Over time, scribal art was perfected, until three different standard versions of
the Egyptian writing became distinguishable. The first version was more
formal and often appeared in religious texts; a second version was frequently
used in literature and official documents; and a third version more commonly
used in private communication. By *c.* 700 BC, Egyptian scribal handwriting had
further evolved to a new, more abbreviated form: its components were still the

same Egyptian hieroglyphs, but they were reduced and simplified so much that they appeared like a whole new script. The more popular, elided script is traditionally called *demotic* (i.e. for the people), and it is more difficult to read than the traditional Egyptian hieroglyphs and the three previous scribal strains mentioned above. Both hieroglyphs and demotic writing remained popular until about AD 400 and had a paramount role in sustaining the Egyptian empire, although even during this later time only a small number of people, who usually ended up becoming scribes, received enough instruction. Those who became scribes usually came from well-off elites; among those who were able to read, there were also those who were in charge of the service of temple, as well as pharaonic and military authorities. While Ancient Egypt was admittedly very close to Mesopotamia, Egyptian writing sports a much different structure and style from that of the Mesopotamian region and must therefore have developed independently, albeit possibly somewhat influenced by the Mesopotamian general idea of writing. Undoubtedly, the early Egypt–Mesopotamia relations were important for the two regions from a cultural point of view, but there is to date no clear evidence to argue for a definitive determination as to the origin of hieroglyphics in Ancient Egypt. What we do know about Egyptian writing is by sheer luck: the serendipitous discovery of the Rosetta stone enabled scholars to decode hieroglyphics in the nineteenth century.

Of course, Egyptian hieroglyphs were not the only ones to appear in the Mediterranean. Cretan hieroglyphs were found on artifacts of Crete, dating from the early-to-mid second millennium BC, overlapping with Linear A, the primary script used in palace and religious writings of the Minoan civilisation. Linear B, which was adapted from Linear A, has been deciphered, while Linear A still remains largely a mystery. The sequence and the diffusion of the three overlapping, but individual, writing systems was as follows. It is believed that the first real alphabetic system appeared in *c.* 2000 BC by adapting Egyptian glyphs with Semitic values. The Ge'ez writing system of Ethiopia is classified as Semitic, but it is thought to have arisen semi-independently, with links that can be traced back to the Meroitic Sudanese ideogram system. Many other alphabetic systems in the world today descend from the Semitic adaptation with a major Egyptian influence. These descendent scripts were later influenced by the Phoenician alphabet, or were directly derived from the original Semitic form. In Italy, there is a gap of about 500 years between the early Old Italic alphabet and Plautus (750 to 250 BC); in Germany, a similar timespan can be identified between the first Elder Futhark inscriptions and early texts like the *Abrogans* (*c.* AD 200 to 750). The following section expands upon the topic briefly touched upon in this last paragraph, focusing on the rise and development of alphabetic writing around the world.

2.2   Rise and Development of Alphabetic Writing

The most remarkable occurrence in the history of writing was probably the shift from pictographic and syllabic systems, based on the representation of objects and concepts via images and forms, to a phonetic system, based on representing sounds in writing. Phonetic systems had the advantage of freeing writing from its traditional mysterious aura, as it often required years of study for scribes to master logographic systems. Phonetic systems thus made writing a great deal more accessible to a wider range of people. The first phonetic alphabets appeared in *c.* 1800 BC in Ancient Egypt as ways to represent the language used by Semitic workers in Egypt. The first alphabetic systems are classified under the term *abjad*, which indicates a type of writing system where each symbol stands for a consonant, and each phone does not necessarily correspond to a symbol. These early abjads did not have a central role in writing for several centuries, and it was only towards the end of the Bronze Age that the Proto-Sinaitic script branched into the Proto-Canaanite (*c.* 1400 BC) and the South Arabian (*c.* 1200 BC). The Proto-Canaanite alphabet may have arisen at least partially upon inspiration from the undeciphered Byblos syllabary and may, in turn, have worked as a basis for the Ugaritic (*c.* 1300 BC). The most remarkable changes towards phonetic scripts came from the trading communities of Phoenicia during the second millennium BC. The Phoenicians spoke a Semitic language, which became the cradle of the new phonetic system. The Phoenician alphabet was based entirely on the Proto-Canaanite alphabet, as it was passed on into the Iron Age.

Departing from Phoenician, the phonetic writing system was later on adopted by the different Semitic groups in Phoenicia and Palestine, for instance, Aramaic and Hebrew, forming distinctive, self-standing versions. These systems are, however, characterised by similar features: vowels are generally never written, and consonants are the main guidelines for the reader to follow (compare present-day Arabic). The writing systems adopted by the different Semitic groups above later gave rise to the writing systems used throughout Western Asia, Africa and Europe. In the eighth century BC, the phonetic system was adopted by the Greeks, who improved the Phoenician system of writing by adding graphic representations of vowels. The letters of the Greek alphabet were comparable to those of the Phoenician alphabet and followed the same order. Initially, Greek was written from right to left, just like the Phoenician alphabet, but eventually the Greeks opted for left-to-right writing, perhaps encouraged by an increased use of manuscripts and a decline in stones for writing. The Greeks, who inherited the Phoenician alphabet, integrated the system with three letters which were placed at the end of the alphabet, and came to be known as 'supplementals'. Over time, different variants of the Greek alphabet made an appearance in Ancient Greece, and at least two major ones are worthy of mention here. The first one, commonly known as Western Greek or Chalcidian, was mostly used in western Athens and southern Italy. The second variant, called Eastern Greek, spread across what we now call Turkey and was also used by the majority of inhabitants in Athens; eventually, this second variant became the most widespread among those who spoke Greek around the world. For some of the graphic representations indicating vowels, Phoenician letters were used; for others, new written signs made an appearance. The name of the twenty-four letter Greek phonetic system derives in fact from the first two letters in the Phoenician system, *alpha* and *beta*.

The Greek alphabet gradually became the basis for the Roman writing system, which then became predominant across Europe through the military achievements of the Roman Empire. The alphabet of the Romans was called Latin after the Latins, a population that lived in central Italy and who departed from Rome to conquer most the Mediterranean lands and a good part of Europe. The Romans first experimented with writing in the fifth century BC, upon immediate inspiration from the Etruscans, who in turn used a script derived from that of the western Greeks. The Roman Empire gained so much power and relevance over the other Italic civilisations during the following centuries, that all of the other Italic scripts that were present in Italy at the dawn of the Roman civilisation did not last for long, and the Etruscan language is now mostly lost. The relative simplicity of the Roman alphabet, combined with an increased availability of primary material like papyrus, wooden tablets and leaves, made writing more popular than it had ever been in the ancient world. During the first few centuries AD, the Greek and Latin alphabets brought about a few new European scripts, like those of the Gothic and Cyrillic alphabets later on, while the Aramaic alphabet eventually became Hebrew, Arabic and Syriac abjads, of which the latter spread as far as the Mongolian region. The South Arabian alphabet was the ancestor of the Ge'ez abugida; the Brahmic family of India, instead, may have stemmed from the Aramaic alphabet.

While the Roman alphabet was becoming established in the Italic peninsula and beyond, the Arabic script had already made an appearance in north-west Arabia, the earliest form being that of the fifth century BC, found on an inscribed column in Tema. The script was developed from the first century BC by the Nabataeans, a group of people who spoke a Semitic language in order to keep counts of their material goods at Petra, on a main caravan route. Unlike the other civilisations discussed so far, writing was initially not an essential commodity for the nomads of Arabia but soon evolved to become a paramount means for spreading the message of Qur'ān by the seventh century AD. It is indeed thanks to Islam that the Arabic script became so widely spread and well known across the world; religion in general was a great motor for development in writing around the world. From the seventh century AD,

Arabic, which had already made its presence felt in the Middle East, became a key scholarly language in the region. Arabic and Persian rapidly began to supplant Greek's role in many areas of literacy. The Arabic script was also chosen as the main script of the Persian and the Turkish languages, and influenced subtly the formation of the cursive scripts of Greek, Latin and other languages. The Arabic language was also responsible for the Hindu-Arabic numeral system which would end up being adopted all over Europe.

Besides the case of Arabic, an interesting script worthy of narrative mention is that of Gothic. Ulfilas went down in history as the first man to have taken up the bold task of inventing, from scratch, a written form for Gothic, a language that had only been spoken up to the fourth century AD. Ulfilas devised a new alphabet in order to represent graphically the Gothic language in its spoken form, and did so drawing on twenty-seven characters borrowed and adapted from letters of the Greek and Roman alphabets. Ulfilas was so committed to the Gothic alphabet because he intended to translate the Bible from Greek into the language of the Goths, for missionary purposes. It remains unclear whether he translated the full Bible, but many sections of the Gospels and the Epistles that he translated came to us as testimonies of his endeavour. The accomplishments of Ulfilas were not the only ones in the European continent. In the ninth century AD, Cyril and Methodius worked to create a writing system that would be suited for representing a previously oral Slavonic language. Cyril and his elder brother Methodius were already well known for being excellent theologians and linguists by 863, when the Byzantine emperor decided to employ them as missionaries to the Slavs of Moravia. The two missionaries were Greek, but they were native of Salonika and therefore spoke the Slavonic language used in that region. Their mission was to find a way to write down the liturgy in Slavonic, and to spread the message of the Bible with their own translation. For this reason, Cyril and Methodius devised a brand new alphabet that would suitably represent the spoken Slavonic of Salonika, on the basis of the Greek letters of the alphabet. The Slavonic alphabet came to be known as Cyrillic, after the more charismatic of the brothers, whose invention is the now extinct Glagolitic alphabet. Admittedly, however, the form of Cyrillic that we have today was probably crafted by Cyril's followers in Bulgaria. Cyrillic is still the script used by all Slavic regions which adopt the Greek Orthodox faith – including Serbia, Bulgaria and, of course, Russia.

Going back to Western Europe, let us now focus on the next pivotal time for the history of writing – the fall of the Roman Empire. From that time onwards, scholarly work became very much an exclusive element of the Eastern Roman and the Persian Empire. Latin, which up to this point had never been the main scholarly language in any case, quickly lost its importance across most of Europe, apart from to the Catholic Church. The main scholarly languages were Greek and Persian, though other languages such as Syriac and Coptic were also frequently used. Many of the letter forms that we use today in most languages, including English, are direct descendants of the forms used in handwriting by the Romans during the last centuries of the Roman Empire. The Latin alphabet found its way to Europe not only through the military conquests of the Romans, but also thanks to Christian culture. Christian monks in Western Europe were particularly keen to write holy books in Latin, and their style eventually gave rise to a relatively new form of the codex. The script they used was that of the Roman Empire, but it was enriched with a few regional variations: in Italy, manuscripts were written almost fully in capital letters between the seventh and the eighth centuries.

In Ireland, the large community of Celtic monks opted for a more unpretentious script. One of the most interesting pieces of evidence surviving from the earliest Celtic monks of the post-Roman period is that of the Cathach of St Columba, the oldest-surviving manuscript in Ireland, and the second oldest Latin psalter in the world. The Cathach of St Columba, which goes back to as early as the seventh century AD, also gives a paradigmatic example of an interesting feature of developing handwriting: in order to draw the reader's attention to the text, the first letter appeared in a larger font than the rest of the text and in a different handwriting style. Occasionally, the words that followed the large-sized letter were more reduced in size, perhaps as an instinctive reaction to over-correction, which eventually went back to normal as the text developed. Texts like the Cathach of St Columba provide evidence for an increased awareness of the distinction between majuscule and minuscule,[1] which would later on, in the print culture, be renamed as uppercase (or capitals) and lowercase letters, as a typically Western European feature. In general, there are two stages during which early Christian texts had an impact on the styles of handwriting and of print, the first was the time of court of Charlemagne in the eighth century, and the second was during the Renaissance, especially in the fifteenth century.

During the reign of Charlemagne, religious scribes made a conscious effort to normalise handwriting into an official style of prestige and simplicity. In AD 780, Charlemagne met Alcuin, a notable intellectual from York, and put him in charge of his palace school at Aachen. A few months after this commission, in 781, Charlemagne requested a copy of the gospels from a scribe called Godesalc. The scribe finished the copy for the emperor in April 783. The Godesalc Evangelistary, as it is known today, was the first manuscript where the script known as Carolingian minuscule was used. The manuscript presented conventional majuscule letters, and the dedication was written in minuscule. It

---

[1] These terms are more closely associated with palaeography and are most immediate for a discussion of handwriting, but *uppercase* and *lowercase*, respectively, are essentially used as synonyms and are more prevalent in everyday speech today.

seems that the writing style used by Godesalc was heavily influenced by Alcuin, who had recently arrived at court when the scribe was writing a copy of the gospels. During the following twenty years, Alcuin made his best efforts to research and improve a new way of writing for Charlemagne's vast reign. In order to craft a calligraphic style that was worthy of Charlemagne's highness, Alcuin went all the way back to Rome to find some inspiration. An effective predecessor of the Renaissance, Alcuin ended up becoming deeply inspired by the Latin culture and the way of writing associated with it, and restored what he believed was a pure classical writing style, perfected by the addition of minuscule letters. The product of his research was impressive. Carolingian manuscripts, most of which were written in a monastery at Tours, where Alcuin worked as an abbot from 796, were by far the prettiest and most legible texts of the Middle Ages. An example of these texts is provided in Figure 2.2 below, which represents an excerpt from Charlemagne's testament from 811.

The later Middle Ages gradually swept away the rigour of eighth-century handwriting, and writing remained chaotic up to the dawn of the Renaissance; indeed, during the fifteenth century scribes strived to restore the long-lost splendour of beautiful writing. By the final part of the Middle Ages, towards the eleventh century AD, a much darker and denser way of handwriting had become distinguishable in northern Europe. The so-called *blackletter* was inspired in some ways by an expressive need to convey a sense of drama with dense, dark and angular pen strokes, mostly motivated by fashion and

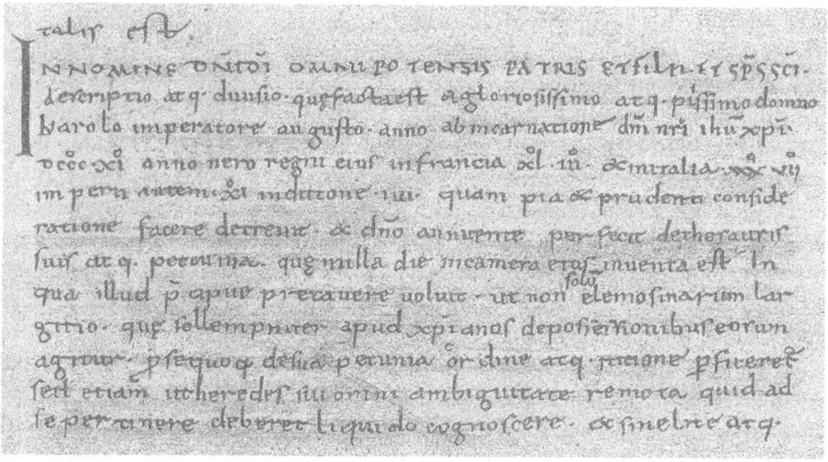
talis est.
IN NOMINE DNI DI OMNIPOTENTIS PATRIS ET FILII ET SPS SCI.
descriptio atq. divisio. quae facta est a gloriosissimo atq. piissimo domno
karolo imperatore augusto. anno ab incarnatione dni nri ihu xpi
dcccxi anno vero regni eius in francia xl iii. et in italia xxx vi
imperii autem xi indictione iiii. quam pia et prudenti considi
ratione facere decreuit. et dno annuente perfecit de thesauris
suis atq. pecunia. quae in illa die in camera eius inuenta est. In
qua illud praecipue praecauere uoluit. ut non solum elemosinarum lar
gitio. quae sollempniter apud xpianos de possessionibus eorum
agitur. pro se quoq. de sua pecunia ordine atq. ratione perficeret
sed etiam ut heredes sui omni ambiguitate remota quid ad
se pertinere deberet liquido cognoscere. et sine lite atq.

Figure 2.2 Charlemagne's Testament, 811, from Vita Karoli Magni (Österreichische Nationalbibliothek) Cod. 529 (Source: ZU_09/Contributor/ Getty Images)

economy. Parchment and papers were not easy to come by, and producing books was quite expensive. In blackletter, all characters were pressed together very tightly, which means that a book could be printed using fewer pages than other fonts. In little time, blackletter became a standard font in German manuscripts, and with the invention of printing in the mid fifteenth century, the font made its way to the first printed book and became the standard typeface for all of the earliest European printed books, including the Gutenberg Bible. Blackletter remained the standard typeface of German books until the early twentieth century, while other parts of Europe experimented with greater variability in style. By the fourteenth century, a wave of revival made its way across Western Europe and brought a renewed taste for the classical languages, especially Greek and Latin, as means of scholarly communication and linguistic inspiration. A similar thing, though to a lesser degree, also happened in Eastern Europe, particularly in Russia. During this time, Arabic and Persian gradually lost their importance as the Islamic Golden Age came to an end. The rediscovery of knowledge and culture in Western Europe encouraged changes in the Latin script and the rise of new strands of the alphabet in order to codify the sounds of the various languages.

During the Renaissance, Italian humanists began to despise blackletter; *Gothic*, as it began to be called, evoked, in their opinion, the dark centuries of the Middle Ages. It is for this reason that Italian poets and other intellectuals of the fourteenth and the fifteenth centuries began a look back at ancient manuscripts, in order to rediscover writing models to imitate. The writing style that mostly struck their interest was a beautiful script that they thought was Roman, but which was in fact Carolingian: the script devised for Charlemagne's monastic workshops in the eighth century was a token of beauty, perfection, clarity and elegance. Two Florentine friends, Poggio Bracciolini and Niccolò Niccoli, were particularly active in adapting the Carolingian script. Bracciolini, who worked for the papal court in Rome from 1403, used the Carolingian script for writing papal documents. His way of modifying the script consisted in adding straight-edged capital letters to the original rounded lowercase characters. Niccoli, on the other hand, worked on the script to make it more suited for casual writing, and he did so by sloping the letters a little. A more sloped shape allowed him to hold the pen at a more comfortable angle so that some of the characters would come together more closely. This effect was already present in mediaeval handwriting, and the writing style that resulted from this way of joining up letters of the alphabet came to be known as *cursive*. While it was not a complete novelty, the scripts of Bracciolini and Niccoli became, over time, very popular among printers of Venice.

The rounded but upright style of Bracciolini was first used by the French printer Nicolas Jenson a little after he moved to the city in 1470. Jenson's typeface was named *roman*, a name that was reminiscent of the long history of the script. In 1501, another famous Venetian printer, Aldus Manutius, who was looking for a new typeface for a 'pocket edition' of Virgil's work, chose the script invented by Niccoli for more casual writing, and called it *italic*, in honour of the Italian Niccoli. The two styles, roman and italic, eventually ended up becoming very popular all across Europe. In handwriting, a version of the italic script ended up becoming the standard way of writing for the majority of people. In addition to handwriting, then, there was also another area where these new forms of writing were applied successfully both for practical and for artistic reasons – that of engraving. By the time roman and italics became popular, writing was an essential commodity for the middle classes, and an art to be learned and taught. In order for the pupil to practise their handwriting skills, sheets and plates were the most popular sources, and these often ended up being bound into manuals. Over time, a few manuals were published explaining the art of doing copper-plate, which involved imitating the forms which the engraver had cut in his copper plate. Some of the earliest publications include the *Essemplare* by Gianfrancesco Cresci, a Vatican writer, in 1560. The most popular collection of copper-plate examples, however, is the *Universal Penman* of George Bickham, which first appeared in 1733 and still represented some useful reference material in some parts of the world up to the twentieth century. Besides engraving and handwriting, there is another area where writing styles were used virtuously – that of printing and modern technology, further discussed below.

2.3   The Rise of Modern Technology

2.3.1   The Printing Revolution

Writing, in its broadest sense, has always been an ever-changing entity; its development, however, was especially accelerated by the technological discoveries which effectively marked the beginning of the modern era. The pen, the printing press, the computer and the mobile phone are all inventions which had a profound impact on the ways in which writing changed over time. The first milestone towards modernity was the completion, in the German city of Mainz, around 1450, of Johannes Gutenberg's movable-type printing press. However, a specific type of printing, called mechanical woodblock printing on paper, had already made its appearance in China during the Tang dynasty before the eighth century AD. The woodblock-based way of printing became popular in Asia, until eventually it evolved to metal movable type in Korea by the thirteenth century. The idea of the printing press eventually travelled to Europe, and Europeans worked on the design with the introduction of the mechanical press. In Europe, the printing press not only changed completely the sheer numbers of books produced but also initiated profound changes in how writing actually worked. The old way of writing by the creation of letters turned into a mechanism of writing by selection from an existing collection of ready-made characters. Scribal writing had, before then, been a major source of creativity: each individual had their own way of approaching handwriting; even for an individual person, writing often changed across different passages according to different variables, like the scribe's feelings, his levels of energy, the way he held the pen and so on. With the movable type, all of the variables above were not relevant anymore. While individual scribes had their own identity in writing, this was not necessarily the case for the modern printer. Especially when they used the same typeface, the *m* in one word would appear, in size and style, like the *e* in any other word in the same book, regardless of who wrote the original manuscript. As one might expect, the modern changes to the way of writing did not find unanimous approval. The holiness of the Bible in particular, some believed, was being threatened by the 'sterilised' way of writing that was typical of the printing press, and this dryness would probably have reflected on the human soul. The economic advantages brought about by the printing technology, however, were far greater than the religious and literary identity worries.

One of the ways in which the cost of labour was reduced during the age of printing was by implementing a series of economy-oriented changes that also had an impact on the mechanics of printing. Manual practices in typography, in particular, were simplified so that less material would be used to produce a larger quantity of books, and black-letter, usually quite expensive and bulky, was increasingly more frequently replaced by roman and italics. Together with the purely typographic changes, the layout of texts also underwent a series of developments, which also contributed to reducing the costs of printing. In printed books, quotations gradually became distinguished, small capitals used, and rules were implemented between portions of text. In particular, printers formulated a variety of presentation solutions, which helped them to actively modify the visual and spatial structures of the text. In order to achieve justification, physical blanks of type were used as spaces in conjunction with word-initial and word-final spellings, replacing the ugly squeezed text of early books, which did not make a flexible use of spaces. When appropriate, extra space was also carved out by breaking words and inserting a hyphen. Some of the other objects of manipulation that favoured cheaper printing, over time, involved decorative borders and ornaments. Other examples include the use of boxed rules from the first few years of the seventeenth century, the implementation of leading between lines for text and, in general, the shift from the page seen as a solid block of text to a more dynamic set of typographic units.

The task of laying out the text was a speciality of typesetters, who would select the pieces of type and put them into a *forme* held together by a frame. The individual pieces of type would then be justified by using spaces of different sizes so that the lines of text would be fixed in the frame. When the *forme* was ready, it was laid on the bed of the press and inked, following a precise series of movements. A piece of wet paper was placed on top of the *forme*, and the metal plate – known as the *platen* – of the press would press the sheet firmly to print the page. Subsequent changes involved the insertion of a parchment frisket which covered the sides of the sheet in order to minimise unwanted ink dripping. *Formes* ended up becoming increasingly more spacious, and a counterweight gradually made an appearance as an essential appendix to facilitate raising the platen. Although there were clearly many changes which followed Gutenberg's first contribution to printing, the basic mechanism of printing remained the same for a long time. What is more, the business of printing did not interrupt the activity of handwriting; rather, handwriting became restricted to more specific areas, and even lived in its own way through printing. Early books imitated handwriting but also added a more rigid, authoritative structure, which had been missing in handwriting until then. Even as we get closer to our present times, handwriting still mimicked type, to such an extent that non-cursive handwriting was still referred to as 'printing', and the authoritative reputation of print became so widespread that the standard shape of roman characters has hardly changed at all over the last five centuries, all around the world. Having made reference to the geographical spread of printing, it seems relevant to also briefly mention ways in which printing uniformised or changed writing across languages.

During the modern age, from about 1500 onwards, continental vernaculars became increasingly more valued as literary languages and competed for a long time with Latin. The classical language of the Roman Empire was conveniently standardised, but it was used only in selected scholarly areas of publication. During the Renaissance in particular, Latin was widespread in the sciences, philosophy and theology, but the mass production of books afforded by the printing press encouraged authors and printers to also experiment with language so that their books could become more accessible to the wider population. Since the Roman alphabet had begun to be used for Latinate languages, however, the characters were almost automatically adapted to other languages, each in their own way. While Latin *c* originally indicated /k/, the other Latinate languages used /s/, for example in French *cinq*, 'five', or /tʃ/, for instance in Italian *cinque*, before the front vowels /e/ and /i/. Latin /kw/, instead, became /k/, reintroducing that sound before front vowels. In order to represent this sound, the letter *k* was used, especially in the Germanic languages, cf., for example, English words *key*, *kind* and *killer*. In the Latinate languages, this sound was represented by *qu*, cf., for instance, French and Spanish *qui*, 'who'. The Celtic languages ended up using a version of the Roman alphabet, and so did a few Slavic languages; the Baltic languages, Lithuanian and Latvian; the

Uralic languages, Finnish, Estonian and Hungarian; Maltese, Arabic, Basque and Albanian – all of which had sounds that Latin had never encountered before, cf., for example, Polish l-like sounds, later developed to /w/, spelled *ł*.

2.3.2   The Industrial Revolution

At the dawn of modernity, the demand for printing and, in turn, the need for paper material, grew exponentially. From the end of the eighteenth century, the mechanisation of the Industrial Revolution brought about a shift from an economy based on a relatively streamlined production of books to one focused on large industries and factory systems. In 1798, Nicholas-Louis Robert patented the first papermaking machine, which allowed him to produce paper as a continuous sheet rather than one sheet at a time. While the papermaking machine took a little time to take off in France, England began to manufacture it from 1807. In addition to paper making, the printing industry itself went through its own mechanisation revolution. Among the most remarkable individuals who contributed to the mechanisation of printing, Fredrich König of Germany is worthy of mention. König was responsible for adding mechanical inking and a steam power mechanism to the printing press, as well as for integrating the machine with a single cylinder appendix. The invention was capable of producing 1,100 sheets per hour and was used for the first time in order to print an 1814 issue of *The Times* in London. With this system, a full batch of daily newspapers could be produced overnight. During the following decades, stereotype rotary presses were introduced: these machines wrapped a cast (the stereotype) of the type around a cylinder and rolled the cylinder across the paper, instead of the other way around. The greatest advantage of the rotary press was the ability to print two sides of the paper at once; by 1863, the new press had further developed to produce both sides of 10,000 sheets of paper in an hour.

Over time, the paper production industry became increasingly more efficient: a machine to grind the wood was patented in the 1840s and, although the resulting paper was of poor quality, the 1870s saw the invention of the chemical process. This new system enabled paper producers to separate the fibrous material from the rest of the wood and produce a better quality of paper. In the meantime, printers had carried on with their quest to find a more suitable type of paper: among the solutions advanced was that of straw paper and even, in one or two eventful occasions, of paper extracted from the wrapping material used for Egyptian mummies. While paper was an object of continuous development and invention, an issue that remained unsolved for a little longer was that of typesetting. By the nineteenth century, using individual pieces of type for composing individual *formes* was becoming a rather clumsy and slow process. It was not until the late nineteenth century that the Linotype and the Monotype machines allowed typesetters to compose texts simply by pressing keys rather than by picking up and laying out single pieces of type. By means of the keys, typesetters had control of the selection of type matrices, and type was cast from the matrices by the line or the complete galley form as it was needed. With this system, composing a text became a lot quicker, not only because laying out type was not necessary anymore, but also because there was no more need to pull type away from the *forme* and place it back on the case that once stored used type. By the middle of the twentieth century, phototypesetting, which later on evolved into digital type, had freed the printing industry from the need to cast any metal type at all. Before metal type disappeared from the scene, though, it became the main component of typewriters.

The typewriting technology goes back a long way in history, and the Industrial Revolution only made this technology a great deal faster and more efficient. The very earliest document written with a rudimentary 'type' system is the Phaistos Disk, a small piece of clay stored in the archaeological museum in Heraklion, Crete. The disk is thought to have been from between 1550 and 1200 BC, and represents an incredibly useful piece of technological evidence. The text is written in 242 individual forms pressed onto the clay using forty-six individual punches – one for each of the forty-six individual characters used. Since the Cretans who lived between 1550 and 1200 BC used Linear A and B, it is possible that the Phaistos Disk was introduced from some other unknown place. Unlike most Linear B tablets, where there is clear evidence of different individual scribes' input, instruments where pieces of type are used, regardless of how rudimentary they might be, may not always provide any straightforward evidence to argue whether one or more individuals were responsible for the typing job. Going back to modern technology, the semi-automatic typewriting machine was patented in 1714 by Henry Mill in England, but it remains unclear whether he actually ended up building a machine. During the nineteenth century, a significant number of attempts were made to create a typewriting machine, and a more tangible achievement was made in 1873 by Christopher Latham Sholes at the factory of E. Remington and Sons. In order to make typewriters, which became popular for private use, type was placed at the ends of metal bars and pulled for printing using levers – in turn linked to individual keys. With typewriting, type was used for writing each individual copy – hence the term *type writing* and not *type printing*.

The machine enabled the typesetter to gain full command of each individual piece of type, while at the same time speeding up the composition process by allowing the compositor to just press the keys (although, admittedly, this initially required quite a bit of physical energy). Towards the end of the nineteenth century, then, touch-typing typewriters, which allowed one to use all ten fingers, first made their appearance (see Figure 2.3). Since typists became quick enough to keep pace with measured dictation, and given that the resulting copy did not need to be recopied for legibility, the new method of composing text inevitably became very popular, even among notable authors. Mark Twain was one of the very first who gave permission for his book (*Life on*

Figure 2.3 Antique illustration of a touch-typing typewriter (Source: Nastasic/Contributor/Getty Images)

the Mississippi) to be typed using the new method in 1874. While he did not go through the typing himself, a secretary of his took care of the business for him. Unlike Mark Twain, other authors got involved directly in typing and bought their own typewriter; nevertheless, typing remained a job exclusive to professionals for a long time. Interestingly, typewriting was seen as something like an art or a handicraft job suited for more artistic individuals, and quite a few of the early typists were women. Female workers generally received a lower wage than men, and the typewriters that they used saved a lot of work. All of the variables above probably contributed, as a whole, to making the industrial changes a revolution indeed – an unstoppable rise of economic prosperity and labour efficiency. As an inevitable result of the advances made in the technology of writing, typing made bureaucracy, administration and commerce run more smoothly.

With the advent of colonialism and an increasingly globalised world, those countries which used scripts that fit into a typewriter keyboard without any issues inevitably had an advantage in the international communicative scenario. Documents printed or copied using a typewriter were cheaper and took about half the time needed for handwriting. Writing longhand was not advantageous to anyone, not to those using Chinese characters nor to those using the Roman alphabet in Western European countries. Likewise, the movable type did not make many distinctions across languages: characters needed a much larger font than the typewriter, and they took up a lot of space for all the sorts. Both the movable type and the typewriter, therefore, were tailored to work using only an alphabetic script. While this problem alone was sufficient to cast a shadow on these technologies, there was another reason why the typewriter in particular was not destined to live for long. The text produced using typewriters was obnoxiously squared and unpleasant to the eye. Every character had to fit into exactly the same allotted space, which means that the letters *m* and *w*, for example, appeared as small and difficult to read, while the letters *i* and *l* appeared as elongated and distended. The relationship between each character and the word and sentence context in which it was placed was never taken into account, nor were any letters allowed to overlap, for example in *fi*. Needless to say, including characters that were not present on the keyboard was not even imaginable, so typewriters were obliged to make the most of what they had available. It was only in the twentieth century that real changes were made to the traditional typewriting system explained above.

2.3.3   The Digital Revolution

The expression *word processing* was coined by IBM in 1964 in relation to a typewriter which stored the typed text on magnetic tape and gave users a margin for editing. Since then, twentieth-century technology has made huge progress: the advent of word processing inevitably introduced a shift from writing as a product of physical endeavour, as in handwriting (or mechanically manufactured, as in typing), to an electronic record that had little in common with the physical boundaries of our everyday world. In computer machines, the writer's action of typing becomes an electronic signal, which is in turn converted to an electronic code. The code underlying writing becomes the language in which the computer stores writing, and it is in this code that a text is sent for printing; concurrently, code is also often displayed on screen and reconverted to writing for the reader to understand. This very book underwent the steps outlined above at draft stage, i.e. while it was being written. This digital writing is very much a dynamic entity: an author can scroll up and down it to make new writing appear before their eyes; a chunk of text can also be wiped out or modified a lot more easily than it could using other means.

Overall, the digital revolution has brought with it an approach to writing that is very different from that of the past. For one thing, the ephemerality of writing has diminished its authority, and books themselves do not have the same value that they did in ancient times. Secondly, the digital world has fostered a renewed taste for fonts and scripts, one that had almost completely disappeared with the typewriter. The Roman alphabet can now be spread out on the sheet while at the same time benefiting from proportional spacing and visual balance. The Greek, Cyrillic, Arabic and Hebrew alphabets, as well as mathematical symbols, are all almost automatically available to the author who uses a computer to write. Chinese, Japanese and Korean, for example, are known by default in our everyday computers and smartphones. Unsurprisingly, more and more systems are now adopting the Unicode standards – which means that any script can now virtually be used to communicate. Despite the infinite number of fonts and font sizes available, the ability to modify the text in real time, and all the other formatting options, however, digital writing still has its own limitations.

The screen often becomes a barrier for a lot of writers, and both writing and reading on screen can become a challenge for concentration more so than paper, while proofreading is still a lot easier on a sheet than on screen. Without a doubt, there is more to our way of thinking than a digital language translated on screen, and being able to have a tangible experience of our writing has its own value. Surely enough, the use of emails, text messages, web chats and tweets allows us to write and deliver our messages with virtually no delay between sender and receiver. This might give us the illusion that we are engaging in real-life conversation, but there are in fact layers of detail that we inevitably miss out in digital written communication. In order to convey some of the layers of detail that are clearly missing in the digital world, our everyday communication is rife with the inventive uses of fonts, standardised logograms commonly called *emojis* and GIFs containing moving images. Typed text carries, ever more frequently, nuances that were once typical only of speech and handwriting, and some of the ways it does this are incredibly clumsy, while others are admittedly genial. Whether these changes will enrich or impoverish our overall history of writing only time will tell.

Further Reading

Christin, A.-M. (ed.). 2002. *A History of Writing: From Hieroglyph to Multimedia.* Paris: Flammarion.

Goody, J. 1986. *The Logic of Writing and the Organization of Society.* Cambridge: Cambridge University Press.

Powell, B. B. 2009. *Writing: Theory and History of the Technology of Civilization.* Oxford: Blackwell.

Robinson, A. 1999. *The Story of Writing*, 2nd edn. London: Thames & Hudson.

Saggs, H. 1989. *Civilization Before Greece and Rome.* New Haven: Yale University Press.

3 Witnesses to Historical Writing

3.1 Early Writing Material

3.1.1 Early Perishables, Stone and Metal

There is no certainty about what materials were used at the beginning of the history of writing. Durable material like stone or metal is what one generally thinks about with reference to early writing. Without a doubt, these examples of early material were among the first witnesses of writing, but the fact that stone and metal are what remains to the present does not necessarily entail that they were the only things that were being used at the time. In order to better inform us about early writing materials, archaeological evidence provides a very useful source of information, most frequently by indirect indications. From indirect evidence, such as cave paintings and other finds, it seems that perishable, relatively softer materials than stone and metal were indeed also used in early writing. The reason was simple: the first forms of writing entailed incising a flat surface with a rigid tool rather than using pigment with a secondary object, one of the pieces of evidence being that of Chinese *jiaguwen* carved into turtle shells. Among the more perishable examples, animal hides were probably also used a great deal for writing or drawing (as further discussed later on in this chapter), even though these may sometimes have had only a decorative or identificatory purpose.

Roughly made pottery shards were also among the first few examples of cheap material, the most notable of which are the *ostraka* used in Greece for banning individuals – mostly politicians – from the city by a democratic vote. Cloth probably had a similar purpose, if it was of a type suited for writing. The outermost layers of stems and roots of woody plants, for example birch bark, were also likely used as early writing material, where birch trees were available, for example in northern Europe and in North America. Writing tablets, especially clay or wax-covered wooden tablets, were instead among the first examples of relatively more perishable materials. They came in rigid flat surfaces used especially for writing. Clay may have been one of the most useful perishable materials for early writing, because it was gradually perfected to become almost as durable as stone, and unglazed pots of clay are very easy to write on. Several other civilisations, for example that of Mycenaean Greece, also used clay as a primary material for early writing, but the clay was not normally cooked; the majority of what we have for the Linear B from Minoan Crete, however, ended up being baked later on by accidental fires. Wax may also have been quite a popular element for early writing, because it has a reusable surface, easily inscribed and erased, and could be supported by wood to make it more long-lasting. While there was undoubtedly a wide range of materials available for early writing, including perishable ones, one cannot ignore the fact that stone and metal were indeed among the most frequently used materials, simply because they were widely available in nature and hardly required any type of processing.

The history of stone and metal as materials used for writing is probably as old as writing itself. Examples of metals are stamped coins, like those surviving from the Romans, and they are usually made of lead, brass and, more rarely, silver and gold. The fact that metal was needed for utensils may have had an influence on how much of it was used as a basis for writing and drawing, in proportion to stone. Quite often, metals were also quite hard and difficult to impress any writing on, but foils or sheets of soft metals like lead were indeed useful and fairly easy to make. Lead sheets were used relatively often for curse tablets, and also for personal communication. Stone, on the other hand, was used for law, death notes, graffiti, poetry, decrees and injunctions, commerce, calendars, and even religion. A general term for stone is used here on purpose because a wide variety of stones was used for writing: the softest and crumbliest ones were used for engraving, while the hardest and sturdiest types of stone were usually painted on. A famous example of stone of the latter type was that of the caves of Lascaux, which hosts prehistoric paintings of animals and humans. In Roman culture, stone was used for inscriptions which were supposed to last for eternity, for example in milestones and monument descriptions.

Among the first examples of portable stone tokens, we have the tables of the Chaldeans, a population from between the late tenth to the mid sixth centuries BC, later annexed to Babylonia. Their tablets look like some rather small shapes of clay, moulded quite roughly into the form of a pillow, and heavily marked with cuneiform characters. Hollow cylinders, or prisms of six or eight sides, formed of fine terracotta, were also occasionally used for writing. The marks were made using a small stylus, which in some examples must have been so tiny that one can read the message printed on the terracotta only by using some magnifying glass. At this early stage in writing history, styli consisted in sticks which were formed in a way that they could press wedge-shaped characters into soft wax or clay tablets. Styli were originally used by the Sumerians several thousand years ago, alongside the wedges that they pressed in order to create cuneiform. The wedge shapes were organised by size, distance and design; the combination of these three parameters allowed for the formation of the first alphabet and system for writing.[1] In Ancient Egypt, the first examples of writing materials are the stone walls of the tombs on which the famous images were drawn. In early Egyptian writing, lime, cement or gypsum were also frequently used along with stone: a common example is that of the Egyptian engravers, who would first of all smooth the stone, and then fill up any cracks in it with gypsum or cement so that the surface of the stone would be most suited for engraving. In order to paint on the stone, brush-pens were frequently used by the Egyptians. As mentioned in the previous chapter, however, hieroglyphs gradually changed to become easier to write and read, while also being adapted to new writing materials. The use of stone was quite time-consuming because it could take days for engravers to smooth out the material well enough for it to be painted on. Soon, a clearer form of writing was needed, and with it, more convenient objects to use as surfaces for writing. The following section focuses on the gradual shift to papyrus, parchment and vellum.

3.1.2   Papyrus, Parchment and Vellum

In western civilisations, papyrus was the material which was commonly used from about 3000 BC. Papyrus is a fibrous material made from the pith of the papyrus plant and, in ancient times, it grew mainly in Lower Egypt. With the introduction of papyrus, brush-writing replaced styli and wedge shapes in most forms of writing. Brush-writing worked by dipping brushes in inks made from water and natural dyes from fire soot. Brush writers were essentially the first ancient pens, and they afforded a different approach to writing – one based on a less forceful relationship between writing instruments and materials. Papyrus leaves, the turning-point ingredient for a more gentle approach to writing, came directly from the papyrus water plant which was found in large quantities in the muddy borders of the River Nile. The papyrus-derived material was extracted from the plant as follows. The stalks of the plant were cut just above the root and the pith was taken out. The sections that were closest to the root were also thrown away because the middle sections were the widest and most refined for producing large papyrus sheets. The remaining stalks were split into thin pieces of about two feet in length using a pointed tool. Subsequently, a number of tissue-thin strips were laid upon a board, one next to the other, forming a tight, slightly overlapping series of fibre strips, which was then bound together using

---

[1] Another early example of Egyptian writing materials was tally sticks, made of wood and bone; much like those used by the Incas, these were used for counting the passage of days, among other things. These materials did not require a lot of work to be used for drawing but did not, of course, have as central a role as stone did for hieroglyphs.

a thin paste of wheat flour, vinegar and muddy water from the Egyptian river. To this base, then, an additional layer of strips was added, making right angles, forming a criss-crossed sheet of papyrus. An example of the way in which papyrus fibre was bound to form a sheet is visible in the fragment shown in Figure 3.1; as shown in this example, the characteristic fibre net remained the same even among the latest specimens of papyrus created at the twilight of the Egyptian era. The fragment of papyrus depicted here is from *c.* AD 600 and was written in Coptic, a language descended from Ancient Egyptian and historically spoken by the Copts of Egypt.

To return to the production process of the papyrus, thus, the sheet was eventually left to dry under a weight of stone or metal and the surface finally smoothed out with a stone or shell. The increasing availability of papyrus in Egypt appears to have facilitated the spread of writing. The earliest evidence of the use of papyrus in Egypt comes from the Theban dynasties, known as the Old Kingdom and spanning the years *c.* 2686–2181 BC. In Egypt itself, and in the wider Mediterranean region from the second century BC, however, papyrus eventually became less popular and gave way to parchment as a primary writing material for writing. Parchment was made from specially prepared untanned skins of animals, mainly sheep, calves and goats. Named after the ancient city of Pergamum in Asia Minor, this innovative writing medium basically antedated true paper. Even though it was believed to have been in use

Figure 3.1 Papyrus fragment of a letter, Coptic, *c.* 600 AD (Source: Heritage Images/Contributor/Getty Images)

as early as 1500 BC, it was the King of Pergamum (197–159 BC) who was likely responsible for its invention. Parchment had become a more convenient material because the papyrus, which had been very popular up to the second century BC, had increased in prestige, also because it had ended up being imported from outside of Egypt. Another disadvantage of ancient papyrus was that it could not be folded up easily without risking causing some cracking in the document – all of which was quite unfortunate, given that papyrus was often used as a roll or a scroll.

Among the reasons why parchment was a more convenient material for writing than papyrus was also the fact that making parchment was a lot simpler than making papyrus. Parchment was traditionally made from the split-skin of the sheep: the wool-side of the skin was turned into skiver, which was a soft but strong piece of leather frequently used in bookbinding; the flesh-side of the animal skin, instead, usually became the parchment. The skins needed to be washed, cleaned and scraped to be made suitable for writing. These steps were carried out as follows. As an absolute first step, the skins would usually be put into vats of caustic lime and water, and they would remain there to soak for a few days until the animal hair had become tender enough to be able to be stripped from the skins. At that point, the damp skins would be stretched tightly, using some leather thongs, and they were left to dry over a large wooden frame. Then, those who worked on the skins would begin scraping away the hair using a long, curved, wooden-handled knife. This scraping would happen while the skin was still on the frame and would end only when the parchment-maker was happy with the quality of the skin surface as a basis for future writing. The skin was left to dry on the frame, and during this time, the material inevitably shrank and became thinner. When reasonably dry, the skin was scraped and shaved again, and when completely dry, it was smoothed out using some fine pumice. At this stage, the hair side of the skin was covered with powdered chalk, so that the surface would become white enough for writing. During the first few decades that it was being produced, parchment was quite thick, but by the thirteenth century AD, it was incredibly soft and thin, and it could be folded up easily. Perfected by the long process described above, parchment was, and still remains today, one of the strongest writing materials. If stored properly, parchment can last for hundreds or even thousands of years.

While parchment eventually supplanted stone and metal in many of their writing-related functions, stone and metal were still used for gravestones, commemoration of the dead and for printing on coins, so the change from one material to another should never be intended as linear but rather as overlapping and mutating in function. Undoubtedly, however, it is possible to trace a process of development from stone and metal to parchment and vellum, and this change happened rather markedly. A testimony of the extent to which different materials were in turn used for writing is to be found in the evolution of writing instruments within the lifespan of the Roman Empire. At the beginning of the Roman Empire, the alphabet was all in capitals and all the letters were very angular: the letter *u*, for example, appeared as a *v*. The reason for the characteristic angularity of the Romans' early writing was a combination of writing instruments and materials: usually, they engraved in stone slabs, using hammers and chisels. Using a chisel and a hammer ensured that the writing would be clearer than, for example, it would have been using styli or wedge shapes; however, it still required a lot of energy, and it had an impact on the number of things that could be written feasibly in stone. Eventually, the Romans turned to scrolls of papyrus, and a new kind of pen, the reed, which was much easier to handle than anything ever seen before. In order to be able to use the reed for writing, a number of practical steps were followed. First of all, one would take a sharp knife and make a diagonal cut on the tip of the reed until a triangular point was obtained. As a second step, a slit was inserted in the middle of the point using the knife, and then the reed was dipped into the ink for writing. While the reed was a great deal more convenient to use than previous writing instruments, it needed continuous resharpening following the technique explained above. The first cut was not a permanent solution for writing: frequently, ink softened the reed with time, which meant that a new pen-point had to be cut with the knife.

An attentive reader will have realised by now that a quick mention of vellum was given in the previous paragraph, but without a definition. The reason for this rests on the fact that the differences between parchment and vellum are a matter of some controversy, which needs to be spelled out carefully in a whole new paragraph. Some suggest that the skins used for producing parchment were not only those of sheep but also those of calves and lambs. Others argue that the skin of any small animal, regardless of its age, could essentially be used to make parchment. For yet others, instead, only the skin of young animals, especially calves, was employed for making vellum, while skins from any other animal were used for making parchment. While all of these definitions may have been relevant from a historical perspective, the terms *parchment* and *vellum* are used today, rather confusingly, to refer interchangeably to the skin of an animal that has been processed for use in writing, printing or binding. Neither parchment nor vellum can be considered true leather, because they are not tanned. There are some differences, however, between parchment and vellum, which can be identified in the way each of the two are processed as well as their intrinsic peculiarities. In general, vellum is produced using the whole skin of the animal; the skin is not broken into two layers as with parchment. Another difference between vellum and parchment consists in the fact that the former has hair marks on the surface, which are responsible for giving it a slightly more irregular surface. Parchment usually has a smoother texture, due to the fact that it is scraped more carefully. Overall, the fact that parchment and vellum were treated with lime makes them both typologically closer to paper than leather, in the way they look and feel.

The description of the basic writing materials given so far provides an informed enough background for an overview of the remaining developments in the writing instruments. From the time in which papyrus gave way to parchment, vellum and eventually paper as a main writing material, the quill was used as the principal writing tool for a few hundred years. The quill was essentially a feather stolen from a large bird, usually a goose; it is interesting to note that the Middle English word *pen* ultimately derives from *penna*, which was Latin for *feather*. Once again, quills were not a writing instrument that could be used 'raw', but rather they required quite a lot of preparation in order to make them suitable for writing. As a first step, the feather would need to be washed and dried. With the help of a knife, the quill would be freed from all the barbs, which are the fluffy parts on the sides of the feather. After the feather was cleaned appropriately, it would usually be buried in sand and then put over a fire. The mixture of heat and sand would make the pen even more rigid and resistant. At this point, the pen would be taken out of the fire, cleaned again fully, and a cut made into the tip in a way that was reminiscent of the reed. The end result of this process was a relatively longer, stronger pen than the reed; a featherless pen was always used and not one with the feathers on, as this would be very inconvenient for writing. Depending on where the cut was made, the tip of the pen could be used for different styles of writing. This flexibility allowed for the German blackletter style to appear in handwriting during the Middle Ages. By making a specific cut on the quill point, the writer would be able to draw wide up–down, and thin horizontal strokes. Some of the most famous historical documents in history, like the Bible, the American Declaration of Independence and Dante Alighieri's *Divine Comedy*, were all written using quills. Together with quills, pen knives were also very popular because they were essential to sharpen the quill point. With some good pen-points sharpening skills, and a little play with ink, some of the more inventive writers came up with new, attractive ways of writing using quills. The elaborate, round, thick–thin styles of handwriting that appeared during the seventeenth and the eighteenth centuries, for instance roundhand, Copperplate and Spencerian, were all the product of experimentation with quills.

By the end of the eighteenth century, a major change had happened in the evolution of writing instruments: the new idea was based on the intuition that pen-points could be made of something tougher, stronger, and that therefore they could last longer. The solution for a more enduring pen-point was based on the use of metal rather than tips of feathers: thanks to the newly invented steam-powered presses, special moulds and sheets of metal, metal pens could be produced easily. By the 1830s, steel-point pens were finally mass-produced and began to be sold in little boxes at stationers' shops. The new pens were easy to make, cheap, hard to break and quick to produce – they were a real revolution for the world of writing. All that was needed in order to write at this point was a box of pens and a pen-holder, which was the shaft that the metal points fitted into. All of this became affordable for an increasingly large number of young school pupils, who used these pens up to the 1930s. Entire book series like the *Sherlock Holmes* stories were written using steel pens, and so were Mark Twain's and Jules Verne's works. The fact that steel pens freed authors from all the mundane worries related to sharpening quills and pens meant that they could become more productive and focus entirely on their writing ideas. While the metal pen was a great deal easier to work with, however, the tool was not entirely problem-free.

As for all writing instruments that had been used up to that point, steel pens were 'dip-pens'; in other words, authors had to remain seated at their desk in order to regularly dip the tip of their pen in an inkwell or a bottle of ink so that their instrument would not run out. Up to this point, there was no way of writing in a way that was not dependent on an inkwell. The steel pen, that is, was a non-portable instrument. The idea of a pen that had its own stock of ink in its own structure had by then become an old one, but early fountain pens had been a failing invention because they were frustrating and unreliable. Early fountain pens went from writing beautifully in one moment to leaking out or writing haltingly one second later. In the 1880s, however, Lewis Edson Waterman, an insurance-broker and inventor from New York, changed forever the history of writing instruments. Waterman's discovery was crucial: air-pressure was a key ingredient in making a reliable portable pen. Without the aid of air-pressure, fountain pens were destined to leak or to stop working all of a sudden, drying out like a well in the desert. Striking a good balance of air-pressure was not easy, because the ink could gush out like a fire-hose as a result of the slightest mistake. By implementing a 'feed', namely a thin, hard-rubber rod with little slits cut into it, Waterman realised that there was a way to regulate the flow of ink using air-pressure if the feed was put right underneath the nib of the fountain pen. Thus, ink flew down two of the channels cut in the feed, and air found its way up the third channel into the ink-reservoir; this system enabled the pen to work with a balanced internal air-pressure so that ink could flow easily.

The ballpoint pen was the last major step in the development of writing instruments, one that lasted up to the present day. The ballpoint pen proved to be most durable, more convenient and adaptable to surfaces like wood, cardboard and even under water. At the end of the nineteenth century, when it was invented, the ballpoint pen effectively ended the ink writing era. American inventor John H. Loud was the first to patent the idea of a ballpoint pen, but the instrument was perfected only in the 1930s by Laszlo

Biro, a Hungarian journalist who ended up living in Argentina during the Second World War. Biro used quick-drying ink combined with a small metal ball that rotated and prevented the ink from drying out completely. In 1943, Laszlo and his brother Georg made the ballpen models more popular, but they still acknowledged the original inventor by calling the new instrument the *Biro* pen. Even today, the Biro pen remains a hallmark writing tool, as it continues to be used by many different people, from school pupils to state presidents. In our present-day society, styli are still used in computers and other digital devices, but these obviously work by applying pressure which in turn changes to digital information rather than by using ink. Words and names are still engraved into objects, for example metal plates attached to memorials, but the tools used for engraving are no longer considered actual writing instruments, and paper is still the predominant writing material despite the advent of digitisation. This last reference to paper encourages us to take a quick step back in the history of writing materials in order to focus more extensively on the two most predominant witnesses of historical writing: these are indeed paper on the one hand, and typographic types on the other hand.

3.2   The Age of Paper

3.2.1   Development of Papermaking

Paper in its broadest meaning, intended as indicating any type of cellulose fibre material, is a primary resource for those working in historical orthography, as it provides layers of information that contextualise our linguistic analyses of orthography. In order to understand what type of information one can glean from paper, let us look into the story of papermaking from the beginning. The invention of paper is attributed to Cai Lun of China, who, in AD 105, announced to Emperor Hàn Hé Dì that his work on fibre material to make paper had borne its fruit. From the eighth century, the Chinese technique for making paper became known to the Islamic world. Before the invention of paper, animal bones, silk, bamboo and wooden slips had been commonly used in China as ancestors of paper. By the tenth century AD, the use of paper had also begun in India, but the traditional birch bark and palm leaf still remained in use alongside paper for more specialised texts like horoscopes, wedding invitations and other cultural uses. The first evidence of paper use in the Indian subcontinent comes from the seventh century AD, particularly in Chinese Buddhist pilgrim memoirs and in the writings of some Indian Buddhists, like Kakali and Śaya. The paper-making technique probably made its way to India from China through Tibet and Nepal, thanks to the Buddhist monks who commuted between Tibet and the Buddhist centers in India. In Europe, the production of paper was not officially established until after a battle in AD 751, when a few Chinese papermakers introduced paper manufacturing in Central Asia. The oldest known paper document from Europe is the Mozarab Missal of Silos, which dates back to the eleventh century AD. The document was made using hemp and linen rags as a source of fibre and may have originated from the Islamic area of the Iberian Peninsula.

By the eleventh century AD, papermaking was established officially in Europe and by the thirteenth century, the technique was perfected in Spain using paper mills with waterwheels. In particular, a paper production centre was recorded in Toledo as early as 1085 and in Xàtiva by 1150. A paper mill was established in France by 1190, and by 1340, there were paper mills in a few northern Italian towns. Paper mills were also present in Holland in c. 1340–1350, in Mainz, Germany, in 1320, and in Nuremberg by 1390; then in Switzerland by 1432, in England by c. 1490, in Poland by 1491, in Russia by 1576 and in Sweden by 1612. Arab prisoners who ended up living in Borgo Saraceno in the Italian province of Ferrara taught a number of workers from Fabriano, Italy, how to make paper manually. Fabriano artisans saw the technique of making paper manually as a prestigious art and managed to improve their skills so much as to be able to supplant the parchment market, which had been most popular before then. The Fabriano artisans implemented stamping hammers in their workflow in order to make better-quality pulp and sized paper using animal glue. While the invention of movable-type printing in Europe had boosted the production of paper, the discovery of America and the European colonisation that followed it brought the European papermaking technique to the other side of the ocean. Until then, the natives had been using mainly a type of bark paper known as *amate* paper. When the North American indigenous people decided to fight back the invaders, they boycotted all British importations, except for paper.

From the late fourteenth century in Europe, papermaking was a fairly slow process which consisted in working on one or two sheets at a time using wire moulds. A testimony of the existence of different moulds may be found in the sheets of paper, and especially the chain-lines watermarks. In the early stages of mechanic paper production, few sizes and grades of paper existed. In general, the fibrous material gives information about the origins and creation of sheets and books, mainly in two different ways. First of all, the mould trays used to make paper had to be repaired or replaced, and this very process of replacement gives a relatively linear chronology of paper. Because of their frequent use, the trays were changed quite often, and very similar but not identical trays were usually fabricated manually as a replacement. Secondly, manufacture-related elements like the chain-lines, wires and watermarks that left their images in the sheet are also informative not only of chronology, but also of the identity of the papermaker. A watermark encoded the place of origin, the mill that made the paper, on what tray it was made in and when it was made. Watermarking consisted in using metal wires to add a thread in the sheet of paper, which would become visible through backlight; this system was initially pioneered by the Fabriano artisans and later adopted by the most prestigious papermakers in Europe, and it allowed hallmarks, signatures, ecclesiastical emblems and other symbols to be displayed as markers of identity.

With the Industrial Revolution, and especially in the nineteenth century, papermaking saw a boost owing to the proliferation of daily newspapers and novels, which required a large quantity of cheap paper. By the end of the eighteenth century, the first Fourdrinier machine had been invented, which allowed for the production of a 60 cm-long sheet. As demand for paper had increased, alternative papermaking solutions to the traditional way (which consisted in recycled fibres from used textiles, made from hemp, linen and cotton) were explored, including the use of wood pulp. By the 1870s, as mentioned in Chapter 2, a machine was invented which extracted fibres from wood for the purpose of making cheaper paper. The wood pulp would some-times also be coloured white to resemble higher-quality paper. The changes brought about by the Industrial Revolution facilitated the manufacture of a lot of cheap paper from wood. At the close of the nineteenth century, the majority of printers in the western world were using wood as a source material for paper.

With the new technological inventions, the cost of paper finally reached a new low, which in turn allowed for paper to become more popular than it had ever been. In England, 96,000 tonnes of paper were manufactured in 1861 and 648,000 tonnes in 1900. The never-seen-before boost in paper production inevitably encouraged an explosion of literacy, especially among the working classes, as more people were able to buy books for self-instruction. At the beginning of the twentieth century, then, paper was so cheap that it could be used for purposes other than writing, as was the case for toilet and wrapping paper, as well as the paper used for toys and interior decoration. The last milestone in paper production was that from mechanical to chemical to thermo-mechanical pulping, all of which occurred between the late nineteenth and the mid twentieth centuries. Mechanical pulping was unable to remove the lignin, the organic polymers in the cell walls of the plant which are the cause of acid hydrolysis. When mechanically pulped paper was exposed to light, heat or moisture would cause it to quickly turn yellow. With chemical and thermo-mechanical pulping, these issues were largely solved, and paper achieved some of the highest standards known in the modern era.

3.2.2   Details about Paper

Paper and its format are an important part of the way in which a text conveys its message: today, the quality of paper is an immediate indicator, together with writing itself, of the prestige of the text written or printed on it. One can usually tell easily whether a type of paper is destined for a newspaper, a prestigious book or as a tissue. There are also many different types of paper: white and brown, laid and wove; there are also various ingredients used in the making, sizes, coatings, thicknesses, weights, shades and many degrees to which paper can absorb ink. Individual sheets of paper also have their own smell, texture and optical brightness, and all of these variables have an influence on the costs of paper. All of the parameters outlined above were also important in the past and played a key role in determining not only how writing should look like but also how much writing should appear on paper. The balance between the brightness of paper and the quality and format of typefaces, for example, and which characters formed a given alphabet, were all important to guarantee good legibility, and prices depended on such a balance. For example, small type printed on duodecimo-sized paper, which is the smallest page size ever made following the Renaissance, was very cheap because it was basically blindness-inducing. The quality of paper was also given by the selection of rags used for papermaking – pure white linens were the most prestigious, while poorer qualities of paper included coloured linens, for example canvas, old rope and even paper made with a percentage of woollens. When wood-pulp paper was invented, the average prestige standards of paper lowered, and the cost of paper began, as mentioned earlier on, a steady decline, but rag paper still stayed at the highest levels of the quality pyramid.

The weight of paper did not really depend on quality, but rather on how much water was diluted in the fibre needed to make the paper; the price of paper, however, normally depended on its weight. Unlike weight, paper sizes were a matter of change and variation over time – the English vocabulary, for example, has about 300 different historical names to indicate paper sizes, but the most common groups of sizes in use at any given time were no more than six or seven. Some examples in use during the early stage of printing were a size called *forma regalis*, which measured *c.* 70 × 50 cm, and *forma mediana*, which measured *c.* 50 × 30 cm. All of the dimensions used in historical paper are approximate, because mould sizes varied slightly. For some historical periods, complexity in paper size was considerably reduced: the sixteenth century, for instance, saw the predominance of the *foolscap* folio size, which was considered the ordinary size, and in the eighteenth century it was the *demy range*. Certain sizes of paper, then, also existed in printing and handwriting varieties, especially from the eighteenth century onwards. Printing sizes were usually larger and of poorer quality than the sizes used for handwriting.

All of the parameters above, and more, are particularly useful for establishing the 'identity' of a sheet of paper, namely its history and who was responsible for producing it. A sheet of manually produced paper can be identified by means of its quality, its weight, its size (which includes length and breadth) and

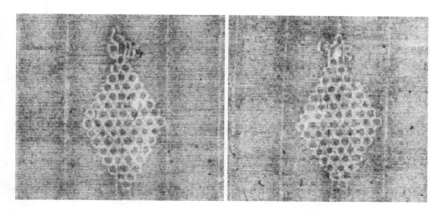

Figure 3.2 Grape watermarks, *c.* 1633–4. Bodleian Library, Oxford,
Rawlinson Poetry MS 31, ff. 8 and 11

its watermark (see Figure 3.2). The quality and weight of historical paper are
not easy to measure, as they are usually simply compared against the average
standards for any given period of time and provenance of the paper. In addition,
one can take a number of micrometre readings of the thickness of individual
sheets, while remaining aware that this can vary within an individual batch of
sheets or even at different parts of a given sheet. An alternative is to measure
the thickness of the full book, but this approach is also not problem-free: the
results can vary according to whether a book has been pressed down by
a weight and also by the temperature, humidity and altitude of the place
where the measurement is taken.

With regard to size, a useful approach is that of classifying paper according
to how sheets were folded in order to make books. Depending on the folding,
different terms are used; once again, only selective examples can be given here,
and the most immediate and simplest ones are those from early print. At the
dawn of the modern era, large books were made of broadsheets, namely sheets
of paper which were not folded at all, while a handbill or a flyer might be in the
form of a half-sheet or a quarter-sheet. For sheets folded once across the longer
side, which gives four pages to the sheet, the usual term was *folio* (abbreviated
2°); when a second fold is made across the first, which gives eight sheets, the
usual term was *quarto* (4°); when a third fold is added to the second, which
makes sixteenth sheets, this was called an *octavo* (8°); when the sheet is folded
twice across the longer dimension and three times across the shorter, which
gives twenty-four pages, this was called a *duodecimo* (12°). While more
complex foldings also exist in historical books, from 16° up to 120°, these
are of course much rarer than the main foldings given above. To return to the

difficulties of measuring paper, there are no two handmade sheets of paper of the 'same' size that will actually look the same, as sheets were often made in small batches. Even if more sheets were made at any one time, a whole book frequently needed paper from a number of different moulds or even from different mills. When analysing a copy of an old book, therefore, one cannot make a description of the book as a whole, unless the full lot of individual sheets is analysed individually and then comparatively. In most cases, the most feasible approach is to analyse a small sample of the paper used for impressing a given book, and the larger the sheet sample under scrutiny, the closer one might get to the whole book.

The length and breadth of the sheet of paper are usually measured from an uncut copy of the book, and then the results are multiplied by the factors appropriate to the folding. If there are no uncut copies, the approximate dimensions of the paper can be obtained as follows: add 0.5–1.0 cm each way to the length and breadth of the leaf of a small book, and 1.0–2.0 cm each way to the leaf of a large book, before multiplying the required factors. With regard to watermarks, these are normally simply named or described, preferably with reference to one of the main collections of watermark patterns like Briquet and Heawood. The watermark's dimensions are given, together with an indication of its link with the chain-lines of the mould. Sometimes, it is useful to provide a photograph or a beta radiograph of the watermark like that of Figure 3.2, as that can help with comparisons with other sheets in order to identify the place of origin, the mill that made the paper, on what tray it was made and when it was made. Given that, as mentioned earlier on, mould trays changed regularly, subtle changes in the watermarks and chain-lines represent useful hints which can be measured, photographed and recorded.

3.3   The Age of Modern Technology

3.3.1   Development of Typographic Style

Much as for paper, the development of typography provides interesting infor-mation for contextualising empirical work in orthography. Of all the elements that characterise typography, type is most relevant: the metal worked as a surface where letter shapes were made to appear, and it was inked and pressed on paper for the letter to be printed. A relatively large number of old types still survive to the present day, which means that we have a lot of primary evidence; however, even through indirect evidence – paper – it is still possible to glean quite a lot about historical writing systems. One of the most memorable features of types, even for those less familiar with the history of the book, is that of typefaces, the design of the letters of the alphabet used for printing, sometimes also commonly known as fonts or styles. There is no generally widespread way of arranging individual letter forms found in a type, and the forms can fall across multiple categories and classifications all at the same time. In the past, distinctions were proposed on a linguistic basis, dividing the Latin alphabet from the Greek and from the other non-Latin alphabets; on a morphological basis, striking a difference between the Latin gothics and the Latin romans; and on a historical basis, taking into account the chronological succession of new forms for roman and italic. This last approach is perhaps most useful for the present overview, though I focus mainly on European printing owing to space constraints.

The first groups of gothic typefaces were inspired from the handwritten versions which existed before the invention of printing. *Textura* was among the first, immediately followed by *rotunda*, which had more round versions of the letters used in the first typeface. The *bastardas* were based on a number of quickly written cursive hands and included both formal and less formal varieties. Unlike the gothic types, roman typefaces, including its cursive variant *italic*, became popular over time for their higher legibility. Typefaces for Hebrew, Arabic and other Near Eastern alphabets were normally a speciality of very few printers, and they were regularly used for printing religious material in particular. Religious printing also made use of *blackletter* and *roman* in a codified way. For quite a long time in England, for example, blackletter was generally used for Protestant material and roman for Catholic publications (see Figure 3.3). Since printing in the classical languages was more widespread in the past than it is today, most printers also owned typefaces for printing Greek. Among the many styles used for Greek in the past, one of the most successful was the cursive Greek type introduced by Aldus in the 1490s and then reiterated and touched up over the centuries by many typeface designers in Europe and overseas.

Roman typefaces remained popular for a long time, and only in the eighteenth century did some of the most powerful type designers come up with a number of innovations. During this time, William Caslon, a type designer from London, worked on a more refined version of the *Old Style* typefaces first developed by Jenson some centuries before. The typeface developed by Caslon was vaguely romantic and pleasing to the eye, and all texts printed in this typeface from the time look exceptionally elegant. A few years later, in the mid eighteenth century, another English type designer, John Baskerville, invented the so-called *Transitional* typeface. The typeface created by Baskerville was characterised by thinner strokes in the letters of the alphabet, known as *serifs*, and a relatively more marked contrast between thick and thin strokes. Baskerville's typeface definitely looked more formal than Caslon's and survived up to the present day. With the Age of Enlightenment in the eighteenth century, typefaces enjoyed

And God ſaw that it was good, † and he ſaid " Let vs make Man to our image, & likenes : and let him haue dominion ouer the fiſhes of the ſea, and the foules of the ayre, and the beaſtes, and the whole earth, and al creeping creature, that moueth vpon the earth. † And God created man, to his

26 ¶ And God ſaid, *Let vs make man in our Image, after our likeneſſe: and let them haue dominion ouer the fiſh of the ſea, and ouer the foule of the aire, and ouer the cattell, and ouer all the earth,and ouer euery creeping thing that creepeth vpon the earth.

Figure 3.3 Book of Genesis, Chap. 1. Comparative passage from the Holy Bible in blackletter (1611) and roman (1609–10)

a new wave of change and development. In France, the Didot family was responsible for one of the first modern serifs, characterised by very thin strokes at the end of each letter and a marked distinction between thick and thin strokes. In Italy, Giambattista Bodoni also worked on some typefaces that characterised the modern age, and some of them are still in use today in some of the fanciest advertisements and magazine designs.

While the eighteenth century saw a climax of artistic expression, the nineteenth century was a serious problem for diversity and growth in typography. The motto of the Industrial Revolution was that of systematisation for mass production – an approach that clashed with the typically complex and varied nature of typefaces. Most typefaces were compressed or stretched for use on posters and newspapers. Different typefaces were used not so much to convey an idea of prestige or beauty, but rather according to how useful they were to fit every available space, thus creating a rather confusing mix of old, new and unconvincingly hybrid styles that characterise that period of history. If the Industrial Revolution simply made use of what existed up to that time, the nineteenth century also saw the invention of the so-called *Egyptian* typefaces. These styles were punchier, bolder versions of existing typefaces, and, much like other modern typefaces, they are still in use, albeit rarely, today. By the end of the Industrial Revolution, typography had become a land of clutter and confusion, where everything and anything was possible; fortunately, however, the chaos did not last for long.

Another William Caslon, the great-grandson of the famous inventor of the first Caslon typeface, decided to remove the serifs from one of his well-known typefaces at the beginning of the nineteenth century. The new interpretation of an old style was not immediately embraced at the time, but, with time, this simpler style did in fact take off and opened the way to a variety of typefaces that came to be known as *sans-serif*. The most iconic early sans-serif is *Futura*, invented by Paul Renner in Germany in the early twentieth century. The German typeface designer became interested in geometric shapes, which is the reason why Futura and its cognates are also known as *Geometric Sans* typefaces. Another sans-serif typeface, Gill Sans, brought a new wave of innovation with its natural curves and forms, inspired from the corporate font used in the London underground in the early twentieth century. Gill Sans and its cognates are now typically called *Humanist Sans* typefaces.

In the mid twentieth century, sans-serif underwent another remarkable development by influence of the Swiss. The so-called *Swiss Style* was characterised by functional and reader-friendly type design. *Helvetica* became the best-known product of the new modernist Swiss development, and it quickly became popular both in printing and in signage design around the world. Modernist sans-serifs were truly an innovation, compared to the range of typefaces that had been inherited until then, but there is more to the history of typefaces. In the twentieth century, computers digitised typefaces, giving birth to the so-called *digital fonts*. With the introduction of digital fonts, traditional typography faced something of a slowdown, and at times even a halt. Early computer technology struggled to render many typefaces with a good enough font and only squared styles were not as greatly affected by the problem. When digital technology advanced, fonts became increasingly more sophisticated and well defined. Suddenly, an eclectic variety of fonts became available to everyone who had a computer at home. With the advent of digitisation, typographic inventiveness was no longer a privilege only for a few artists, but a commodity available to all would-be writers, either as mere users or as outright inventors.

3.3.2   History of Typemaking

Types were three-dimensional representations of letters of the alphabet reversed left to right. They were cast in an alloy of lead, antimony and tin called type-metal, which never shrank nor expanded when cooled. The art of making types changed quite markedly during the centuries that followed the invention of printing, especially with the advent of increased professionalisation and modern technology. However, much of the early typemaking technique remained fairly similar for a very long time and consisted in comparable practical steps across countries. As a first step, a relief pattern of each letter of the alphabet was cut by hand on the end of a steel punch that was about 44 mm long. The punches were then hammered into small blocks of copper, known as *matrices*, each of which was patiently trimmed so that the bottom of the impression of the punch was square to the sides and to the bottom of the block and was set at the right depth from its top surface. At this point, each matrix would be fixed in the mould, which was a steel box made in two halves. The type-caster would put the two halves of the mould together, while also holding the first matrix in between the two moulds, and then fill the mould with molten metal. The metal would become solid almost immediately and, after a few seconds, the type-caster was able to open the mould and retrieve the new letter. Even at the earliest stages of type-casting, a professional could make about 4,000 types per day, which equals to a type every ten to twelve seconds. The early printing process of typemaking described above is usually taken as a reference point for most diachronic comparisons across types from later centuries.

Now, with reference to what a type looked like: a piece of type was made of a number of different parts, and each of these parts usually had a precise name. The two most important parts were the face, which, as discussed above, is the most visible side of the metal character; and the body, which is the physical block on which each metal letter was placed. A relatively secondary, but still important element is the x-height, which refers to the height of the lowercase letters, disregarding ascenders or descenders. All of the parameters above were important for determining the shape of the letters on the page during printing. In order to print the letters, type was pressed deep into sheets of paper which had been softened by damping. The ink impression of the letter made on the page usually blurred at the edges as the type sank in, and then changed when the paper dried and shrank down in size. As a result of the difficulty of altering the gauge of mould, types gradually varied less and less in size. Very early on in the history of printing, however, individual printers often had many series of sizes, and the international trade in typographic material led to the proliferation of a variety of standards. In order for printers to use alphabets of different sizes, types were made in different bodies; since letters of the same alphabet also differed in width, types of the same body also varied in a similar way. A group of letters of the same alphabet, comprising a range of punctuation marks and other symbols, all of one body and design, was called a *font*; each type in a font was usually purchased in proportion to how frequently it was generally used during printing.

A typical way of describing historical type is by including the original designation for the whole font that the type belonged to, for example Pica roman, Caslon No. 2, together with measurements of the apparent sizes of its body and face based on the printed image of the type on the sheet of paper. With regard to the type-specific measurements, caution is always warranted when all that we have is indirect evidence from paper. As mentioned earlier on, paper often shrank in size, and so did the appearance of letters on the sheet. Thus, when measuring body size in a set of solidly printed lines, one should always account for a reduction in dimensions between 1 and 2.5 per cent for the reasons established above. The apparent body size of type is taken by measuring twenty lines of type vertically, possibly a few times across different pages, and the results must be drawn as precisely as possible to the nearest millimetre. The distance is measured from a given point in a line to the corresponding point in the twenty-first line above or below. Where possible, lines should always be measured where they were set firmly, that is to say without the printed image of any strips of type-metal, wood or card which could be slipped in between each line of type. As for measuring the size of the face, all that is required is a finely graduated scale and a magnifying glass. The vertical distance of type is taken on the printed image from the ascender of a letter, which is the part of a lowercase letter that extends above the mean line of a font, and the bottom of a neighbouring descender, which is the part that goes below the mean line of a font. If the result is multiplied by twenty, one will get the approximate twenty-line measurement of the minimum body on which the face could be cast, which is often slightly less than the apparent body size of a font of type. Then the x-height and the capital height are measured in millimetres and the result would be presented as follows: [face height × 20] × [x-height] : [capital height]. The measurements of the apparent size of a typical Pica roman might therefore read as follows: Body 82. Face 80 × 1ˑ7 : 2ˑ5.

When one comes to grips with the apparent size of a type, the next possible step for the analysis of type consists in the identification of its intended standard size, simply by making reference to the tables existing in key bibliographic material such as Gaskell (1972: 15), which has incidentally provided very useful material for informing my overview of type analysis here. A final, perhaps most complex step in the description of type is the identification of its face, among and beyond all of the different typographic styles outlined in section 3.4.1. Sometimes it is necessary to make reference to the historical founders' and printers' type specimens, but even when comparing a typeface with a wide range of catalogued specimens, there exist endless variations, touch-ups and revisions to each individual style. Identifying individual typefaces is a skill that goes beyond the beginning level of knowledge in book history, and readers are encouraged to refer to some of the references below to learn more about this aspect, if interested.

Further Reading

Basbanes, N. A. 2013. *On Paper: The Everything of Its Two-Thousand-Year History.* New York: Alfred A. Knopf.

Bland, M. 2010. *A Guide to Early Printed Books and Manuscripts.* London: Wiley-Blackwell.

Feldherr, A. & G. Hardy (eds.). 2011. *The Oxford History of Historical Writing: Beginnings to* AD *600.* Oxford: Oxford University Press.

Gaskell, P. 1972. *A New Introduction to Bibliography.* Oxford: Oxford University Press.

Roe, G. E. 1996. *Writing Instruments: A Technical History and How They Work.* Stockport: G. E. Roe.

Part II

Elements of Orthography

4   Orthographic Components

4.1   Types of Writing Systems

Writing systems convey linguistic information that does not always consist only of a transcription of speech. Sometimes, historical linguists are faced with a series of discrete signs, which reflect meanings unrelated to sounds created over the course of time, and which their users have found effective. By virtue of the diversity across writing systems, there are different approaches to classifying them. The most widespread is that based on identifying the types of linguistic units represented by the signs of a writing system. In other words, much of the task of classifying writing systems consists in *decoding* its signs. Crucially, most historical writing systems make use, in a more or less harmonious way, of a combination of different ways of representing linguistic units. A large number of historical writing systems use a mixed representation system: they combine a phonemic writing system with symbols used to indicate numbers (e.g. 1, 2, 3 and so on). While it is rare to find a historical writing system that uses exclusively one type of unit representation, a reasonably neat distinction can be made between at least two groups of writing systems – those largely made of *logographs* and those largely made of *phonographs*. A logograph is a sign that stands for a word or a morpheme.[1] Since morphemes have both a meaning and a pronunciation, logograms are also associated with both a meaning and a pronunciation (though the above definition of a logogram is not unanimous; cf., e.g., Daniels, 2018: 155). An example of a logogram still used today in the English writing system is &, which indicates the conjunction 'and' and represents the sound /ænd/.

Logographic systems work on the basic requirement that written signs stand for morphemes, which may or may not be full words, and they do not account for words independent of their morphemic make-up. In principle, a truly logographic writing system would use four different signs for the four morphologically related words *smile*, *smiles*, *smiled* and *smiling*, but instances like this were frequently not the case in writing systems of the past. What happens in all

---

[1] A morpheme is defined as the smallest meaningful unit of a word; e.g. the word *spellings* has three morphemes, *spell* + *ing* + *s*.

historical writing systems that we know so far is that one sign is used to indicate the common unit, so in the example above, *smile*; in cases like this, the label *morphogram* would be more precise. More frequently, the root morpheme of a word is represented by a logogram, while any additional inflectional morphemes are represented by phonograms. In cases like these, the term *logogram* is used as a means to indicate writing systems where the root morpheme had considerable weight. The majority of the early writing systems were indeed heavily logographic. In early Sumerian cuneiform only lexical roots were represented by a sign, never inflectional morphemes, which gave the writing system somewhat of a rudimental, but characteristic early-writing appearance.

Now, we will move on to the group of writing systems made of phonographs. Phonographic writing systems were made, as the word suggests, largely of signs that correspond to one or more sound elements in the language – typically without specific semantic values. A phonogram may be pictorial, for example the Egyptian hieroglyph ![glyph], or linear, involving exclusively arbitrary lines, for instance in <F>. In these examples, the object indicated by the sign is not a word or a morpheme, but rather a phonological unit free from any semantic message. For both the examples above, this is the phoneme /f/. In general, three main types of phonograms can be distinguished in historical writing systems. A *syllabogram* is a sign that indicates a syllable, especially vowel or consonant-vowel syllables, though vowel-consonant and consonant-vowel-consonant syllabograms are also attested historically (e.g. in Mesopotamian cuneiform). Writing systems primarily made of syllabograms are called *syllabaries*. One of the most famous examples of a syllabary is that of the Linear B, used for Mycenaean Greek well ahead of the rise of the Greek alphabet. When the sound unit indicated is a phoneme,[2] then the signs are termed *letters*. Since the phoneme is occasionally called a phonological segment, these writing systems are also known as *segmental systems*.

A third type of phonogram consists in the use of phonemes in semi-decomposable clusters. This type of phonogram, mainly found in the native scripts of South Asia, is called *akshara*. An akshara represents either a vowel that is not preceded by a consonant or a consonant followed by an unrepresented vowel, which is usually /a/ for many of the relevant languages. Instances from the Devanāgarī writing system, found in Hindi, Marathi and Nepali, are उ *u* and त *ta*. Occasionally, a diacritic[3] mark may be needed to signal that no vowel follows the consonant, as in त् *t*. In complex aksharas, a dependent sign is integrated with the simple akshara to substitute the default vowel with another

---

[2] A phoneme is a perceptually distinct unit of sound in a specified language that distinguishes one word from another.

[3] For diacritic mark, I intend a sign such as an accent or cedilla, which when written above or below a letter indicates a difference in pronunciation from the same letter when unmarked or differently marked. See Chapter 5 for more about diacritics.

vowel, for example in Devanāgarī ते *te*, to merge sequential consonants into a single consonant cluster, as in स्त *sta*, or both solutions, as in स्ते *ste*. In general, a new akshara can be identified following every vowel, which means that a vowel and a following consonant are never in the same aksharas even when they sit in the same syllable (but there are some exceptions if the following consonant is a nasal). With reference to phonograms more generally, a writing system may feature signs without a specific sound correspondence, as mentioned above, or where pronunciation is dependent on that of other signs. Example signs for this category are *phonetic complements*, *semantic determinatives* and *punctuation marks* (the latter category is discussed in detail in section 4.2.3). A phonetic complement is a sign employed as a complement to an additional sign in order to clarify or emphasise the pronunciation of that other sign to which the first is added. The complements are indeed phonograms but they do not carry with them a separate pronunciation from that of their host sign. Much like the phonetic complement, a semantic determinative is a sign added to another sign, but this time it signals the semantic category of the referent of the sign, as a way to disambiguate the sign. Both of the categories above were present quite frequently in Egyptian hieroglyphics. The word 🔲ᴀ (*pr* 'go'), for instance, has a 🔲 phonographic function because it indicates the sounds /p/ and /r/; ⌒ has a phonetic complement function, as a way of reiterating the /r/ of the previous sign, and ᴀ has a determinative role and signals that the word relates to the idea of movement.

In addition to all of the terms discussed so far, there are two labels which also need mentioning: *ideogram* and *pictogram*. The first term refers to a sign that indicates an idea, for instance the barred circle, ⊘, normally used to indicate a prohibition. The second term refers to a sign made of a somewhat conceptualised image of an object, for instance the marks that we find on the toilets/restrooms 🚻. To all intents and purposes, emojis like ❤ are also pictograms, because they represent a heart, but they may function as ideograms in some contexts, for instance to indicate the idea of love. Ideograms and pictograms are key elements of early writing systems, because they provided iconographic foundations from which writing arose. For instance, a drawing of a sun could indeed mean 'sun' and maybe also indicate 'day' or 'time'. However, it was only when ideograms and pictograms turned to logograms, phonograms and determinatives that true writing began. The terms *ideogram* and *pictogram* do not indicate whether a sign is writing or not, nor do they accurately describe the purpose of a sign in a writing system or the type of a given writing system. Owing to their particularly vague nature, these terms should not be used by students of historical orthography, but they are mentioned here by way of clarification.

The confusion surrounding the two terms discussed above had an impact on the way some early writing systems were labelled in the past. Egyptian hieroglyphs, for example, were long believed to be ideograms, in the sense that they were thought to indicate ideas rather than to mediate language. These difficulties may have arisen from the complex relationship between hieroglyphs and pictorial decorations in Egyptian ruins (see, for example, Figure 4.1). Hieroglyphs themselves actually had a certain pictorial quality, especially when they appeared in monumental inscriptions. The term *hiero-glyph* simply indicates the visual characteristic of a sign and, much as for the terms ideograph and pictogram, is not a way of classifying writing systems. A hieroglyph may assume different roles in writing: the Egyptian hieroglyph ⌷, for instance, which visually indicated the basement of a house, could

APOTHEOSIS OF RAMESES II.

Figure 4.1 Example of Egyptian hieroglyphs in the context of a pictorial representation (Source: benoitb/Contributor/Getty Images)

function as a logogram (meaning 'house'), a phonogram (representing the consonants /pr/) or a determinative (signalling that the preceding word referred to a building). On a similar note, Mayan hieroglyphs were initially misunderstood as a system for calculating and recording numbers instead of a typical writing system. Chinese characters – which are sometimes still called ideograms – were also initially thought not to represent speech.

From the examples provided so far, it will hopefully have become clear that historical writing systems are anything but simple to classify, and theoretical concepts and definitions may not always capture the full complexity of historical writing. It is perhaps due to complexities inherent to historical perspectives that little theoretical work has so far been pursued in historical orthography, and most of the knowledge existing to date has to be borrowed and reinterpreted from present-day studies on writing. While what has been provided in this chapter will be immediately applicable to historical writing, therefore, it should be kept in mind that what comes next in this chapter may be a readaptation from academic thinking that largely reflects on present-day writing systems. These considerations naturally lead to the more general question of whether orthographic components can be determined from both a synchronic and a diachronic perspective concurrently, or whether they should be studied as distinct yet complementary elements – which is not only an empirical but also a theoretical issue. Luckily for most readers, this remains a question for future scholars to concentrate upon, and the theoretical material discussed in the remaining part of this chapter and the book as a whole is simple (or, alas, simplified) enough to be applicable to historical writing systems without glaring conceptual problems.

4.2   Orthographic Units and Elements

4.2.1   Graphemes and Allographs

The definition of the term *grapheme* is rather controversial in the literature, and an overview of the different theories is helpful for a more enriched approach to understanding historical writing systems. The word was first mentioned by Baudouin de Courtenay in the early twentieth century, by analogy with the term *phoneme*. Today, the word *grapheme* indicates at least four different definitions, namely a written unit that corresponds to exactly one phoneme; a minimal contrastive unit in a writing system; the smallest segmental unit within a graphemic hierarchy; and, simply, a letter. The last of these four definitions, that of a letter, will not be discussed here, as the concept of the letter is developed in detail in section 4.2.2. Let us take a closer look at the three other definitions of the grapheme, following an increasing order of complexity, and beginning with that of the written representation of a sound. This first concept responds to the idea that writing stems from speech and represents a secondary system of language representation. According to this definition, graphemes are identifiable only in phonographic, i.e. alphabetic, writing systems. The range of graphemes identifiable following this first approach differs from that stemming from the idea that writing systems are made of autonomous units. According to the *autonomous* (or autonomistic) model of writing systems, the identification of individual graphemes is language-specific and depends on the distributional rules in a given system. In English, for example, the letter *x*, which, for the autonomous approach, is a grapheme, represents two individual sounds, /k/+/s/, and would therefore represent an issue for an approach that aims to exclusively match an individual phoneme with a graphic unit. Conversely, for <qu>, as in *query*, which is also considered an individual grapheme according to the autonomous approach, the one-writing -unit-one-phoneme approach would see <q> → /k/ and <u> → /w/.

The second definition of the grapheme, that of a minimal contrastive unit in a writing system, stems from the autonomous principle established above and refers to the idea that the analysis of each writing unit can be conducted internally within a writing system. With this approach, the grapheme is usually seen as analogical to the phoneme, in the sense that graphemes can also be identified, just like phonemes, by drawing on minimal pairs. If we compare the words *seal* and *zeal*, for example, which differ only by one sound and change meaning because of it, we will identify <s> and <z> as individual graphemes. According to the principle explained above, sequences of vowel letters like <ea> in English would be intended as two separate graphemes, as each of them can be separated to form other minimal pairs (e.g. *be̱ast – bo̱ast* and *mea̱t – mee̱t*). If we take into account the graphemic syllable, however, these sequences of letters can be interpreted as complex graphemes and as inseparable in the process of word division, i.e. <ea>, <oa>, <ee>. While the approach explained here seems reasonably straightforward, there are some language-specific complications that need to be taken into account. These complications have undermined unanimity in the way in which the grapheme is defined across languages following this second definition. Some approaches, for instance, consider as valid only those graphemes that are used in the spelling of native words, while others are more inclusive to borrowings and allow for the identification of a wider spectrum of graphemes. In German, for example, <ph> for /f/ appears only in loanwords and has frequently been replaced by <f> over the course of time; compare, for example, the spelling *Telephon* (early twentieth century) → *Telefon* (present-day version). According to the same principle, the spelling <qu> in English is defined as a complex grapheme because it represents the smallest inseparable unit usable for making minimal pairs, for example in *quote – note* or in *quite – bite*. Crucially, a graphemic minimal pair does not necessarily have to be phonological, as the latter of the two examples above indicates.

The definition of the grapheme which stems from the autonomous principle, as discussed above, is clearly not purely and wholly based on a correspondence between graphemes and phonemes, but rather it also takes into account morphological or syntactic principles. For example, the spelling <ä> in German frequently responds to the morphological principle as <ä>, pronounced as /ɛ:/, establishes a morphological link across words in <a>, such as *Mann* 'man' and *Männer* 'men' (both items being connected with the morpheme {mann}). As a result of the fact that graphemes may or may not have explicit links with pronunciation, a distinction may be drawn, in the autonomous definition, between segmental and non-segmental graphemes, namely units that do and do not have a counterpart in pronunciation respectively. All together, segmental and non-segmental graphemes thus include a wide range of orthographic units, belonging to an impressively large number of languages. These are, for instance, alphabetic letters or a pair of letters such as <a> and <qu>; syllabograms like <カ>, which indicates /ka/ in Japanese *katakana*; morphographs/logograms like <马>, which in Mandarin Chinese means 'horse'; punctuation marks like <,> and <?>; and numeral signs like <5> and <∧>.

The third definition of the term *grapheme* rests on the idea that the graphemic system is structured in a hierarchy, much like the phonological system. Underlying this third definition is the hypothesis that spoken language, sign language and written language are three different communicative routes interlinked by a number of factors. The connections between the three routes entail the fact that the hierarchical levels which make up spoken and written language have correspondences in writing and must be defined autonomously, without the aid of phonology. According to this approach, graphemes represent the smallest suprasegmental units of writing, which means that they are found one level above letters, the individual segments of writing. Graphemes are structured in syllables; syllables can in turn form higher-level units, forming the so-called *graphemic foot*, which is a linear group of graphemic syllables, and the *graphemic word*, which is a sequence of graphemes identified by a space on the left and on the right side and can include the graphemic feet. With this approach, the idea of a graphemic syllable takes a central place in identifying which units are actually graphemes. Much like the phonological syllable, the graphemic syllable features a vowel position, i.e. the syllable peak, which indicates a vowel letter, and optional consonant positions. For example, the word *band* features one graphemic syllable, where the <a> takes the vowel position.

The graphemic syllable always responds to a length-sequencing principle, which regulates the way in which a graphemic syllable looks. In *band*, the longest letters, *b* and *d*, are found at the two ends of the word, while the short letter *a* takes the syllable peak position (more about this in section 4.2.2). At a lower level, the syllable is made of an onset, a nucleus and a coda. The nucleus of the strong graphemic syllable, which is the only syllabic component in monosyllabic words and the first unit in bisyllabic ones, branches into two structural grapheme positions. Grapheme positions are not always individual graphemes, since letter sequences such as <oa> or <ea> in *mean* or *moan* have within the framework of this approach, one grapheme only, even if they each represent a grapheme-position. Figure 4.2 exemplifies and hopefully also integrates the hierarchical description given so far for the word *band*. Interestingly, this third definition of the grapheme does not necessarily exclude the autonomous definition given earlier on. The approach to establishing graphemes using minimal pairs can still be used while viewing the grapheme as a hierarchical entity. Within the context of this third approach, though, the elements which create minimal pairs inevitably depend on their position in the graphemic syllable structure of a word.

What the above indicates is that the three definitions of the grapheme are really quite separated from each other, but nonetheless they are not always mutually exclusive. Given its important role in orthography in general, the grapheme is the object of extensive discussion, and there is no consensus about whether the idea of the grapheme is even necessary at all. Some scholars (e.g. Daniels, 2001: 67) have even gone to the extreme end, arguing that the idea of

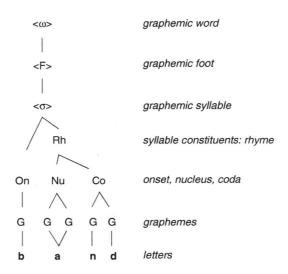

Figure 4.2 Hierarchical graphemic system (from Berg et al., 'Buchstabenmerkmal, Buchstabe, Graphem'; in B. Primus & U. Domahs (eds.), *Laut – Gebärde – Buchstabe*, Berlin; New York: Walter de Gruyter, 2016, p. 351)

the grapheme, particularly in connection with the sound-related aspects of a language, need not to exist at all. This claim is based on the assumption that writing systems do not function like linguistic systems and cannot therefore be defined by analogy with phonological elements. In spite of some occasional strong claims like these, there is value in working with the grapheme by analogy with the phoneme, as long as comparisons are made conscientiously and conclusions are drawn on the basis of empirical, demonstrable results. Because of the relative novelty of historical orthography, there is in effect a state of legitimacy of trial which all scholars interested in theoretical aspects of orthography should take advantage of, in order to glean different, yet hopefully complementary perspectives on elements of writing systems. Separate understandings of graphemes yield different hypotheses about the historical changes affecting writing systems, all of which can enrich our understanding of orthography as a whole.

A concept immediately related to that of graphemes is that of the *graphemic inventory*. The graphemic inventory of a writing system consists in the full collection of graphemes available in a specific language where the writing system is used. The shape of graphemic inventories depends not only on language, but also on which definition of the grapheme is used. To return to the example mentioned earlier on, if we understand the grapheme as a letter, then *q* would of course be a grapheme in English. If, however, one takes the definition of the grapheme as the smallest distinctive unit that is an autonomous part of a graphemic syllable, *q* cannot be considered a grapheme any longer, as it only appears together with *u* in the English vocabulary. It is for this reason that Berg (2019: 32) indicated two basic distinctions in English:

> simple: <a, b, c, d, e, f, g, h, i, j, k, l, m, n, o, p, r, s, t, u, v, w, x, y, z>
> complex: <qu>

For Berg, *q* is not a grapheme, as it cannot be an autonomous component of a syllable without the *u* in *qu*. From this perspective, *rh*, *sh*, *ch* and *wh* are each formed by two graphemes, because each letter in the four sequences can also appear on its own to form a syllable, for example in *rule*, *city*, *heck*, *weird* and so on. This way of understanding graphemes, however, clearly detaches itself from the way in which diphthongs are understood in phonology, where two units of a diphthong are always considered one phoneme, e.g. /oʊ/ in *boat*, regardless of whether they can appear independently or not; both /o/ and /ʊ/, can, as single units, form a syllable peak in English. As opposed to the framework proposed in phonology, Fuhrhop et al. (2011) view the same units discussed as complex graphemes.

If one defines graphemes as elements of a graphemic syllable, then punctuation marks, numbers and other key orthographic elements will be automatically banished from the graphemic inventory. In principle, however, capital letters may be seen as graphemes on some occasions if written minimal pairs are a means for distinguishing graphemes (see, e.g., Meletis, 2019a). According to Rutkowska (2012: 232), for example, one could, theoretically, count fifty-two instead of twenty-six graphemes in English. Historically, the number of individual graphemes in English would be even larger, as it would encompass lost graphemes such as <Þ>. The same applies to other languages. In German, for instance, <ä>, <ö> and <ü> stemmed from the blend of the units <a>, <o> and <u> with a superscribed e-letter, i.e. <å, ů, o̊>. Another example from German is that of the <h>, which does not have its regular sound within a wordc (<h> ↔ /h/), cf. *drehen* /dRe:ǝn/ 'to turn over' or *dehnen* /de:nǝn/ 'to stretch'. The unit of <h> only signals vocalic segmentation and the quality of the vowel before it, i.e. long /e:/.

Without a doubt, more space would be needed in this chapter in order to give an exhaustive overview of the grapheme; the information provided above, however, should hopefully give the reader enough information to be able to move to the next component of historical writing systems – the *allograph*. In broad terms, allographs are variants of graphemes, but they are essentially tied to how we intend the grapheme. Under the first definition of the grapheme, different ways of indicating the same sound can be regarded as allographs, e.g. <o> and <oo> in *move* and *moon*. Under the second definition of the grapheme, and, tangentially, also the third definition, an allograph is a non-contrastive graphemic variant. From this perspective, it might be useful to refer to a difference existing between *graphetic* and *graphemic allographs*. Graphetic allography is defined by visual likeness, which means that graphetic allographs can be identified according to more idealised categories. For instance, different typefaces like Verdana |a| and Rockwell Extra Bold |**a**| are identifiable as graphetic allographs on the basis of their connections with the basic shape of <a>. Graphemic allography, instead, is based on common traits. In particular, there are three categories of graphemic allographs, namely (1) intra- vs. inter-inventory allographs, which are allographs found within one inventory or across individual inventories; (2) free vs. positional allographs, the former occurring in free variation, and responding to stylistic factors, the latter being in complementary distribution; and (3) externally independent vs. externally determined allographs, which are allographs dependent or not on other linguistic levels, like syntax and pragmatics.

Allographic variation usually occurs for three main reasons. The first factor is the presence of stylistic variants, so either because different hands write the same grapheme or because different typefaces are used. Allography can also arise by the presence of serifs, which, as briefly discussed in the previous chapter, are small lines closely connected to the letter stem, at its top or its bottom. To return to the widely used example of <a>, |a| would be a serif-font allograph of |a|, which instead is a sans-serif-font version of the same grapheme. This type of variation is present in every type of writing system. In Chinese, for example, there are older and regional allographs of individual graphemes, like the traditional form |馬| and the simplified form |马| to indicate 'horse'. A second factor underlying the presence of allographs is that of script-specific positional conditioning. An example comes from Greek, where <σ> has an allograph |ς| word-finally. In Arabic, the majority of graphemes have allographs: see, for example, the grapheme *tā'*, which appears as |ﺗ| word-initially, |ﺘ| word-medially, |ﺖ| word-finally and |ﺕ| as a stand-alone form; for the grapheme *dāl*, instead, a bound allograph |ﺪ| and a stand-alone form |ﺩ| are available. Capitalisation – more extensively defined in section 4.2.3 below – can also be a distributionally conditioning factor for allography, particularly in those writing systems where it is driven by the grammatical function of the unit in question. In several writing systems, word-initial capitalisation is a useful marker of a new sentence. Sometimes, though, capitals function as graphemes as they can indicate two semantic units, e.g. in *turkey* vs. *Turkey* and *titanic* vs. *Titanic* in English.

A third factor behind the occurrence of allographs is that of a 'universal' distributional conditioning, i.e. independent from a given writing system. Examples include the spellings |y| and |ie|, which alternate in a non-idiosyncratic, predictable way across many languages, including English and German. Overall, the difference between allographs and graphemes as such can be blurry and associating phonemes with graphemes does not always work. A key factor distinguishing phonemes/allophones from graphemes/allographs, for instance, is that some graphic units are sometimes graphemes, sometimes non-graphemes. Fuhrhop et al. (2011: 284), for instance, suggested that <c> and <k> may be seen as graphemes when preceding <e> and <i> and allographs elsewhere. Admittedly, the idea of allographs explained so far is fairly widespread, particularly in empirical work tightly linked to correspondence theory (as in Fuhrhop et al., 2011; Berg, 2019). However, nobody agrees on the definition of the terms graphemes and allograph, which are still a hot topic in the field (see Klinkenberg & Polis, 2018; Meletis, 2019), and the term allograph in particular definitely requires further theoretical work (Meletis, 2019: 42).

4.2.2   *Letters, Graphs, Characters and Glyphs*

Letters are the basic symbols of many writing systems and, in alphabetic scripts, they constitute the smallest separate elements of a writing system. Since there is much complexity involving scripts from around the world, let us concentrate here on the Latin alphabet, so as to keep our focus on orthographic concepts, rather than on languages more broadly. While there are language-dependent variations, like, for example, the letter *ß*/ẞ in German, the present-day Latin alphabet is generally made of the following uppercase and lowercase letters:

A, B, C, D, E, F, G, H, I, J, K, L, M, N, O, P, R, S, T, U, V, W, X, Y, Z

a, b, c, d, e, f, g, h, i, j, k, l, m, n, o, p, r, s, t, u, v, w, x, y, z

The way in which each of the letters above appears may change, but those given here are, in broad terms, their idealised forms. The individual realisation of each letter above is subject to a complex cosmos of variability, so that one can even identify an internal hierarchy of smaller individual components in each letter. Just as in morphological units, letters of the alphabet can also be considered organisms with their own individual parts. The parts are mainly two: the head, which is the longer, more prominent part of a letter, and the coda, which is the shorter and more dependent part. The compartmentalised way of understanding letters explained here rests on the assumption that the graphemic space can be split into three spatial areas, namely a central space, an upper outer space and a lower outer space. Heads may occupy the largest part of the central space, while the coda can be found in one of the upper or lower spaces – but this is not really always the case. For the letter *p*, for example, the head will be | and the coda Ɔ; for the letter *z*, the head will be / and the coda ⊐; for the letter *m*, the head will be | and the coda ⋔; and for the letter *e*, the head will be ⊂ and the coda –. There is one remarkable difference between upper- and lowercase letters: the former category always takes a good portion of the graphemic space, while the latter shows a lot of variation in how much space its units usually occupy. Lowercase letters' spatial development is influenced by the quality of their heads, which can be classified as long (*f, t, j, h, p, b, k, g, d*), slant (*z, v, w, s, x*), short straight (*m, n, r, l, i, u*) and short bent (*e, o, a*). The length of the heads determines the so-called *length hierarchy* of letters, which influences the organisation of the graphemic unit. In this hierarchical organisation, long-headed letters are found at the very bottom of the structure. Slant-headed letters come just above long-headed letters, followed by short-straight-headed letters and short-bent -headed letters, in this order.

Length hierarchy can be a useful means to gauge rules behind graphemic syllables, as briefly outlined in section 4.2.1. In a typical graphemic syllable, graphemes appear following the length-sequencing principle. That is to say, the centre of the syllable is inhabited by the least spacious grapheme; the outer character positions, which move away from the core on both syllable edges, increase in length linearly following the same principle. This phenomenon seems to have provided ideas to scholars for explaining spelling conventions in historical writing systems. To return to the allographic example of |y| and |ie| in historical English mentioned earlier (e.g. in *agency – agencie*), it could be explained by virtue of the following length hierarchy principle: the form |y| usually appears word-finally, where open syllables may be found; if, however, the syllable ends with an <s>, for example in *bellies*, then a |ie| usually appears. While the example above is one of the most outstanding for English, the importance of the syllable structure for understanding graphemes has so far been discussed only in relation to the Latin alphabet. It remains unclear, for instance, whether the principles discussed and the type of graphemic syllable have a comparable importance in the Cyrillic alphabet, which is made of fairly central units that take in large part the core graphemic space (e.g. *п, т, к, г, ж, ч, ш*).

So far, it is quite obvious that the letter and the grapheme are two entities conceptually intertwined and mutually interactive; within the context of this relationship, however, there still remains an important question to answer: what is the role and relevance of the graph? A *graph* is the smallest unit of writing and consists in the single occurrence of a letter of an alphabet in any of its various shapes. Examples of graphs include letters, syllabograms, punctuation marks, numerals, spaces and special symbols such as £ and @. Graphs become graphemes when they carry some specific functionality. For instance, a graph *c* is a grapheme <c> in *cat*, as it essentially distinguishes this semantic segment from others, e.g. *m* in *mat*. In other examples like *corner, cricket, crocodile* and *critical*, the graph *c* does not represent a grapheme as such. For other graphs like *h*, a more complex set of graphemes may be involved, for example in *rheumatisms*, where <r> and <h> become a digraph, <rh> (note that there also exist trigraphs, for example German <sch>, but these are rare in historical languages). A similar thing happens in written Chinese, as the word 垃圾 (lājī), 'rubbish, garbage', is formed by two units, 垃 and 圾, which cannot be pulled apart and, jointly, indicate a single grapheme.

Graphs are the object of study of *graphetics*, a scientific area in linguistics that focuses on the physical properties of written signs, their visual and mechanical aspects (Coulmas, 1996: 177; see also Chapter 6). The classification of letters provided in the previous paragraph is an example of the types of properties analysed in graphetics, since the dissection of individual parts reveals, for instance, the core elements of the graphic renditions of a given letter. Many of the concerns in graphetics are related to how written marks are made, beginning with the basics, i.e. orientation. For most of the letters of the alphabet discussed so far, the head and the coda have to be written, for example, from left to right. For Chinese writing, the matter is slightly different: they are

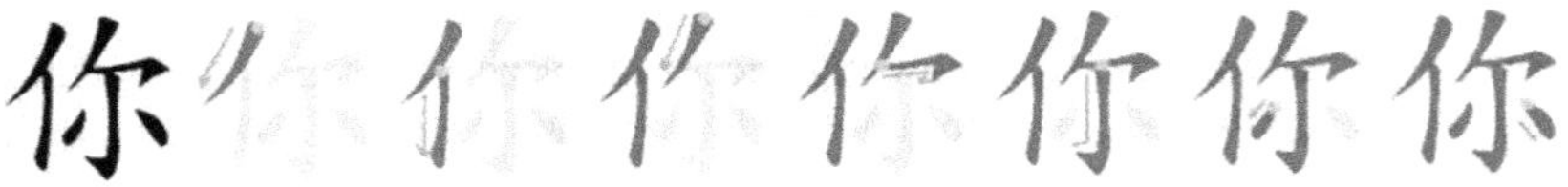

你 你 你 你 你 你 你 你

Figure 4.3 Stroke order for 你 'you' (after Berkenbusch, 1997: 6)[4]

made of smaller elements, symmetrically positioned across a centralised area and have to be drawn from the upper left to the lower right. There is, therefore, a stroke order for writing Chinese characters, which is top to bottom; horizontal before vertical; outer before inner; left to right; middle before sides; and close bottom. Figure 4.3, shows the order in which 你, 'you' (Chinese pīnyīn *nǐ*), is drawn.

Before moving on to segmentation markers, and in order to close the overview of the central graphemic units there is another distinction that needs to be introduced at this point – that between characters and glyphs, distinction that is most frequently encountered in typographic discourse. The difference between the two can be broadly compared to that between the grapheme and the allograph, with the only difference being found in the following definition: characters are "the abstract representations of smallest components of written language that have semantic value" (Allen et al., 2012: 11). The properties of a character encompass several traits, including that of providing alphabetic, numeric, ideographic or punctuative information, in addition to other features like whether the direction of character placement is vertical or horizontal, and, in the latter case, whether it is from left to right or from right to left. The term *character* serves to cover a wide variety of elementary signs of a written language: unlike the grapheme, for example, a character can also represent diacritics (e.g. ´, which indicates the acute accent and can be combined with another character, for example *o*) as well as different types of separators (e.g. ·, which is a single interpunct, as further discussed in Chapter 5).

The definition of a character is intrinsically close to that of a glyph, which has not yet been discussed in this chapter: the *glyph* is defined as a symbol used in a writing system to represent a character and, more generally, as a collective way to indicate a logogram, a phonetic sign or a compound sign. In writing systems whose units are not as easily identified as for the Latin alphabet, the term *glyph* is normally applied to indicate morphographs (or logograms), phonetic signs and compound signs. One character can be represented by a number of different glyphs which are linked together by a reasonably high level of comparability in form. Examples of glyphs for

---

[4] Source: https://commons.wikimedia.org/w/index.php?curid=195461, user: M4RC0, CC-BY-3.0.

the character *A*, for example, include A, *A*, **A**, A and A ; for the character *a*, instead, we can find glyphs like a, *a*, **a**, a, and *a*. While the explanation above should be sufficiently clear in its own right, a rather more extensive definition of the glyph can be given by proposing a distinction from the character. One major difference between characters and glyphs is that characters are abstract, while glyphs represent the practical form that characters can take when rendered or displayed. The glyph consists of a specific rendition of one or more characters, and a repertoire of glyphs constitutes a *font*. A range of characters can also correspond to one glyph, since letters used in different languages are grouped into individual scripts. While most of the characters representing the same graph will be graphemically the same and will have corresponding semantic values, they are understood as different characters in Unicode.[5] To give an example, there are three units relatable to the letter <Đ>, i.e. 00D0 (Latin capital letter eth), 0110 (Latin capital letter d with stroke) and 0189 (Latin capital letter African d).

4.2.3 *Punctuation*

The term *punctuation*, sometimes occurring in alternation with *interpunction*, refers to the use of conventional signs, like dots and horizontal, vertical or oblique marks, in order to structure graphically historical writing. Punctuation is also seen as more broadly relating to typographic devices like boldface, italics and even capitalisation. Occasionally, the uses of spaces between words, and line breaks within a word, have also been referred to as examples of punctuation. A more formal, reader-oriented definition of punctuation encompasses the idea that punctuation marks are one-element features, in the sense that they take one shape, without a distinction between uppercase and lowercase forms. Additionally, punctuation marks never merge or combine in form and in meaning; they occur independently (this excludes diacritics, which require merging), they cannot be equalled to speech, and they can be written without the need of neighbouring text (this last parameter means that blank spaces are not included). The formal definition of punctuation allows one to zoom in on a range of punctuation marks, i.e. < . ?, () ... : ! ' – " " >, in addition to language-specific marks like ¿¡ for Spanish and «» for Italian. Note that the more formal definition of punctuation does not include /, since the slash can actually be spoken out, e.g. in *his/hers* 'his or hers'.

---

[5] Unicode is an information technology standard for the consistent encoding, representation and handling of text expressed in most of the world's writing systems.

Punctuation marks are intended as graphemes in some theoretical perspectives, but not always, depending on the elected understanding of the grapheme. Whatever their relationship to the concept of the grapheme, punctuation marks are an important orthographic category in alphabetic writing systems, and although they are a typical feature of western scripts, they are also present in eastern historical and present-day scripts. While western histories of punctuation are more or less known, eastern punctuation has been more neglected. There are, however, some remarkable early examples of punctuation in historical Eastern cultures: Sinitic scripts developed markers specifically aimed to guide the reader from as early as the Warring States era (475–221 BC); in early China, scribes made use of written marks, together with spaces and indentation, in order to signal key parts of the text, like the beginning and the end, as well as to distinguish between main and accompanying text. An additional, interesting example comes from the Dunhuang texts, which provide early evidence of Tibetan writing and which feature a large number of punctuation to indicate glosses. Some of the East Asian punctuation marks differ from the western ones only graphicaly but not functionally. For instance, 、 is used in Chinese for listing items, while · is employed for juxtaposing items in Korean. Other examples of script-specific punctuation marks include ~ in Armenian and ؛ in Arabic.

A detailed account of the inherent features of punctuation was provided by Bredel (2005, 2008, 2009). The author mainly discusses issues related to German, but some of the points developed in her work are also relevant to other scripts where the same marks are used. According to Bredel (2005), there are three properties which make punctuation marks different from graphemes, all of which are based on the graphemic space framework outlined in section 4.2.2. The first property, [+/– empty], describes whether or not the marks overlap the line that separates the central space from the lower outer space. The second property, [+/– vertical], refers to the upper space and indicates whether punctuation marks have vertical features in the upper space or not (see the example given in Figure 4.4). The third property, [+/– reduplication], describes whether or not the punctuation marks can be split into identical subelements. For example, : and ... can be taken as repetitive examples of a dot; likewise, () and "" can also be considered examples of reduplication. The properties identified above have mechanical and practical outcomes: for example, [+ empty] punctuation marks guide the eye movement, while [– empty] help to guide the inner speech that is sometimes used for reading. The feature blending [– reduplicated, + empty], i.e. the en-dash and the apostrophe, can be useful for the reader to process information lexically when these marks signal broken or fragmented entities. Finally, the . , : ; ? ! marks, which have the [– reduplicated, – empty] features, work above the lexical realm. Punctuation marks with the quality [– reduplicated, + empty, + vertical], namely ? and !,

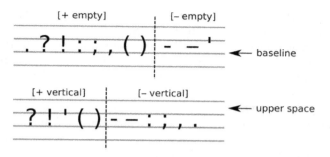

Figure 4.4 [+/− empty] and [+/− vertical] features (from Bredel, 'Zur Geschichte der Interpunktionskonventionen des Deutschen – dargestellt an der Kodifizierung des Punktes', *Zeitschrift für Germanistische Linguistik*, 33 (2005), pp. 179–211)

have particular epistemic roles, while [+ reduplicated, + empty, − vertical], like parentheses, help the reader to decode when the writer intends or not to reveal himself or herself to the reader.

 An important remark to make about the model above is that it focuses on the role of punctuation on the receiving rather than the creative process. Historically, the study of punctuation has paid greater attention to the writer's perspective, with specific reference to the distinction between prosodic and grammatical functions. Prosodic functions are correlated with intonation, stress and rhythm in speech, while grammatical punctuation refers to structural differences. Initially, punctuation in Latinate languages was thought to have been more prone to prosodic features, while other languages, such as Germanic ones, were believed to lean more towards structural features. This view, however, has recently been revised to support a mixed perspective, where traditionally prosodic punctuation marks are described as structural devices. The comma in English, for instance, has been interpreted by Kirchhoff and Primus (2016) not only as a means for expressing inflection, but also, and especially, as a means for signalling grammatical conventions. Despite the recent attempts to establish a systematic framework for understanding punctuation, this element of orthography would definitely benefit from more research, especially from a historical point of view. To this end, future researchers will need to consider the variety of elements which, over time, have shaped rules up to the present day, including the role of the printing technology (references to this last topic are also made in Chapter 8 of this book). Some recent publications have begun to tackle historical punctuation research that integrates typological, sociolinguistic, pragmatic and didactic aspects from a comparative way (e.g. Claridge & Kytö, 2019; Rössler et al., 2021), but the topic is yet far from being exhaustively covered.

One final note about punctuation which deserves a spot in an introductory discussion of components of historical writing systems is that of its connection with word division (further elaborated on in Chapter 5). The expression *word division* indicates the ways in which words in historical texts usually appear, which is in one of the following three ways: joined, hyphenated or separated – the last being much more widespread than the other two. The identification of words by separation from one another can be tracked back to as early as the sixth century, when Irish and Anglo-Saxon scribes introduced the so-called *distinctiones*. Early scribes required visual signs in order to read their texts more easily in their own time, and one of the solutions for them to achieve this was by introducing the practice of word separation, using spaces for the majority of words and hyphenation for those words found in line-final position, which is when a word breaks at the end of a line. The practice of these early scribes, however, has been forgotten for a long time, and in fact the majority of those who have commented on word separation have complained about the absence of a systematic approach to actively identifying individual words up to the first half of the sixteenth century (see, e.g., Denholm-Young, 1954: 70; Petti, 1977: 31). The reason why not much has been said on the topic may be found in the complexity of the orthographic phenomenon and its frequency: word division in line-final position, for example, was a feature found in almost every piece of written material. Despite its frequency, word division seems to be remarkably under-researched in diachronic orthography to date, perhaps due to its apparent haphazard nature.

While line-final word division in particular may have been driven, historically, by phonological and morphological factors, there is to date no consensus on the matter, largely due to the absence of any serious empirical work, either for a specific language or cross linguistically, on the matter. For handwriting in particular, splitting individual words at the end of lines has been considered (e.g. by Hector, 1958; see also Denholm-Young, 1954: 70; Petti, 1977: 31) a rule-free practice, with the exception of the fact that, normally, no fewer than two completing letters would be broken down to the second line. Scholarly discussions from our previous generation have discredited the earlier proposals, proposing the existence of conventional patterns clearly derived either from phonology or from morphology. For Old English, for example, it has been proposed that the main word division principle is essentially morphological, encompassing suffixed, prefixed and compound lexical items (Hladký, 1985: 73). Concurrently, however, it has been suggested that the division of polysyllabic words is evidence for the sound division into syllables, thus assuming that line-final word division is based on the syllabification of Old English (Lutz, 1986: 193). Clearly, opinions about line-final word division are contrastive and reflect a rather fragmented view of scribal practices.

More recent research has continued to address the phenomenon from the point of view of individual scribal choices, providing something of a new reference point for future scholars to compare their data against (Calle-Martín, 2009; 2011). These investigations have followed Hladký's work for the understanding of word segmentation in some historical texts, suggesting a ranking based on the reasons underlying word division, i.e. morphology or phonology. Items falling in the first category are those that follow a traditional word-formation principle of prefixation, suffixation and composition, e.g. in *vn-doable, moan-ing*, and *somwhat*, respectively. Words belonging to the second category, instead, are those split on the basis of their actual pronunciation, according to the following phonological rules: (i) the CV-CV rule, in other words, the split after an open syllable, as in *sy-newes*; (ii) the C-C rule, the split between two consonants, as in *mer-curye*; (iii) the V-V rule, the split between two conjoining vowels, as in *api-um*; (iv) the ST rule, involving either the division or the retention of the pair -*st*, as in *sub-stance* or *was-tyng*; (v) the CL rule, the keeping together of a consonant and a liquid on the basis that they are both part the same syllable, as in *par-brakynge*; and (vi) the CT rule, the splitting of the pair -*ct*, as in *elec-tuaryes*. In addition to the two categories above, a third group was also identified where any other unusual segmentation options, for example in words like *ointme-nt*, find a home.

4.2.4   *Capitalisation*

Much like punctuation, capitalisation can be used as a text-structuring aid in alphabetic scripts. For example, it frequently fulfils the task of marking the onset of a sentence or individual words inside a sentence. Unlike punctuation, however, capitalisation entails a difference between uppercase and lowercase letters – one which historically derives from the use of different scripts. As briefly mentioned in Chapter 2, the distinction between uppercase and lowercase letters was reinforced over time by the gradual change of materials used for writing, with early evidence showing a more marked use of uppercase letters for the full text and more recent scripts using lowercase letters on parchment and, eventually, paper. During the shift to different writing materials, uppercase letters did not totally disappear, but rather they acquired a more specialised role, which became that of marking the onset of sentences and, typically in mediaeval manuscripts, even whole portions of texts. The functional features of capitalisation have quite a lot in common with punctuation, and that is, in fact, one of the main reasons why capitalisation is sometimes considered part of punctuation. Sentence-internal capitalisation in particular seems to have been a rather widespread feature among some historical languages, so much so that nouns often appeared capitalised in the past. Both in present-day and historical English, capitalisation is used, among other reasons, for marking a sentence boundary and for placing emphasis on a word or a group of words. Examples of word units that would fall under this category are names of persons or things, for instance the *Great Pyramid of Giza*, or in any case expressions with a similar purpose. In historical English printed prose, sentence-internal capitalisation seems to have been quite a common feature, while there are of course also exceptions, for example religious books, which show a much less marked likelihood to align to mainstream literature.

In other historical writing systems, and especially those of German and Luxembourgish, sentence-internal capitalisation was a conventionalised modernising trait. In German, capitalisation, particularly in sentence-internal position, was interpreted as a set of graphic units that "convey additional information, supporting the interpretation of the basic textual content, by marking and thereby classifying certain textual structures" (Gallmann, 1985: 63). Capitalisation can help the reader to decode the basic textual content, by identifying specific textual structures. In particular, three classifier subclasses have been argued for in relation to capitalisation, that is the grammatico-lexical classifier, i.e. noun capitalisation; the semantico-lexical classifier, i.e. proper nouns capitalisation; and the pragmatico-lexical classifier, i.e. the capitalisation for politeness reasons, like for example polite *Sie* or, occasionally, the word *Du* 'you' in German. In this language in particular, which is where most research on capitalisation has been conducted so far, sentence-internal capitalisation seems to have been the product of different linguistic factors. Previous corpus-based work (e.g. Bergmann & Nerius, 1998; Barteld et al., 2016) has shown that, in printed material, proper names and nouns referring to gods and saints became capitalised first, then nouns for persons and objects underwent capitalisation soon after. Outside the remits of German, Danish appears to have established a pattern for noun capitalisation by the end of the eighteenth century (as discussed, e.g., in Ruus, 2005: 1286).

Patterns of historical capitalisation have also been noted in languages outside of the Germanic family. In French, for example, the phenomenon became more frequent in the seventeenth century, under the influence of specific language-internal variables. In particular, uppercase letters were frequently used to indicate respect, for example with reference to religious ideas or items (*l'Ecriture sainte*, 'the Holy Scripture', *l'Eglise catholique*, 'the Catholic Church'). Likewise, other categories of words, for example the word *Droit*, 'right' and *Justice*, 'justice', which are sometimes used metaphorically, were occasionally capitalised (see Meisenburg, 1990). For Polish, Bunčić (2012: 242) suggested that "[c]apitalization was far more widely used in the 16th century and is now restricted to certain names and proper nouns and to the first word of a sentence (as in English)". Overall, these examples show that the use of uppercase letters within sentences was nothing less than the norm in some periods of history. There is clearly more work to do on the matter though, both language-internally and comparatively. Future research would also need to shed light on some of the contradicting claims existing in the literature (compare for example Maas, 2007 and Nowak 2019 on matters relating to religious books).

Further Reading

Claridge, C. & M. Kytö (eds.). 2019. *Punctuation in Context: Past and Present Perspectives*. Bern: Peter Lang.

Coulmas, F. 2003. *Writing Systems: An Introduction to Their Linguistic Analysis*. Cambridge: Cambridge University Press (see especially pp. 18–88, which correspond to three individual chapters: Chapter 2, 'The basic options: meaning and sounds'; Chapter 3, 'Signs of words'; and Chapter 4, 'Signs of syllables').

Daniel, P. 2018. *An Exploration of Writing*. Sheffield; Bristol: Equinox.

Crystal, D. 2015. *Making a Point: The Pernickety Story of English Punctuation*. London: Profile Books.

Meletis, D. 2020. *The Nature of Writing. A Theory of Grapholinguistics* (Grapholinguistics and its Applications 3). Brest: Fluxus Editions.

5   Structure and Presentation

5.1   Orthography as a System

Historical writing systems always have an internal structure, and written symbols frequently distribute each other following some kind of predictable order. Structure and presentation are quite complex topics, which would need much more room than one chapter in order to cover the breadth and variety of nuances related to the two issues. For the sake of simplicity, this chapter focuses mainly on alphabetic writing, for which one can borrow, once again, plenty of information from synchronic studies on writing. The idea that there are different principles governing a given writing system is, in fact, quite old; it goes back to the late nineteenth and twentieth centuries and can be related to the influence of Jan Baudouin de Courtenay. He elaborated a number of rules governing writing systems based on three principles: phonetic, etymological and historical. Thus, Baudouin de Courtenay related orthography to what he thought were its principal determining factors, namely pronunciation, origin (with special reference to morphology) and tradition. The idea of a multilayered principle system behind orthography was further elaborated upon and modified by a number of scholars. Among the most relevant names, Firth (1935: 61) was the first to mention the idea of a *polysystem*, or *system of systems*, with reference to the existence of and interaction between phonological, grammatical and lexical systems of orthographic representation.

Since these early contributions, the interaction of multiple principles underlying orthography has been the object of discussion and empirical investigation in a number of subsequent publications; for the English language, the most frequently mentioned are those by Ruszkiewicz (1976), Sgall (1987) and Liuzza (1996), which provide something of a foundation for understanding the rules governing English orthography. The following quote from Sgall summarises the interaction of principles as follows: "In the literature, one often speaks about an orthography being based on several principles, the main among which is the phonetic one, while the others underlie the deviations from this basic principle and can be classed more or less exactly in accordance with the levels of the language system" (1987: 12). In addition to the principles underlying orthographic structures, there are also conventions for the arrangement of writing, which can in principle be changed. For instance, the lines appearing in the largest size of type on the first page of a book would usually be the title; smaller-sized lines immediately following the title, instead, usually indicate the author or the editor. Writing at the bottom of the first page frequently devotes space to the details about book production, such as the name of the publisher, the city and the place of publication. These conventions are, once again, not set in stone, as there are many examples of exceptions to the rules, but finding the book title at the bottom of the front page and the publisher's name at the top would indeed be unusual exceptions. The rules relating to language and orthography tell us which symbols have to be used in order to express a concept or an utterance; the principles regulating the internal structure of a writing system, instead, establish how these symbols should be written down, in relation to each other and to the material where they are written.

Other examples of conventions for the arrangement of writing are those which govern linear continuity in a text, namely the features of *orientation*. These are *axis*, i.e. horizontal or vertical; *lining*, i.e. whether the lines, in a horizontal script, succeed one another downwards or upwards or, in a vertical script, from right to left or from left to right; and *direction*, i.e. left-to-right and right-to-left or down and up. English, for example, along with many other western languages, was traditionally written in horizontal lines of symbols from left to right and the lines have almost consistently followed orderly on the page from top to bottom. Hebrew and Arabic, instead, are historically written in horizontal lines, from right to left. Chinese was traditionally written vertically in columns starting at the upper right, while Mongolian was written vertically in columns starting at the upper left. While all historical writing systems have a straightforward general sense of linear direction, there are also some slightly more complex cases. In Aramaic, for instance, writing still appeared horizontally from right to left, but it was only consonants and long vowels that were written down. Short vowels, instead, were usually not written in Aramaic; if they were written, they appeared as symbols above or below the consonant phonologically preceding the sound in question. In ancient Mesopotamia, clay cuneiform tablets were made in such a way that one side would appear flat and the other side more curved. While both sides could be written on, writing conventionally began on the flat side, as a way to signal direction to the reader.

In addition to direction, there are, of course, many other conventions and ways in which writing is structured, which work in synergy or independently from other linguistic levels of development. Some of the ways in which the orthographic elements laid out in the previous chapter can combine within a given historical writing system include the interrelation between graphemes and other orthographic units, like tildes[1] and accents, the recurrence of graphemes in well-established clusters and the use of ligatures across orthographic units. While it is difficult to establish the specific rules whereby these elements organise themselves across languages, structural levels are quite straightforwardly identifiable. Starting with graphemic systems, words combine elements from an individual set of characters that often represent discrete, contrastive elements. In turn, graphemes can be considered a set of graphological features, which combine in lexically specific permutations to form digraphs or larger agglomerates and also merge together to form morphological affixes, suffixes or whole words; individual words are in turn combined forming compound word spellings and entire phrases. All of these elements work together following a set of language-internal constraints, which, as argued earlier on, govern the quantity and quality of spellings permissible in a given historical alphabetic writing system. Symbiotic examples of language-internal conventions can also occur via diglossia, a situation in which two languages – or two varieties of a language – are used under different conditions within a community. The coexistence of different orthographic elements, and the complications that these may bring to the way in which orthography is structured, falls beyond the remits of this chapter but is a topic that deserves further attention in specialistic book-length contributions.

5.1.1   Segmental and Morphological Structures

For this chapter, let us begin our overview of the structural levels outlined above with the smallest single unit, as discussed in Chapter 4 – the grapheme. A *free grapheme* is one which occurs independently. In English *dog*, for instance, each of the graphemes, <d>, <o>, and <g>, is a free grapheme because each can be found freely in other contexts. Diacritics, on the other hand, are *bound graphemes* and are found only in combination with other graphemes. In French, for instance, there are diacritics like the grave accent ˋ, which appears only in conjunction with other graphemes, and in particular the vowels <a> and <e>, i.e. <à> and <è>, e.g. in *frère*. The combination of a free grapheme with a bound grapheme, as in <è>, is normally seen as a complex symbol. The Indian scripts represent a particularly interesting additional example. In these scripts, consonants are written from left to right and some vowels are written after the consonant in this horizontal order, as one would expect. Other vowels, though, are written before, below, or above the consonant that they follow in pronunciation. Figure 5.1 provides examples of this kind from Sanskrit: the consonant

---

[1] The tilde ~ is a diacritic mark that can indicate a particular pronunciation for the letter to which it is attached.

<k> क	<kā> का	<ki> कि
	<ku> कु	<ke> के

Figure 5.1 Position of diacritics to write Sanskrit vowels (from Rogers, 2005: 12)

<k>, क, in the first column from the left is a free grapheme because it is found by itself. The forms का कि कु के, on the other hand, are complex symbols, made of the symbols for the vowels in <ā>, <i>, <u> and <e>, ा ि ु े, which are diacritics occurring together with the consonant क.

In addition to the combination of free and bound graphemes, historical writing systems also show examples of individual graphemes joined together and appearing as one unit – the result is known as a *ligature*. For aesthetic reasons, the sequences <fi> and <fl> in the Roman alphabet are often printed as ligatures (illustrated in Figure 5.2). This kind of combination has no structural meaning in the framework of the writing system, and it is often referred to as *non-structural ligature*. English readers, for example, normally consider the ligature version of <fi> to simply represent <f> followed by <i>. The case of Danish, instead, exemplifies a second category of ligatures, one in which ligatures *do* make a difference in the graphemic inventory. The ligature <æ> In Danish is made from the combination of the graphemes <a> and <e>. Since <æ> is considered a separate grapheme in the Danish writing system, and it is alphabetised after <z>, it is an example of a *structural ligature*. These examples of ligatures behave in the writing system like a single grapheme, while non-structural ligatures are treated as a sequence of two graphemes.

In addition to structural and non-structural ligatures, there are also *quasi-ligatures*, namely sequences of graphemes which behave like a ligature even though the individual letters are not visually joined together. In older Danish, for instance, <aa> represented the vowel /ɔ/ and, much like <æ>, it was alphabetised as a unit and placed before <æ> and after <z>. Today, <aa> is still a separate unit and has become <å>; the spelling <aa>, though, is still occasionally present in the vocabulary, for example in some Danish proper names like *Kierkegaard*. Another interesting example can be found in Spanish, the historical form of which had <ch> and <ll> as quasi-ligatures; with the invention of computerised writing, it was decided officially by normativist Spanish linguists that the two quasi-ligatures would become sequences of individual graphemes, in order to simplify typing. This decision had an effect on the Spanish alphabetical ordering in recent dictionaries compared to older

Non-ligatured	Ligatured
Fi	Fi
Fl	Fl

Figure 5.2 Non-ligatured and ligatured <fi> and <fl> (from Rogers, 2005: 12)

ones which indicate <ch> and <ll> as quasi-ligatures. Importantly, a quasi-ligature is different from a sequence of graphemes because it is actually treated as a single grapheme. The sequence <ea> is traditionally a way to indicate the vowel /i/, for example in *beam* and *eagle*, but this is only a sequence of graphemes and not a quasi-ligature, because, structurally, <ea> is simply made of two individual letters, <e> and <a>. The alphabetic ordering in English also never treated <ea> as an individual, self-standing unit. In historical Spanish, however, <ll> is indeed a quasi-ligature, because it acts as a separate grapheme in its writing system and has its own place in the alphabet. Thus, the sequence <lla> would appear, in a present-day Spanish dictionary, after <lu>.

Moving on to the other levels of orthographic organisation, a primary consideration for the reader to make at this point is to determine what linguistic level graphemes represent. In the Roman alphabet, the letters are connected to some level of the phonology, while the numerals <1>, <2> and <3> are all related to morphemes.[2] All writing systems feature some degree of variation as to the linguistic level involved, but the linguistic level mainly related to the graphemes of a writing system is normally one of the most immediate ones for us to usefully address some of the possible additional levels of structural organisation in orthography. In a historical writing system where each of the characters is more or less explicitly connected to the phonemes of a language, one might expect something like an immediate one-to-one relationship between sound and letter. This, however, is not often the case, and a difference in the number of units in a specific linguistic-graphemic relationship (e.g. a greater number of graphemes than phonemes or vice versa) is normally known as a *unit discrepancy*. It is indeed because of the presence of unit discrepancies, and on the basis of the phonemic framework of a given language, that one can speak of groups of graphemes that frequently 'go

---

[2] More about the phonemic and the morphemic principles will be discussed in Chapter 7, with reference to some of the main possible levels of orthographic analysis.

together' in a given writing system. The simplest case in which a mismatch between sound and spelling can be noted is that of a polyphone, which indicates a single grapheme representing two or more phonemes. In English, for example, the grapheme <x> is a polyphone when it is used to represent two individual phonemes, namely /k/ and /s/ together, i.e. /ks/.[3]

A *polygraph*, on the other hand, is a sequence of graphemes representing a linguistic unit usually identifiable by means of a single character. Normally, in an alphabet, a polygraph consists of two or more letters representing a single phoneme. In English, for example, the sequence <sh> is a polygraph, because it indicates the single phone /ʃ/. When there are two graphs forming a polygraph, these are normally identified as forming a *digraph* – a special case of poly-graphy which we have already seen, albeit briefly, described in Chapter 4. The English polygraph <sh> is not a quasi-literature, as it is not considered equiva-lent to a single letter. The digraph is alphabetised between <sg> and <si>, as one would normally expect for any sequence of <s> followed by <h>. The French word *chaque*, instead, contains a digraph, <ch>, and a so-called *tri-graph*, <que>. Trigraphs are also a special case of polygraphy; they usually occur less frequently than digraphs, and, as the name suggests, they are made of three graphs lined up in consecutive succession to form a polygraph. The <que> in the French word *chaque* is a trigraph and represents the sound /k/, while the digraph <ch> indicates /ʃ/. In traditional Spanish, instead, <ch> would be a quasi-ligature, rather than a digraph, because it is deemed to be equivalent to a single grapheme and it is not alphabetised as a sequence of two individual graphemes.

The next level of structural organisation of orthography is that of morph-ology, where a group of individual graphemes can be identified with a certain degree of regularity across a wide range of vocabulary in a given language. *Morphological spelling* occurs when there is a degree of consistency in the orthographic representation of particular morphemes, which increases grad-ually during the process of standardisation and is therefore especially evident in orthographies from the relatively recent past. Morphological spelling is a rather systematic parameter for the investigation of orthographic develop-ment: in *morphographic* systems, symbols are mainly related to morphemes. As briefly shown in Chapters 4 and also, to some degree, earlier on in this chapter, some of those morphemes may actually make up entire words and give rise to historically different morphemes – and different words – with identical sound but different spelling. The more that different morphemes are distinguished in spelling, the higher the level of morphography a writing

---

[3] Polyphones are relatively infrequent in alphabetic writing systems, but they are quite common in moraic systems, where each grapheme corresponds to a mora, i.e. "either a syllable-initial CV sequence or a codal (final) consonant" (Rogers, 2005: 272). Moraic systems, like Japanese *katakana* and Cherokee, have traditionally been called, rather imprecisely, syllabic.

system will have: for example, in English, different spelling forms exist for *you*, *yew*, *u* and *ewe*, as well as for *right*, *rite*, *wright* and *write*, each form having its own, unrelated meaning. Within the context of morphography, the notion of *orthographic depth* (also commonly known as *opacity*) is quite useful in order to measure how spelling structure falls at the interplay between the morphological and the lexical level of analysis. Orthographic depth is greater if different allomorphs of the same morpheme are written the same. Thus, for example, word-final *-ed* in English can easily be related to the concept of 'past tense', as it does not feature systematic differentiation between its allomorphs /ɪd/ (e.g. in *gutted*), /d/ (e.g. in *played*) and /t/ (e.g. in *washed*). Consistent spelling of a morpheme, independent of its spoken variables, can also be found in words that sound different but are etymologically and semantically interrelated, so, for example, in *child-children*, *south-southern* and *sign-signature*.

Generally speaking, the examples of spellings outlined above defy the alphabetic principle of a writing system because they encourage increased complexity behind sound–symbol correspondences, and, for that same reason, they contribute to the opacity of a writing system. For example, for a number of etymologically related words, like those given above, the grapheme <i> may indicate /aɪ/ or /ɪ/, <ou> may correspond to /aʊ/ and /ʌ/, and <g> to /g/ or zero, and there are, of course, many more possible correspondences than just those given in these examples. For these reasons, English orthography is more 'deep', while other writing systems, like that of Spanish, have traditionally been more 'shallow', but these are, once again, no black-and-white distinctions. In Sampson's words (1985: 45), "the deep/shallow contrast is a gradient rather than all-or-none distinction", and morphemic and morphophonemic spelling – which is how the examples discussed in the previous paragraph are formally known by linguists – does have exceptions in most historical languages. English is, once again, an object of particular interest in the context of this discussion, because it includes an intermediate depth between the phonemic and the morphophonemic level. For instance, the vowel in the plural suffix, as in *pitches*, is represented by <e>, but there is no way of distinguishing graphically between voiced and voiceless features (so for instance, between /s/ and /z/ in *bats* and *gods*). A maximally deep orthographic form would have **pitchs* rather than *pitches*, but the sequence <tchs> is not allowed in present-day English, as it would violate the *graphotactic principle* of its writing system, i.e. the possible letter sequences allowed in English orthography. Interestingly, there are numerous examples of historical English when the spelling actually subverts both of the rules established above, such as the form *pitchs* itself, for example, but it is difficult to establish whether the examples inherited from the past are meaningful enough to advance any hypothesis on the historical development of orthographic depth.

The formation of compound phrases and more complex structures is an issue that overlaps with not only orthography but also a few other linguistic levels of analysis, including phonology and syntax. For the present chapter, however, let us focus specifically on the elements of compounding that are more strictly related to writing: these will be the correlation between compound forms and punctuation marks – the latter often playing either an active role in joining together individual words or a passive role, when its absence causes words to merge. When separate lexemes are joined together to form compounds, a formal distinction has to be made in writing that is not necessary in speech for a simple reason. In real-time utterances, varying vowel and consonant length, different degrees of loudness or pauses of different length may not necessarily help one to identify word boundaries or even full sentences (compare, for example, the difference between *a nice drink* and *an ice(d) drink*). In writing, however – and this applies also to historical writing – there are visual indicators of word limits which permit no gradience and help writers to make an absolutely clear distinction between different types of compounding. Most western languages, including English, have developed a tradition of signalling compounding following the principles of total separation, hyphenation and total juxtaposition. The constituents of so-called open compounds, which follow the principle of separation, are each identified by using spaces in between the words: examples include *cable television* and *central nervous system*. In hyphenated compounds, the constituents are separated by one or more hyphens, depending on the number of constituents; examples include *hunter-gatherer* and *forget-me-not*. Solid compounds, for instance *software* and *twentysomething*, are orthographic words and thus uninterrupted sequences of letters.

5.1.2   Suprasegmental Structures

In addition to segmental (i.e. pertaining to discrete elements of sequential speech, such as consonants and vowels) and morphological information, historical writing systems often provide information that is not immediately linked to speech but is still helpful for structuring and organising writing. Word and phrase boundaries are among some of the most important elements worthy of mention here, but they are not a constant in history. In several ancient texts, especially those in Latin and Ancient Greek, word boundaries are regularly unmarked – lexical spellings appear as simply written one after the other without any space or breaks (a phenomenon known as *scriptura continua*). There is, of course, a historical reason for the absence of word identification markers in these early Latin and Ancient Greek: before the advent of the book culture, Latin and Greek script was used on scrolls by scribes who often wrote not for the sake of writing as an art, but rather because it was their duty. The role of the scribe was just that of writing down everything they were told to, in order to create written evidence of whatever piece of information had to be recorded. The most natural way in which speech could be transposed to writing was, for them, that of writing in a continuous string of letters, just as they would hear them in speech. Ensuring clarity for the reader was not a major concern for early scribes: readers were usually trained performers, for example actors or orators, who would memorise the content of the texts and the way in which it was to be interpreted. During these reading performances to the public, the piece of continuous writing was simply used as a cue sheet, and it therefore did not require any careful reading.

In most historical texts, however, as briefly mentioned in the previous chapter, punctuation elements are normally used to identify words, whole sentences and groups of sentences, and their distribution on the page. The use of punctuation marks to signal word and phrase boundaries varies according to language, and even within individual languages, punctuation is not always used consistently. Part of the confusion arises from the fact that many punctuation marks have several functions all at the same time, depending on where in the sentence they are found and the intentions of the writer. A full stop, for example, may mark an abbreviation as well as the end of a sentence. Sometimes, especially in monuments and inscriptions, an *interpunct* is used; this punctuation mark, also known as *interpoint* or *middle dot*, consists of a vertically centred dot and is often used in ancient Latin script (though word-separating spaces did not appear until sometime between 600 and 800 BC). In most western historical writing systems, however, a short blank space, inserted at both ends of a word, is normally used as a boundary to identify a lexical spelling form. In English, some phrases are separated by a comma, others by a semicolon and others are not separated at all. Sentences, on the other hand, are often marked twice: the first letter of the first word is capitalised, and a period, a question mark or an exclamation mark is frequently inserted at the end.

An interesting case is that of Spanish, which marks sentences with an exclamation or a question mark by placing the relevant punctuation marks both at the beginning and at the end of a sentence. Inverted marks were originally prescribed by the Real Academia Española (Royal Spanish Academy), which recommended the use of the symbol indicating the beginning of a question in written Spanish (e.g. *¿cómo estás?*, 'How are you?') as early as the mid-1700s. The Real Academia also encouraged the use of the same inverted-symbol system for marking exclamation both at the beginning and at the end of a sentence, using the symbols *¡* and *!*. At the opposite extreme, phrase and sentence boundaries were not marked in Chinese for a very long time; quite recently, however, the western influence seems to have encouraged the introduction of punctuation marks for phrases and sentence boundaries in Chinese. Beyond phrases and sentences, paragraphs are also traditionally identified using elements that come directly from orthography. Paragraphs in particular are often marked either by indenting the first word of the paragraph a bit to the right, much as occurs for paragraphing in this book, and/or by adding a line break in between paragraphs. In historical texts, spaces between paragraphs or larger sections within a chapter are occasionally split by decorations, depending on the type of text and the amount of funding that was invested in its production. In languages written from right to left, indentation occurs on the right-hand side. Zooming further out in our structural understanding of writing systems, we arrive at a point where it is difficult to distinguish between what is purely linguistic and what belongs to the structure of the page, and it is this very grey area of inquiry that the remaining part of this chapter will discuss.

5.2   Display and Layout

The connection between layout and writing system structure has important implications for our overall understanding of orthography: if we choose to ignore the structure of the page, there is a chance that we will miss out on some of the reasons why orthography appeared the way it did. The orthographic conventions used by those responsible for producing texts in the past were often complemented – and at times even contradicted – by the visual and material reality of the page. The *visual programme* of a text, i.e. its layout, decoration and illustration, would usually hold the task of acting as a cohesive and structural framework for writing of all types, regardless of its purpose and its language. Because of their interrelated functions, orthographic and visual textual markers are sometimes difficult to tell apart. A chapter title is an excellent example to illustrate this point: not only is it placed on the page somewhere that has over time become conventional for titles, but it is also signalled by specific font style and size. Clearly, though, there is a lot more to the visual and material reality of the page than just conventions for titles – the layout of the page is a complex process, which has attracted some long-standing academic attention. One of the landmark contributions to the topic is Malcolm Parkes's work (1976) on the interrelation between page layout and information structuring. Parkes elaborated on the concepts of *ordinatio* (the organisation of material) and *compilatio* (the process of combining and rearranging material from different sources), and how these two practices are interrelated.

In his study, Parkes made frequent reference to the term *mise-en-page*, intended as the overall arrangement of the verbal and visual elements on a page. In orthographic literature, however, perhaps due to its technical air, the term *mise-en-page* is hardly ever used, and instead the words *display* and *layout* are often preferred. Aside from display and layout, which to all effects are convenient synonyms of *mise-en-page*, there are different levels of understanding of text visualisation. Among the most recent research in the field is that by

Tjamke Snijders (2015: 429), who referred to the "communicative potential" of layout and prefers a highly comprehensive definition which describes the units in which the material text "has been subdivided . . . illuminated, and written down". Snijders did not include palaeographic 'micro features' of script and individual letter forms in his definition of communicative potential, but the range of elements which make up layout otherwise includes an impressively large variety of verbal, visual and material characteristics. Examples include, among many, the codicological structure of the book, the size of the page, the quantity of writing and its relationship to space, use of colour, titles and rubrics, types of initials and their sizes and shape, punctuation, tables of contents, different types of illustrations, and the type and quality of written material. While it is impossible to cover all of these elements in detail, the following section will focus on a few of them, giving an example of what to look for in the context of a *mise-en-page* analysis.

5.2.1   Mise-en-Page

The *mise-en-page*, the general placement of the different elements which contribute to the layout of the page, can be described using some pre-established parameters as a guideline. Consider the example in Figure 5.3: the description reported below from Tesnière (2020: 625) corresponds to the general details usually given for describing the *mise-en-page*.

Elegant use of the hierarchy of script to construct the first page of the *Vita Martini* of Sulpicius Severus dating to the second quarter of the ninth century: *mise-en-page* where the writing goes in 'diminuendo', as in Irish manuscripts. Page measurements 230 × 177 mm; dry point ruling; justification: 177 × 125 mm. The title in Capitals (7 mm) written on every other line, with alternating black and red; the beginning of the text is marked by a large ornamented initial jutting out in the margin; copied in Capitals mixed with Uncials (5 mm) every other line in red ink and then in a black ink; the text in Caroline minuscule follows.

Now, not every linguistically trained reader is expected to understand every single detail of the description provided above, but there are some ways in which this section can help towards getting a better grasp of it all. Details about layout and distribution are often quite technical, or they refer to a set of standard parameters which are considered something like an analytical paradigm. While technicalities are beyond the remit of this book, I will focus on the paradigm used for describing the distribution of text on the page; this framework can be applied to any type of text (though rarely is it applied to folios) in any kind of book item, whether it is manuscript or print. Let us begin with the basics, which are needed in order to understand the rationale behind the standard parameters: the purpose of the *mise-en-page*.

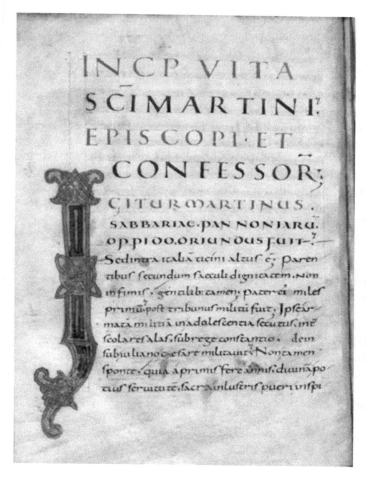

Figure 5.3 Paris, BnF, lat. 10848, fol. 5v (Severus, 2nd quarter of the ninth century; from Tesnière, 2020: 625)

The visual approach to studying the page entails the assumption that the physicality of the book can be used effectively as a means to shape the meaning and the interpretation of a text. The physical form by which text establishes a connection with the reader – a connection that is the backbone of all written texts, since they can rarely exist as separate from their material condition – is by necessity historically contextualised, shaped by the technologies of paper, ink, print, illustration and binding existing at the time of its creation. Texts are also historically contextualised in their participation in, imitation of, or opposition to a set of handwriting or typographic conventions shared and agreed to by those who made, purchased and read the texts. The *mise-en-page* is one of the features that scholars use in order to reconstruct the output of scriptoria and printing houses, establishing patterns for what was produced and in which quantities. Put in connection to the text or the illustration, the *mise-en-page* may also provide details on the norms of reading and the aesthetic codes of the time of production.

All elements which belong to the text's physical appearance are the product of conscious choices made in the past. The selection of parchment or paper, format, type, ornament, illustration, binding and page layout were made by one or more individuals, either alone or in conjunction. Examples of those likely involved in deciding the *mise-en-page* were authors, compositors, scribes, printers, publishers, editors, buyers and readers (the last two especially in the case of bindings). Decisions about the distribution of text and page layout were largely made on the basis of the funds available for producing the text. In his study of Cambridge University Press, for instance, David McKitterick (1992: 280) suggested that the "cramped effect, of small sizes of type occupying as much of the page as possible" of seventeenth-century Cambridge printed items was caused by the "penny-pinching" of its printers. The 1629 Cambridge Bible, he also argues, "embodied a series of typographic decisions whose principal intention was . . . to economize within a framework established by convention" (McKitterick, 1992: 280). These decisions were characteristic of an English trade whose main income came from small-format books like school books, ABCs, almanacs and prognostications, as well as a growing number of cheap printed items such as pamphlets, ballads, newsbooks and jobbing printing. Large and fine paper, larger formats and copperplate engravings, instead, all suggest that an item was exceptionally allotted more funding than the average book, and this was often not from the scribe or the printer.

Whatever material was used – parchment, papyrus or paper – carefully preparing the writing surface ahead of writing was paramount for using the material to its fullest capacity. Gauging distribution and layout in both manu-scripts and paper usually followed a programme prescribed by the head of a workshop or printing house, and either it was based on an existing model or it may be an original creation – the latter usually being in response to some specific commissioning request and dependent on the quantity of funding. The *mise-en-page* was usually decided for manuscripts, before the copying of the texts, and for printed books, before Typesetting. The goal was to establish the way in which the written area should appear in relation to the page format and size, thus maximising readability and identifying the extent to which illustra-tions could relate to the text. The way in which the layout of the page appears usually depends on a wide number of parameters, which may contain some technical details and require careful description. For these reasons, what follows over the remaining part of this subsection is borrowed more closely from Tesnière (2020), and copyright permissions were of course obtained prior to printing:

(1) The organisation of the space written in the centre of the page is contingent upon:

- The format of the support, i.e. the dimensions of the page, which vary according to economic indicators, the envisaged readers, the type of text and other factors;
- The relationship between the parameters of justification, i.e. the dimensions in height and width of the written surface, and the margins. In historical manuscripts and early printed books, the wider the margins, the more prestigious the text was usually perceived as, since this format usually required more paper and made the item more expensive;
- The structure of the written space, which is defined by the ruling, which contains an outline of the *mise-en-page* at the same time as it serves as a guideline for the copy. The establishment for the scheme of the ruling is the first thing to do in describing the *mise-en-page*. The ruling may be done with dry point, lead point or ink. The structure of the written space may be in long lines or in several columns, depending on the style of the book in question. Columns began to make an appearance in historical writing very early on, though they were eventually supplanted by layouts with long lines under the Italian humanistic influence. In principle, there is not an immediate correlation between the chronology of writing and the use of columns, just as there is no link between the use of columns and text formality. There is nevertheless some connection to be made between columns and particular registers and genres, especially in texts with a relatively high level of formality. With reference to genre, the use of columns is particularly frequent in highly esteemed literary compositions, for instance in poetry, often accompanied by copious decoration and coloured specimens.
- The special case of text with commentary, which adds layers of complexities to the *mise-en-page*. Much of the commentary that one finds for books printed soon after the invention of printing is directly inherited from the manuscript tradition. Antiquity had two types of commentary: the marginal commentary in the form of scholia transmitted in the manuscript of the classical author, and the autonomous commentary with lemmata. In the early Middle Ages, instead, the written material that was to function as commentary was copied following a layout that creates an explicit association between the authoritative text and the commentary. The layout depended on whether one saw it as primarily serving the goals of the authoritative or of the commentary text. Subsequently, *glossa ordinaria* further developed the organisation of

the *mise-en-page*. Text and commentary were welded together little by little on the page. The hierarchy between the Bible and its commentary was established by the contrast between the scripts and their interlinear placement: the text of the Bible filled one interline in two; the intermediary line remained empty. There were three sizes of writing: the largest for the biblical text, the middle for the *glossa ordinaria* and the smallest for the interlinear gloss. Often, particularly in legal manuscripts, the commentary encircled the authoritative text, and the different modules of script indicated the level of importance accorded to each text.

(2) The degree of "readability" on the page takes into account the following parameters:

- All aspects of writing: its form (Caroline minuscule, Gothic, cursive, *bastarda*, etc.); its module; its position in relation to the space between the lines; its degree of leaning. For example, the readability of Caroline minuscule (e.g. as in Figure 5.3) has often been praised. That is one of the reasons for which its later form was imitated by the humanists in the fifteenth century;
- The separation of words;
- The punctuation;
- Abbreviations, which make the page more dense;
- All the elements which organise into a hierarchy and structure the text to facilitate reading and comprehension: the hierarchy of scripts, the colours (e.g. red ink for chapter titles and biblical lemmata) and their variations (e.g. blue and red, or black and red, violet and red); underlined words; decorated or filigree letters cutting into or separating the text; the succession of paragraph marks (which are called in French *pieds de mouche*);
- Anything else that makes the page more spaced out, and in particular the ends of line which suppress empty spaces.

(3) The relationship of text and image:

- The placement of the image in the text and the way it relates to the text is governed by multiple constraints and, for this reason, it was usually determined before the text was copied or typeset. The illustration, whether it was a miniature, a drawing or anything else, was for a long time inserted in the columns of the text – the space it occupied in ancient rolls. Associated with a decorated letter, and sometimes with a rubricated title, the miniature became, from the thirteenth century, a sign marking the beginning of books or chapters. From this moment, the decoration entered into a closer relationship with other elements of the page, such as side panels or full-frame vegetation. Consequently, depending on the importance given to the illustration, the illustration would sometimes spread out through the two columns of text. Freeing itself from the antique model, the illustration gradually occupied the margins, too, particularly in Italian regions. The title page in its true sense does not exist in mediaeval manuscripts. Nevertheless, the picture inscribed on the first page of the deluxe manuscript would often serve in the final centuries of the Middle Ages as a title page.

5.3   Orthographic Elements of Visualisation

The previous section has briefly made reference to the interrelations between page layout and orthography, and has provided a description of some of the main parameters used in order to study the *mise-en-page* of historical texts. The beauty of the study of the visual distribution of orthography, and its connection with the strictly bibliographic and palaeographic features of the text, rests in the fact that details about the physical form of a book, and its connections to orthography, can be contextualised in broader social, intellectual and political issues behind the production of the given object of study. The meaning of the historical text resides in its typographic expression, the selection of type, and the sheer amount of orthographic variation – all of which can be studied not just for its meaning and content within the remits of writing itself, but also for its embodiment of orality. By displaying prestigious formats and types of paper, alongside carefully selected spelling variants or an impressively consistent orthographic standard, a book can signal its high status. By means of para-textual features like prefaces, and the way in which these are embellished by illustrations in the cover page, the book even clearly indicates its social position and its function. The end result of the many decisions made by those who planned the *mise-en-page* and fleshed it out on paper are permanently visible, and can thus be interpreted and studied in their entirety and inescapable complexity. The visual part of the book tells the story of an often complex negotiation of the text's meaning within the economic, social, political and cultural contexts, one the one hand, and the writing conventions socially accepted or expected at the time of production, on the other hand.

Despite its undeniable epistemological value, and its unarguably interesting facets, the study of the relationship between the visual display of a text and orthography remains, to date, one of the most underrated areas in historical orthography. Thus, if on the one hand orthography is an overlooked area in historical linguistics, the *mise-en-page* is the 'Cinderella' of book history. The *mise-en-page* of manuscripts, for example, is rarely ever described in the catalogues of libraries; likewise, codicological or bibliographic manuals hardly devote an entire chapter to the *mise-en-page*. Instead, they usually describe in a minute way each of the individual elements of which the page is composed, taking into account the way in which the artist has placed them successively in place. The fact that neither the visual display of orthography nor the *mise-en-page* have received their deserved empirical space in the academy is certainly not owed to the absence of topics which require more extensive scholarly attention. Among the linguistic elements more closely connected to the *mise-en-page*, margin conventions, frame and line ruling, as well as the use of paragraphs and columns all seem promising venues for exploring connections with the orthographic components of the text.

Among the relevant elements on the page which are closest to the linguistic realm, instead, spacing, justification and abbreviation, for example, still require some extensive attention from those interested in the visual arrangement of historical writing systems. It is undeniable, however, that the elements more closely related to the *mise-en-page* outlined above are also somewhat relevant in orthography. While it is impossible to provide a full history of each of these orthographic elements, this last part of the chapter aims to provide a brief description of spacing, justification and abbreviation, integrating the discussion about the *mise-en-page* provided in section 5.2, and the linguistic descriptions provided for these same elements in Chapter 4. The aim of these brief descriptions is not that of being exhaustive, but rather to provide snippets of each of the three topics' historical developments, as a way of identifying fertile areas for future discussions on the topic. The hope is that some of this information might rouse the readers' interest and encourage them to explore some of these topics in their own further reading.

5.3.1   *Spacing, Justification and Abbreviation*

First, *spacing*. As mentioned earlier on in this book, spacing conventions were not always consistent in antiquity and the Middle Ages, whereas they have changed relatively little from the early printing era to the present day. Between the end of the sixteenth century and the beginning of the seventeenth century, however, more marked changes occurred in the layout of the page as a result of developments in compositional practices, which led to a wider, large-scale shift from an understanding of the page as a solid block of text to a more flexible organisation of typographic elements. In particular, space gradually took a pivotal role for a revolutionary approach to ordering the text with more precision and rigour, to replace the unpredictability of older texts, which were often squeezed together. The increased awareness of space as an element of printing likely also enabled compositors to rethink spelling consistencies. Typesetters began to adopt the habit of using spaces of different widths according to the characters that they separated between words. For example, the type *f* in word-final position in English normally required one of the wider spaces due to its stretching shape, but not if the following word featured a *j* in word-initial position, as the hooked tail of the type would take some of the room usually filled in by the space. On the other hand, spaces were narrow in the vicinity of round types like *v* and *u*, and there was a finer difference between word-initial *v* and *u* depending on the character in the preceding word, as *u* sometimes required an even narrower space than *v* due to its rounder shape. With the introduction of those changes, typesetting across most European languages began to enjoy a more widespread use of spaces of varying widths for the express purpose of enhancing readability. From the eighteenth century onwards, American, English, French and other typesetting style guides – explicit lists of rules to help printers follow an in-house standard – were really quite detailed and precise. Early English language guides by Jacobi in the UK (1890, 1892) and MacKellar (1866), Harpel (1870), Bishop (1895) and De Vinne (1901) in the USA, for example, established that sentences should be separated by more space than that of a normal word space. Spaces between sentences were to be em-spaced, and words would normally be 1/3 em-spaced, or occasionally 1/2 em-spaced.

In the history of the modern book, the use of spaces was, both in manuscript and in print, an essential ingredient of *justification*. Text alignment, which is another term for justification, consists in the setting of text and/or the placement of images relative to a page, column, table cell or tab. The edge of a page or column is known as the *margin*, and a gap between columns is known as the *gutter*. In handwritten documents, justification was a matter of scribal choice, depending in most cases on the value of the copy at hand. Even though there was a general commitment to make the most of the writing space, it was a fact that valuable copies were particularly respectful to the inner and outer margins, and line-fillers were frequent devices to avoid a blank line after the closing of a paragraph. Less valuable copies, in turn, were more concerned with the importance of the writing space and, as a consequence, showed frequent use of margins for the running text – to the detriment of word division – together with a wider use of abbreviations. Through the history of printing, instead, justification has been the preferred setting of type in many western languages: the reason for this is that the classic Western manuscript book page was built of a column or two columns, and justifi-cation in this context was important in order to enhance text readability and to maximise the use of type in a given typesetting day. The classical western column did not rigorously justify but came as close as possible to it when the skill of the penman and the character of the manuscript permitted. In early printing, justification was part and parcel of the overall process of imposition, which entailed combining pages in a *forme*. Given the fact that printers operated with a limited supply of type, pages were often set and prepared in the combination required for the formes to be put on the press. The printer would calculate the required amount and quality of type based on the *exemplar*, the material form of the text chosen to be the basis for the composition. Whether for half-sheet or for full-sheet printing, the forecast of the contents of each page, i.e. the *casting-off*, was usually made on the exemplar by counting words and marking the future pages. Casting-off was a process which did not usually take place in the order in which the book was to be read, but rather in small, isolated and often independent sections. It was, in fact, quite rare for a printed text of any length to be prepared in sequential order by one person for a sustained period of time, without any interruption at all. As a result of the compartmentalised approach to casting-off in a *forme*, a text was perceived, during the production process, as a construction in which content, and even the internal coherence of the text, had only secondary significance; the ways in which the text appeared visually, instead, including the distribution of the text across the page, were paramount.

Among the solutions used for making the text fit in on the page, there were indeed *abbreviations*. Short word forms were usually created so that spelling out a whole word could be avoided. In its most simple definition, abbreviation consists in the use of fewer graphemes or symbols than the original form to express the same meaning. Average abbreviations consist of noticeable modifications to the word structure, but their shape sometimes depended on the individual scribe and the region of the text in which they are embedded was produced. Occasionally, abbreviations also occurred by truncating letters at the end of words, or from the body and the end, or by taking away the letters from the middle of a word, leaving in the initial and final letters. Abbreviations became popular in early printing as expedients to save time and space, and also to provide secrecy, but they actually go a long way in history. In both Greece and Rome, the reduction of words to single letters was common practice: in Roman inscriptions, words were commonly abbreviated by using the initial letter or letters of words, and most inscriptions have at least one abbreviation. Some of these early abbreviations often had more than one meaning, depending on their context. The letter <A>, for example, was, among other things, an abbreviation for *amicus*, *annus*, *Aurelius*, *aurum* and *avus*. In general, abbreviations made an appearance in order to make writing easier for the scribe, though it is not to be excluded that, among other reasons, writers also wanted to help the reader to run their eyes faster across the page, especially when the subject matter that was being dealt with on page was repetitive and conventionally familiar to the reader (as was the case of religious prayers and well-known sections from the Bible).

An interesting characteristic of abbreviations is that they occasionally act as a bridge between text and image: sometimes, they are based on individual letter shapes, sometimes they are modified by additional strokes, and at other times they are completely detached from letter-like elements – this last characteristic usually leaving the reader with no chance but to guess their meaning. Some of the abbreviations were so cryptical to the modern eye that they justified the need for abbreviation dictionaries, the most influential of which were written in the eighteenth and the nineteenth centuries. Key titles for the use of those normally working in philology and interested in understanding more about abbreviations are the dictionaries compiled by Cappelli (1899), Chassant (1846) and Trice Martin (1892). Just as the Latin of the Roman Republic (with which the increasingly widespread use of abbreviations is typically associated) bears little semblance to the Latin of the mediaeval church, so the system of abbreviations used in the legal documents of late antiquity was different from that of religious texts of the high-to-late Middle Ages, and this in turn was different from the way in which words were abbreviated in the modern world, all the way up to the present day. The standardisation of English between the fifteenth and the seventeenth centuries involved considerable development in the use of abbreviations. Initially, abbreviations were frequently marked using various suspension signs, including full stops. Thus, sequences like <er> were replaced with a <ɔ>, for instance in *mastɔ* for 'master' and *exacɔbate* for 'exacerbate'. While these abbreviations may seem of little use, they were clear evidence of an attempt from those manually copying academic texts to minimise copy time. In the Early Modern English period, between the fifteenth and the seventeenth centuries, the letter thorn, *Þ*, was used for abbreviating *th*, as in *Þᵉ* ('the').

During the growth of philological linguistic theory in academic Britain, abbreviating became very widespread, not so much in order to facilitate the display of language, but simply because it was fashionable. Probably for similar reasons, in the mid nineteenth century in Boston, a fad of abbreviation started that swept the United States, with the globally popular term *OK* generally credited as a remnant of its influence. Over time, the lack of convention in some style guides has made it difficult to determine which two-word abbreviations should be abbreviated with periods and which should not. In our modern times, widespread use of electronic communication through mobile phones and the Internet has fostered a great number of colloquial abbreviations. This was due largely to increasing popularity of textual communication services such as instant and text messaging. The original SMS, supported message lengths of 160 characters at most (using the GSM 03.38 character set), which means that abbreviations were useful for making the messages cost-effective. The close connection between brevity and price economy in text messages resembles that of faxing services, which were often notoriously – sometimes hilariously – ridden with enigmatic abbreviations. More recently Twitter, a popular social networking service, has begun driving abbreviation use with 140-character message limits, reiterating the principle of economy that is at the heart of most elements that sit at the intersection between orthography and the *mise-en-page*.

Further Reading

Peikola, M., A. Mäkilähde, M.-L. Varila, H. Salmi & J. Skaffari (eds.). 2017. *Verbal and Visual Communication in Early English Texts*. Turnhout: Brepols.

Rogers, H. 2005. *Writing Systems: A Linguistic Approach*. Malden; Oxford: Blackwell Publishing (and especially pp. 13–18 in Chapter 2).

Mountford, J. 1989. 'Language and writing-systems'. In N. E. Collinge (ed.), *An Encyclopedia of Language*. London: Routledge, pp. 701–39.

Sampson, G. 1985. *Writing Systems: A Linguistic Introduction*. Stanford: Stanford University Press.

Tesnière, M.-H., 2020. 'The *mise-en-page* in Western manuscripts'. In F. Coulson & R. Babcock (eds.), *The Oxford Handbook of Latin Palaeography*. Oxford: Oxford University Press, pp. 619–32.

Part III

Analysing Orthography

6   Investigative Approaches

6.1   Traditional Methods

6.1.1   *Philology and Pragmaphilology*

The first half of this book has mainly discussed theoretical aspects of historical orthography, laying out the historical and material context of writing systems, as well as individual orthographic units and how they are ordered and structured to work as a system. This part of the book sets out to cover a range of analytical methods, with the hope of defining benchmarks useful to the student of historical orthography for the most promising empirical approaches in the field, drawing on some of the knowledge and habits inherited from the past. Since the age of cultural nationalism in the late eighteenth and nineteenth centuries, language history has become a nationally constructed object, and supraregionally unified orthography turned into a national monument. This development has entailed consequences, especially for orthographic research, for example the focus on language-oriented philologies. Philology, one of the best-known ways of studying historical orthography, is probably the oldest example of an empirical approach in linguistics and was shaped, over time, by the ever-changing approaches to studying language more broadly. In order to better illustrate this point, let us indeed begin our discussion of empirical methods in historical orthography by focusing on a short history of philology.

The word *philology* stems from Greek φιλολογία, 'philologìa', which means 'love of reasoning, love of learning and literature', and is strictly connected with the word φιλόλογος, 'philòlogos', an adjective meaning 'fond of words'. Philology involves a wide range of practices that are generally connected with the study of texts and languages, and has changed considerably, as an empirical practice, in the history of modern linguistics. Initially linked with the process of curating works from ancient authors, philology has branched out to include not only classical philology but also comparative philology (or historical linguistics), manuscript studies, *Altertumskunde* (the study of ancient cultures through their artifacts) and literary criticism. Because of the many branches of philology existing, there is no univocal understanding about what it entails;

philological methods, that is, differ from discipline to discipline. What is common to all philological practices, however, is the orientation towards the *bibliographic context* in which the languages and literatures of the past are found. While philology is now one of the best-established methods of inquiry in historical linguistics, appreciation of it has fluctuated over time. Jacob Grimm (1785–1863, portrayed in Figure 6.1) was one of the first to speak very highly about philology, as he famously claimed that "none among the sciences is prouder, more noble, more pugnacious than philology and more implacable against mistakes". This view contrasts with that of the first half of the twentieth century, when the term *Buchstabenphilologie*, meaning 'philology of letters', was used to indicate, in a sarcastic way, research which relied too heavily on writing.

During the past decades, philology has enjoyed a new wave of attention, particularly on account of its rediscovered connection with historical sociolinguistics and pragmatics. In the second half of the twentieth century, a renewed

Figure 6.1 Portrait of Jacob Grimm (Source: ZU_09/Contributor/Getty Images)

interest in manuscript studies, with special emphasis on the Middle Ages, gave birth to what came to be known as *New Philology*. The rise of New Philology was the product of a scholarly response to the concern that the Middle Ages – once considered the heart of the philological method – had lost momentum in the face of newer approaches and discoveries, especially in literary criticism. In a special issue of *Speculum*, Stephen G. Nichols (1990) introduced New Philology as an exciting attempt to return to the ancient splendour of manu-script-based research. The renewed interest in philology entailed a focus on the text as an artifact, while previous research had placed emphasis on reconstruct-ing an 'original' version of the text, one that would get as close as possible to the form intended by the author. New Philology was essentially a radical change from older philology: while previous philological work had considered orthographic variation as 'noise' to get rid of, something inevitably resulting from the availability of multiple versions of a text, New Philology took into account variation as a valuable piece of evidence for understanding manu-scripts better. Variety and variation began to be interpreted as *qualities* of writing inherent to the Middle Ages.

In other words, the existence of multiple variants of a text was not evidence of poor linguistic skills from the past, but rather the product of a taste for diversity, which was cultivated and protected. The new way of seeing philology lay at the intersection between the interests typical of literary studies and those of more traditional, linguistically orientated approaches to manuscript studies. More recently, philological research has returned to the question of manuscript transmission and how different versions of an original text can be mapped out by drawing on the evidence available from orthography. Those working in historical linguistics have also emphasised the need to return to the study of the manuscript text as a primary, untouched source of evidence. One of the most notable statements on the matter is probably that of Roger Lass (2004), who, in the context of choosing material for a collection of primary sources, made a convincing case for including only texts that were available in their original, manuscript form. According to Lass, a true historical linguist should always prefer text material that offers untouched spelling, capitalisation and punctu-ation, and should refuse working with texts containing language manipulated in any way by curators, editors and compilers. Creating a corpus using edited texts, Lass argued, will inevitably allow for a number of editorial changes to affect corpus originality, and thus its historical validity.

While the last generations of scholars have reinforced the need for focusing on manuscript transmission, through the mediation of orthography, there is another branch of philology that has recently made an appearance – that of *pragmaphilology*. This branch of philology focuses on accessing the pragmatic and philological variables, i.e. the physical arrangement of the text and the selection of linguistic material underlying the history of the transmission of an individual text. In other words, it draws on both aspects of organisation already introduced in Chapter 5 in relation to structure and presentation in historical orthography, namely the *mise-en-page* and the visual display of orthography. The emergence of pragmaphilology as a cognate branch of philology is proof of the growing scholarly appreciation of text materiality and form. Among the pioneers of pragmaphilology were Andreas Jacobs and Andreas H. Jucker, who affirmed that "adequate (i.e. pragmatic) analysis of historical texts must study these texts in their entirety, including socio-historical context, their production process and – crucially – a faithful account not only of the syntactic/lexical level but also the physical and orthographic level" (1995: 11–12). In broad terms, pragmaphilological work establishes connections between orthography, palaeography, morphosyntactic features and wider concerns such as the social contexts of the text's production, with a view to gleaning a fuller understanding of the communicative event that is a full text.

Pragmaphilology, in line with New Philology and other recent branches of philological investigation overlapping with historical sociolinguistics, rests firmly on the study of original, non-edited texts. For Taavitsainen and Fitzmaurice, "a prerequisite for the conduct of historical pragmatics is the acceptance of written texts as legitimate data" (2007: 18). Thankfully, high-quality digitised copies of original texts, and online scans of manuscripts, are making it increasingly easy for researchers to avoid relying on poor-quality resources, while further encouraging first-hand manuscript-centred approaches. By drawing on digitised copies of original material, one can gain access to a few layers of orthographic analysis – but of course digitised material is never to be intended as a full substitute for the physical book. On the plus side, the increasing availability of digitised copies of original material has widened the angles from which to study orthography and expanded the range and the sheer quantity of primary material available to the modern researcher.

Probably thanks to the advent of pragmaphilology, empirical research in philology has seen an increasing use of corpora. The chief reason behind the rapid growth of corpus-based work is the growing interest in the compilation of structured and systematic collections of texts from historical varieties of languages, most of which have now been digitised and made publicly available. While old-generation corpora were available mostly in physical form and could be analysed only manually, the last three decades have seen an upsurge of digitisation in linguistic corpora. Over the last few decades in particular, the use of corpora has become the standard, most widespread means of accessing orthography of the past worldwide. Corpora have reduced the time required for finding evidence of orthographic phenomena from past centuries and have exercised a significant influence in bringing theoretical and use-based analyses closer together. Corpora have also encouraged a more systematic typology of writing communities, intended as a broadly agreed set of public goals expressed by a category of texts, and articulated by the operations of community members.

For issues related to historical orthography, the discoveries brought about by the use of digital corpora have initiated a revolutionary outlook on the mechanisms behind change, the causes of diachronic developments and more. Approaches based on corpora have afforded rapid access to data and widened the scope of research questions, which has encouraged a growing number of new research methodologies. The development of research programs geared towards enlarging the size of digitised data has led to the dynamic growth of individual corpora, some of which can be used for informing orthographic analysis with additional linguistic areas, including syntax, phonology and morphology. Today, empirical work in orthography can hardly ever be understood as a separate entity from computer-aided work, and in fact theoretical advances and methodological developments are becoming increasingly interconnected, inspiring scholars to discuss and theorise about the nature, purposes and uses of corpora. One of the most notable products of the growing interest in corpus material is the work of McEnery and Hardie (2012), written with a view to provide a typology of linguistic corpora, and to classify them according to several features like mode of communication, data collection regime, annotated versus unannotated material, total accountability versus data selection and monolingual versus multilingual content. Unfortunately, an extensive discussion of computer-aided approaches to studying orthography is yet to be entertained in historical linguistics.

Among the many types of digital resources available to those interested in historical orthography, *facsimiles* are probably least frequently talked about in discourses about corpora. A facsimile is a copy or reproduction of an old book, manuscript, map, art print, or other historical item that is as close to the original material source as possible. A facsimile is different from transcriptions because it provides an exact copy in scale, color, condition, and other material qualities of the original item that it represents. Facsimiles of books and manuscripts, for example, usually have a full copy of each individual page, and if they do not, they are called *partial facsimiles*. Exact copies of original manuscripts are very useful to scholars who otherwise find it very difficult or impossible to access the original item, and there are many instances where only facsimiles survive and the original item has been lost. The majority of facsimiles are sold commercially, and some of them contain editorial notes and addenda. While most facsimiles are now in digitised format, those in print also exist but they may be in limited editions and, indeed, quite expensive. Overall, facsimiles are very precious material for researchers who work in historical orthography, but they are not flawless; those who have worked with facsimiles are well aware of their limitations and pitfalls. The potential issues are manifold and sometimes serious: they range from sheer mistakes in photography, parallax effects, problems with contrast thresholds and rendering for the digitised copies to the impossibility of retrieving the material in which the original text was produced for the printed copies. A conscientious use of facsimiles, and of corpora more broadly, is therefore in order; where possible, original material should always be preferred to a copy, regardless of how faithful to the original the latter may be.

6.1.2   Intratextual, Intertextual and Cross textual Analyses

In the previous section, we have seen how philology places considerable stress on the bibliographic framework of orthography. While this approach is reasonably straightforward, theoretically, how researchers go about studying textual material and orthography in practice still remains unclear. The methods discussed in this section are well-known philological methods, and while they will be rather straightforward to understand, there is a caveat that needs to be made about the illusion of linearity of some of the steps to be followed within each method: data collection and interpretation, the two main stages that usually characterise empirical work, are always intertwined, rather than sequential. Data collection is predetermined and controlled by prior findings or by one's research objectives; and the modes of description used during data collection lead to a preference for a specific set of interpretations. Today, a large number of researchers make use of data that has been collected and processed by others, but even in these cases, one needs to adopt analytical reasoning, formulate a hypothesis and propose some valid interpretation of their data. That said, there are three methods that are most worthy of attention here, all of which are useful for recording and interpreting orthographic *variability*. These methods consist in the comparison of variants in a single text, the comparison of two or more texts and, as a sub-variant, the comparison of different copies of the same text. Naturally, each of these methods has advantages and disadvantages, depending on the research objective of an individual researcher, and they may also be combined together.[1]

The *intratextual approach* consists of comparing variants in a single text and is the most suitable way of determining possible text-internal factors which may contribute to the selection of a specific orthographic form. Examples include syllable boundaries (Early New High German *menner* 'men' but *man* 'man'), adjacent sonorous segments (Turkish *düğün* 'marriage') or assimilations (Hungarian *egyben* 'in one piece', *hatban* 'in six pieces'), issues of word shape (weight) (Late Middle English Chancery Standard *theyre* 'their')

---

[1] Most of the examples provided below in the context of each of the three methods are from Voeste (2020), to whom I am most grateful.

and lexical category (New High German function words *in/*inn*, *dir/*dier* 'to you'). The intratextual approach also accounts for language-external factors, which means that the overall regional context, the level of education of the author and the text's individual writing characteristics are still relevant for explaining the appearance of orthographic features. The usefulness of the intratextual approach lies in the possibility for the researcher to glean very focused insights into the orthographic patterns of an individual text. While it may not be the only or the most promising method for all research projects, the intratextual approach can be used as a tool for a preliminary study.

The method can generate preparative material for a broader study on a full corpus, for example in order to understand the diachronic development of an individual author's piece of writing across the full corpus of authored work. If, instead, it is true that intratextual approaches are often the main starting point for exploratory philological research, they are not necessarily simple to carry out. On the basis of the analysis of a relatively small dataset, in particular, it is difficult to claim that one has enough evidence to make any strong argument that falls outside the remit of the history of the individual text that is being analysed. If idiosyncratic spelling is spotted in a given text under analysis, for instance, it is impossible to tell, on the basis of that individual piece of evidence, whether the idiosyncrasies were used consciously, i.e. with full awareness that the spellings stood out as unusual, or whether they were unintentional. While these considerations are inevitable limitations of the intratextual approach, they would nevertheless be a sufficient starting point for a more comprehensive study.

The *intertextual approach* to the study of orthography is a method that involves at least two different texts and aims to investigate the influence of a given variable between the two texts under analysis – the variable usually being the influence of a language-external factor, like the text's chronology or its place of production. In a study that follows the intertextual approach, the analysis should follow a structure that accounts for one variable, which is usually known as the independent variable, to become the object of investigation as a possible causal factor. Much like intratextual analysis, intertextual analyses are not as easy to undertake as one might think. In order to discover the extent to which the independent variable has any influence on the dependent variables, one must also ascertain that there are no potentially confounding variables that disturb the investigation. This means that all other variables have to be fixed for the approach to work effectively.

Arguably, the initial assumption that all elements between the texts are equal or very comparable is difficult to measure and to prove empirically, and it is in fact often the case that there are many compromises made at the onset of a study that follows the intertextual approach. For instance, texts written or produced in the same region or during the same decade or the same quarter of a century are sometimes considered to share sufficiently 'equal' variables. While finding comparable texts is difficult to begin with, focusing on a very specific set of data can also reveal difficulties that make the use of the intertextual approach ineffective. It would not be surprising, for example, if orthographic patterns from individual writers were inconsistent over time, but rather they varied in their degree of consistency and variability from time to time or even from text to text. Most philological work actually backs up the claim that there is hardly any consistency at all in an individual's spelling, morphological and syntactic systems. A corpus study of Thomas Mann's works (Grimm, 1991), for instance, showed that his linguistic features are sometimes more consistent when engaging with his brother Heinrich than in his other writings. The argument provided so far leads one to an inevitable truth for all those wishing to benefit from using the intertextual approach: this approach to investigating an orthographic variable requires aprioristic certainty that the texts being compared are actually sufficiently similar to each other.

So far, the overview of the intertextual approach has shown some rather straightforward ways in which the method can be used for asking questions about historical writing systems. However, if on the one hand the analysis of an isolated determinant, on the basis of sufficient comparability between the texts, is useful and convincing, there are, on the other hand, more complications that warrant a third empirical approach. In particular, a causal link between a spelling variable and a language-external or a language-internal factor may not be as easy to identify as one might think, because linguistic variables can often be interlinked in complex, dynamic ways. Various factors may all be at play concurrently and influence the selection of an individual orthographic variant – all of which means that isolating a single causal determinant for a given spelling feature might be short-sighted, if not outright naive. Thus, for the analysis of larger collections of texts, researchers often work with the assumption that multiple factors, such as text-type, dialect or social rank of the author, are in fact interlinked. Building on this assumption, then, they attempt to determine which of the variables involved in the diachronic study of orthography shows up as particularly dominant in a given corpus.

The *cross textual approach* involves a comparison of different versions of the same text, and is, in essence, a subtype of the intertextual analysis. Unlike the intertextual approach, however, which involves studying exact copies of a text, cross textual analyses always involve different copies, reprints, editions or successive textual records – e.g. a draft, a first complete manuscript and a fair or final copy. The cross textual approach follows strictly the rule of *ceteris paribus* ('all other things being equal'), as it requires the author and the text to be not just similar but identical in order to make the variable analysis possible. This third approach is especially useful if one wants to investigate changes that appear to have been made on purpose from one version to the next, introduced by the scribe, the editor, the proofreader or the typesetter. Variables identifiable using this third approach may also indicate an underlying sound change or some regional or local features. Sometimes, changes might even encourage a reinterpretation of spelling variants, and be accompanied by a better understanding of underlying morphosyntactic features. A study that uses the cross-textual approach will usually look for *possible* and *actual* spelling variants, by determining not only the actual space of a given spelling form across multiple textual copies, but also its possible space, i.e. the sum of all imaginable combinations of graphemes that were actually used in the spellings of a word.

6.2   Synergic Perspectives

6.2.1   A Short Note about Terminology

So far, this chapter has introduced some well-known approaches to investigating orthography – all of which, in the traditional spirit of philology, are usually used for investigating an individual language. The second half of this chapter focuses on some recently developed lines of analytical inquiry, where philological elements are of course still present, but where efforts are made to achieve a more explicit synergic perspective on historical writing systems. All of the topics discussed in this second section of the chapter are aimed to facilitate a comparative study of orthographies over time, at a moment in history where researchers are increasingly more interested in international perspectives. In the concluding chapter of *Advances in Historical Orthography*, Anja Voeste and I made reference to the fact that, for comparative perspectives on analytical methods to become effective, it would be desirable to agree on some generally accepted terminology (Condorelli & Voeste, 2020: 249). Merja Stenroos also suggested that "the description of orthography is a field undergoing development and so far there seems to be no one established system of terminology in use" (2004: 263). While a full-blown set of terms and definitions has yet to be established for historical orthography, a nearly inescapable theoretical requirement for comparative, cross-linguistic routes of analysis is that of *Schriftlinguistik* (also known as grapholinguistics), a young linguistic subdiscipline that deals with the scientific study of all aspects of writing. Grapholinguistics has, in recent years, grown to establish itself as a linguistic subfield, mainly covering those aspects in the present book that are parallel and comparable to the study of purely linguistic structures. The development of the field is mostly tied to Germany, and the only comprehensive textbook on the subject to date was indeed published in German (Dürscheid, [2002] 2016). The history of grapholinguistics, however, can be traced back to the research topics of interest and traditions that arose in German universities as early as the 1970s, and which culminated in many instances of research into the German writing system and its historical development.

The achievements outlined above have more recently been integrated with organised efforts to create synergy in the theoretical aspects of orthography and have encouraged, among other things, the publication of a special section on grapholinguistics made available within an otherwise 'mainstream' dictionary, i.e. *Wörterbücher zur Sprach- und Kommunikationswissenschaft* (Neef et al., 2012). The dictionary provides some compelling evidence for some of the contradictions existing in the field, as it contains many multiple definitions of seemingly identical terms. The reason for the existence of multiple definitions is that most of the terms in grapholinguistics are in fact objects of contention from various disciplines and languages simultaneously – an issue that takes us back to the problem of the lack of generally accepted terminology in historical orthography. Without a doubt, many of the current problems may be linked to grapholinguistics' immaturity. In addition to terminology, the current state of grapholinguistics is evident from how much information we have available about various writing systems. Most importantly, a mature linguistic-based theoretical thought, which needs a sufficient level of breadth and complexity to be able to cover historical writing systems comprehensively, is also lacking. In addition to the existing difficulties, most of the work that has been done in grapholinguistics relates to present-day writing systems, which means that those working purely on historical aspects of orthography have to filter through or reinterpret existing knowledge in order to evaluate its applicability to historical parameters.

While a great deal has yet to be achieved in grapholinguistics, this subfield of linguistics does indeed provide a basic 'universal' language for approaching orthographies synergically – and the newest generation of researchers seems to be increasingly interested in making this universal language a more solid framework for all to use.[2] The purpose of grapholinguistics is that of exploring and defining the relations between the spoken language and the written language, in addition to the overlap between concrete units and abstract units of linguistic communication. The field of grapholinguistics aims to achieve the goals outlined above following two different routes, *graphematics* and *graphetics*. Graphematics is concerned with the description of writing systems (as opposed to *orthography*, which is concerned with the standardisation of writing systems). Graphetics, on the other hand, has already been briefly discussed in Chapter 4 (section 4.2.2), but a definition is provided here again for convenience: it concerns itself with the materiality of writing, explored by recourse to such systems as languages or cultures or by experimental methods. All of the

[2] One of the most promising general theories provided recently on grapholinguistics is that of Meletis (2020).

elements inherent in the two routes of grapholinguistic theory mentioned above are important for comparative, cross-linguistic perspectives, but it is especially the graphematic part that allows for different lines of analytical inquiry to be made possible across languages. In what follows, some of the most widespread of these strands will be introduced, and, for all of them, the grapholinguistic framework should be held as an unspoken, yet crucial foundation for guaranteeing a level of discursive comparability across languages. The sections follow the Romance and Germanic linguistic strands on the one hand and the Slavic route on the other hand, reflecting the language groups where the lines of analytical frameworks were originally experimented in and discussed. While a distinction between language groups has been retained below to reflect the broad original context where the frameworks were developed, the sections are not to be intended as restricted only to the reference languages discussed below. Neither, of course, are the topics discussed in this second section of the chapter meant to be fully exhaustive. Rather, they are to be taken as examples aimed at encouraging comparative frameworks in historical orthography, at a moment in history where researchers are more focused on international perspectives.

6.2.2   Insights from Romance and Germanic Frameworks

The comparative study of diachronic writing systems is an investigative perspective that has become popular among Romance and Germanic languages. Technological development, the implementation of new analytical approaches, as well as theoretical and methodological innovations and discussions are among the most relevant factors responsible for encouraging a comparative perspective on the development of historical writing systems. The comparative approach has followed different analytical frameworks which, in turn, reflect the different definitions for the term *grapheme* (some of which were discussed, in a simplified way, in Chapter 4). The strands followed to date are indeed many, but they can all be grouped into at least three major categories: the comparative model of Romance *scriptologie*, the cultural history of comparative orthographies and the comparative graphematics of a single orthographic unit. The comparative model of romance *scriptologie* is distinct from *scriptology*, which instead corresponds to the general area of writing theory that contemporary linguists call grapholinguistics, as discussed above. Traditionally, *scriptologie* seeks to trace down the diachronic development and the structure of mediaeval spelling, which was the period of time preceding the rise of a widespread orthographic standard across many languages. The term *scriptologie* refers to a description of variation in historical writing systems following a *diachronic*, *diatopic* and *diastratic* route (i.e. across time, space and socio-cultural variables). This approach has seen a surging interest in its application to mediaeval orthography, for natural reasons: romance-speaking Europe featured some remarkable dialectal fragmentation throughout the whole of the Middle Ages. In particular, languages belonging to the Gallo-Romance, Ibero-Romance, Italo-Romance and Balkano-Romance groups all had in common the presence of dialects with semi-idiosyncratic peculiarities.

Over time, some of the regions where these dialects were spoken developed their own standardised systems for writing the dialects. More often than not, these dialectal writing systems were anything but perfect transcriptions of the spoken dialects and, for this reason, they were dubbed *scriptae*. Dialectal *scriptae* are basically a blend of different graphic features all co-existing in the same writing system and represent a treasure trove in historical orthography. They include *diatopic* features, that is to say regional and dialectal marks, *atopic* features, which means that they are not dialect-specific but rather shared by the full linguistic domain, and lastly, *sociolinguistic* features, in the sense that a graphic feature became a marker of the social status of those who used it. Within the Gallo-Romance area of the twelfth century, for example, the *langue d'oïl*, present-day French's ancestor, consistent in a few oral dialectal variants, rather than a unique systematic language. Some of these dialectal variants had their own *scripta*, hybrid writing systems made of particular features specific to that dialect mixed with features shared by the whole *langue d'oïl* dialectal corollary. These and similar examples constitute key areas of work in *scriptologie*, a framework of analytical inquiry that lies within the umbrella of the comparative method and that seeks to examine orthographic variation in individual manuscripts.

Generally speaking, *scriptologie* has been used as a framework of inquiry for studying the Gallo-Romance and Italo-Romance dialectal areas and, although less comprehensively, the Ibero-Romance area. To date, *scriptologie* is almost entirely missing from the Germanic areas of academic work, perhaps because these languages never reached complex enough dialectal variation to justify this framework of analytical inquiry. There are, however, other ways in which *scriptologie* can become a useful tool for scholars interested in Germanic languages: its comparative perspective can provide a basis for analysing variation across several sister languages belonging to the same language group. What is more, *scriptologie* can also be applied to languages from periods of time other than the Middle Ages, and there are virtually no geographical boundaries on the focus of analysis. It could, for example, provide an excellent framework of inquiry for a pan-European study of orthographic developments in eighteenth-century Europe (covering the area represented in the eighteenth-century map in Figure 6.2). In a sense, *scriptologie* could act as a first stepping stone for an understanding of pan-European orthography on the basis of the development and interaction of individual *scripta*. Metaphorically speaking, the said framework could provide an outline of the whole house that

Figure 6.2 A map of early modern Europe in the eighteenth century (Source: www.loc.gov/item/98687161, Contributor: Frederico de Wit)

is the European continent as well as a description of the individual bricks – the *scripta* – which make up the full house (Goebl, 1995: 315). A testimony of how effective the framework discussed so far can be may be found in the extensive treatises of Romance linguistics available to date, which present a comparative survey of all written varieties relevant to the language family. A key title is, for example, the *Lexicon der Romanistischen Linguistik* (1995), which provides a summary of all the *scriptae* attested in mediaeval French. Typical texts analysed as a basis for writing treatises like the one mentioned above are non-literary ones; these, by virtue of their ephemeral nature, are more likely to inform scholars about non-standard writing systems. The orthography of non-literary documents usually represents more closely the characteristics of the time in which they were produced, as well as the speech sounds of the place where they were created.

While *scriptologie* focuses on variation, the *cultural history of comparative orthographies* studies similarities across writing systems. This second framework of analytical inquiry studies diachronically the norms that constrain and order the graphemic inventory of a language, and the connections between those norms and societal changes. The analysis of individual graphemes, i.e. the history of spelling, represents the core of the said framework of analytical inquiry. Within the remits of European orthographies, most of the languages in the European continent have in common the use of the Latin alphabet, which effectively represents a strong interconnecting factor for languages that otherwise have quite distinct writing systems arising from regions that are geographically remote. Recent collective research endeavours have presented a relatively new way of understanding the comparative history of orthography across Romance and Germanic language groups (but also, albeit to a lesser extent, Slavonic and Finno-Ugrian). The relationships between different language communities and patterns of orthographic standardisation across Europe, for example, have recently received more attention from a synergic perspective by Baddeley and Voeste (2012b) and Condorelli (2020d). The perspectives afforded by these synergic efforts point to a development of historical writing systems in Europe as a process of convergence towards parallel, if not at times identical, standardising conventions. Crucially, some of the socio-historical factors involved in this univocal process of development are quite comparable across Europe: these include the mobility of scholars, the flow of intellectual ideas and the spark of technological innovation in the printing industry of the European continent. From comparative work of the type above, it is possible to derive some parameters that can be used for future comparative insights into diachronic developments, as follows.

The first parameter is that of a *typology of writing systems*, encompassing both traditional semiographic systems of spelling, frequently including etymological spellings (like the French language), and additional systems more detached from Latin, i.e. phonographic systems of spelling (like Italian or Spanish). Another parameter is that of a comparative view of the *graphic expression* of each vernacular's phonetic characteristics, especially with reference to the creation of letters for 'new' phonemes absent from the Latin phonological system – for example, palatals and fricatives. A third parameter is the assessment of the extent to which *language contact* may lead some languages to have influence over others. A clear example would be that of the role of French for written communication in England after the Norman Conquest of 1066, which led to the French respelling many English words (e.g. <qu> instead of <cw> in *queen*, <gh> instead of <h> in *night*, <dg> instead of <cg> or <gg> in *bridge* and so on). There are many other potential parameters that could be identified from the cultural history of comparative orthographies, but many more are yet to be found and agreed upon by the scholarly community, both implicitly – by means of additional synergic work on the lines established so far – and explicitly – by way of open discussions about planning and policy in historical orthography.

Moving on, let us now focus on the third and last framework of inquiry to be introduced in this section – that of the *comparative graphematics of a single orthographic unit*. Recent years, for example, have seen a growing excitement in the comparative study of punctuation, first of all from a palaeographic or a codicological point of view, and also as a unit of orthographic structure that takes the role of a useful marker for syntactic, semantic, enunciative and pragmatic elements in a historical language. The comparative history of punctuation is not only a strictly 'materialistic' subject, but also a means to detect the extent to which different texts served the reading experience and the ultimate goal of a given text. At least two different research routes in the topic can be identified to date. The first research strand is that of the so-called *white punctuation* – the history of how words became identifiable using a blank space or graphic sequencing. White punctuation was a widespread feature across most European languages, especially those with a writing system based on the Latin alphabet. An interesting feature that has arisen from studying white punctuation across Latin, Irish, Spanish and French, for instance, is the presence of a twofold option pattern. One option was for grammatical words to be joined together so that they would become full words; for example, Latin *deparadiso* coming from *de paradiso*, Old Irish *isaireasber* coming from *is aire as-ber*, French *laueintre* coming from *la ueintre*, and Spanish *conderecho* coming from *con derecho*. Another option was for words to be split into two or more visual units, like for instance Latin *reli quit* coming from *reliquit*, French *ar gent* coming from *argent* and Spanish *di sputar* coming from *disputar*.

The second research strand in historical punctuation is that of *the linguistic and comparative history of punctuation in European languages*. Borbála Keszler, who was among the first to put forward this idea (2003, 2004), placed emphasis on the wholesomeness of European punctuation as a full, all-encompassing subject touching many languages, and provided some significant information about the cultural history of European punctuation. One of the landmark volumes that have heralded the subject, however, is the *History of Punctuation Marks in Europe* (Mortara Garavelli, 2008), which gives a comparative perspective on historical punctuation across more than twenty languages. In the introductory chapter to the volume, Lepschy and Lepschy (2008: 3) indicated that punctuation across Europe has both unitary and divisive traits concurrently. This is because punctuation marks are highly comparable across languages, and yet at the same time they are embedded in the chronological development of each language and the inherent differences of the individual language groups. These two individual but complementary aspects of punctuation make punctuation features mutually understandable across many – if not all – writing systems in Europe, while at the same time preserving interesting language-specific differences that are worthy of empirical investigation.

If we approach present-day writing from the point of view of orthotypography (i.e. the rules that came about for identifying 'correct' orthography today), several noteworthy differences across languages come to mind. Consider, for example, the following: French punctuation marks are always preceded by a space, but the majority of other European languages do not have this feature. In addition, quotation marks are not the same for all languages; so, for instance, Italian has «these quotation marks» whereas English uses "these" or 'these'. In the case of embedded quotations, Spanish and French feature a mixture of quotation marks («quotation 1 ... "quotation 2 ... 'citation 3' ... " ... »), while Hungarian punctuation behaves slightly differently („quotation1 »quotation 2» quotation 1"). Computer-aided writing systems usually account for conventional differences across quotation marks, but they are not necessarily automatically applied in series, unless more complex rules have been built specifically prior to using the pieces of software.

Another interesting difference relates to the rules that allow splitting words at the end of a line: in English, words are usually split between the prefix or suffix and the root, for example in the word *question-able*, but Italian and Spanish split words on the basis of their syllables, for instance in Italian *que-stione* and Spanish *cue-stión*. A fourth interesting point that is worthy of mention with respect to differences across languages is that of punctuation used for word contraction. In Spanish, letters are always spelled out in full in every word; so, for instance, the word *oeste*, is always spelled out like this, but Italian contracts words quite often. Thus, the words *lo amico* never appear like that in writing, but rather *l'amico* is always the preferred norm. All of the differences established above call for more historical evidence to unearth the reasons for their existence, accounting for factors like translation, scribal copying of texts, printing, manuscript circulation, the history of reading and the interaction between all of these things together. Interesting insights may also come from applied linguistics, with specific reference to the passing on of rules across generations, the perception of them across the society and the way in which the rules are understood across different age groups within the same generation (see also Chapter 9). The ever-growing quantity of material available to researchers from historical corpora makes the attainment of these research goals increasingly easier.

6.2.3   *Insights from Slavic Frameworks*

The term *biscriptality* refers to the use of two or multiple writing systems for the same language and entails that this peculiarity of writing is approached from an empirical point of view. In the literature, biscriptality has been referred to under different names, but the most frequently used one is that of *digraphia*. In recent years, biscriptality has actually been incorporated in the definition of digraphia, and the two are not synonymous anymore. Bunčić et al. (2016: 54) defined biscriptality with a definition that represents a slight modification of the definition of digraphia: "[b]iscriptality is the simultaneous use of two (or more) writing systems (including different orthographies) for (varieties of) the same language".[3] Biscriptality can occur on at least three different orthographic levels: the first level is that of the script (*bigraphism*), in other words, the use of two or more scripts for the same language – for instance, as it happens in present-day Serbian, which is written in both Latin and Cyrillic scripts, and Tatar, written with Arabic, Cyrillic and Latin letters. The second level is that of orthography (*biorthographism*), that is to say, within a given writing system, the co-existence of two or more inventories and/or arrangements of the written signs. Russian 'pre-reform' orthography, as opposed to present-day Russian orthography, or the use of the *taraškevica*, in opposition to *narkomovka* in Belarusian, and again the use of traditional, as opposed to simplified *hanzi* for standard Chinese, are all excellent examples of this second level of biscriptality. The third level is that of the glyph (*biglyphism*), that is to say, the appearance of two or more glyphic variants within a given writing system. Examples are the use of blackletter glyphs as opposed to other continental glyphs like italics or antique for German. Each of the three manifestation levels is never fully detached from the others. For instance, within a given script (say, the Latin one) one may be able to analyse biscriptality at the level of orthography and the glyph concurrently, while orthography or glyph distinctions between different scripts are not as useful to discuss, even if they occur as examples of bigraphism. There are also instances of biscriptality where multiple manifestation levels exist; compare, for instance, Russian Cyrillic for perspectives on both orthography and glyph. During the early eighteenth century, Russian Cyrillic allowed for the coexistence of the 'new' westernised letter forms and orthography with the older 'Church Slavonic' letter shapes and orthography. Further to the manifestation level differences, biscriptality situations may occur according to a few different perspectives, as follows.

The first perspective refers to chronology. Within certain scholarly strands, a distinction has been established between the use of two or more writing systems for the same language concurrently (synchronic biscriptality) and the

---

[3] This definition excludes diachrony from biscriptality, but this of course does not mean that this chronological dimension cannot be applied to it. Bunčić et al.'s understanding of biscriptality (2016: 20) accounts for the definition of *script* as a "set of graphic signs for writing languages", that of *writing system* as a set of graphic features working together to write a given language and that of *orthography* as a standardised way of writing the graphic signs that make up a particular writing system – reflecting the definitions used for the present book as a whole.

use of two or more writing systems for the same language *at different times* (diachronic biscriptality; cf. Dale, 1980; Berlanda, 2006). From a sociolinguistic perspective, instances of synchronic biscriptality are of greater importance, as these situations refer to complex linguistic links within existing language communities during specific time spans. However, from a historical viewpoint, the study of the use of two or more writing systems for the same language at *different* times is without a doubt quite important. Diachronic biscriptality is frequently associated with a period of synchronic biscriptality, when writing systems of different eras are used concurrently in a language community. Thus, for work in biscriptality, it is a good idea to make a complex study of both synchronic and diachronic levels of biscriptality scenarios. Cases of diachronic biscriptality are, for instance, the switch from the Arabic to the Latin scripts in twentieth-century Turkish, the shift from Scandinavian runes to the Latin script and, finally, the change from Glagolitic to Cyrillic in Old Church Slavonic.

A second perspective relates to geographical and political identity. A difference has been identified between cases of biscriptality existing within an individual geographic or political situation (termed *monocentric biscriptality*); and arrangements where the same language is written drawing on different scripts in different geographic, social or political groups (*pluricentric biscriptality*). Instances of pluricentric biscriptality are cases of bigraphism, involving, say, the connection between Hindi, written in Devanāgarī characters, and Urdu, written in Arabic letters; Romanian, written in Latin characters, and Moldavian, appearing in Cyrillic letters; Bosnian, written using Arabic characters and in Latin or Cyrillic graphic forms. There are also cases of biorthographism, examples of which are the relationships between Post-reform Russian in the early-twentieth-century Soviet Union and Pre-reform Russian migration texts during the same period; Catholic and Protestant Upper Sorbian; and Warsaw and Cracow-centred Polish more than a century ago.

A third perspective characterising biscriptality relates to the level of formality. In some cases, a difference may be established between cases where more than one writing system is seen as a standard for a given language, such as present-day Serbian, where both Cyrillic and Latin scripts are official, and arrangements where the standard language only formally accounts for one script, but additional scripts are also used informally, for example on TV commercials and the Internet. Instances of informal bigraphism that may be relevant here include the existence of Glagolitic graffiti in pre-modern Russia and the co-existence of Latin and Cyrillic standard and non-standard orthographies on Serbian websites.

A fourth perspective relates to the textual context. In particular, a difference may be established between scenarios where the same text features multiple writing systems (*hybrid-script texts*) and texts featuring only one script, which still relate to other similar material forming biscriptality scenarios (*monoscriptal texts*). While monoscriptal texts are most frequent and do not need explanation, an example of a hybrid-script situation would be that of personal ads. When a distinction is established between hybrid-script and monoscriptal texts, one may conduct an investigation into whether the assumed readers of each of the two groups of texts are the reasons behind different biscriptality situations. Hybrid-script texts may be preferred by readers who know more than one script, while monoscriptal texts, even in biscriptal situations, may be destined for those who can read only one script.

While biscriptal situations usually occur within a society or a community, there are also situations where biscriptality arises from the presence of two or more writing systems for a given language by an individual (known as *individual biscriptality*), in contrast to the system used within a given community where the individual is situated (called *societal biscriptality*). The community level has so far received most empirical attention, drawing on a range of theoretical and empirical frameworks. Bunčić et al. (2016: 30–50), for instance, identified more recent analyses of biscriptality situations which lean on socio-linguistic paradigms, that is, taking sociolinguistic empirical approaches for studying speech and adapting them to writing, and more recent studies with a solid trajectory of academic development, like numismatics. With reference to individual practices, the attention has frequently been on situations where different writing systems are linked to different languages, in other words to situations where two or more monoscriptal languages are employed by the same person. Biscriptality at the level of the individual, however, which is admittedly not as widespread as for the community level, is found more frequently among many individuals educated in modern Serbian or earlier Serbo-Croatian (see, e.g., Feldman & Barac-Cikoja, 1996).

The analysis of biscriptality from a historical point of view, especially from a sociolinguistic perspective, frequently focuses on community-related situations, but there are indeed some examples where interesting insights can be gleaned also from the perspective of the individual. For diachronic orthography, biscriptality at the individual level represents an interesting area of potential work especially for sixteenth- and seventeenth-century languages, where the co-existence of Greek, Latin and English, for example, was a fairly common feature of individual book publications of the time (especially in books that dealt with scientific subjects or held prayer-related functions). Other relevant examples include the reading abilities of individuals in Ancient Egypt, or even mediaeval Slavic scribes writing texts using both Glagolitic and Cyrillic (further discussed below). Occasionally, when the focus is on the individual's perspective on the orthographic phaenomenon, a difference can be established between the *producer's perspective*, that is when the same person is responsible for writing texts using more than one script, and the *receiver's perspective*, which refers to the condition of the reader at whom the text is aimed (the reader can in fact be literate in one or more scripts).

Since some of the pieces of information provided so far stem from synchronic linguistics, let us now take a step back and focus briefly, as a way of closing this chapter, on examples of historical biscriptality, with specific reference to bigraphism, biorthographism and byglyphism. The case of Glagolitic and Cyrillic Old Church Slavonic is an interesting instance of bigraphism. The first script used to write Old Church Slavonic was Glagolitic, while Cyrillic was introduced a little later (the oldest examples of Glagolitic texts are in fact from the tenth century AD). The shift from Glagolitic to Cyrillic is in effect an instance of diachronic biscriptality, but there was also an important period of time in history where both scripts were available concurrently, not only within the same society but also occasionally even by the same person. Old Church Slavonic, therefore, is one of the rare cases where both diachronic and synchronous bigraphism are attested, at different levels of formality. A curious example of bigraphism may be found in the use of Glagolitic graffiti on the walls of St. Sophia cathedral in Novgorod. This script is in sharp contrast with the Cyrillic script normally used in many different situations during the same time in Novgorod.

A second example of bigraphism may be found in the use of Glagolitic, Cyrillic and Latin in the Croatian and South Slavic areas. In Croatia, the Glagolitic script was present until the nineteenth century. This situation caused a rather longstanding bigraphic situation between Glagolitic and Latin scripts – a relationship also interfered with by the Cyrillic script. The co-existence of different scripts goes back a long time: already in the mid sixteenth century, translations of the New Testament and other titles were published in Croatian using the Glagolitic, the Cyrillic and the Latin scripts. Each of the three versions were conceived to address the largely monoliterate population of the time, who were familiar with only one among the Glagolitic, Cyrillic or Latin scripts. The three writing systems were so successful that, eventually, the Propaganda Fide in Rome used all three scripts in their books. A third example is that of the Arabic and Cyrillic alphabets co-existing in mediaeval Bosnian. At the time, especially in written material aimed at Muslim readers, a revised form of the Arabic script had made an appearance. Arebica – so the writing system was called – was based on the Ottoman interpretation of the Arabic alphabet for Turkish. The Slavic language of Bosnia often appeared in a version of the Cyrillic alphabet called *Bosančica* or *Western Cyrillic*. The bigraphism situation occurring between Arebica and Bosančica was, in effect, not monocentric, because Muslims usually used Arebica while everyone else preferred Bosančica. Over a century ago, Arebica even began to be used in newspapers as a contrastive means for headings and other elements of the page.

Moving on to biorthographism, an example of that is Russian Cyrillic in the period immediately before and after the First World War. The years 1917–18 marked the beginning of Russian writing reforms, officially used by the emerging Bolshevik government, which resulted in the production of printed books using the revised orthography; the earlier orthography, on the other hand, continued to be used in material printed outside of Russia until the early twentieth century, thus creating a case of pluricentric biorthographism. A second example is that of Russian 'everyday' orthography in Novgorod birchbark documents from the eleventh to the fourteenth centuries. In several Russian birchbark texts, discovered especially in Novgorod from the mid twentieth century, a peculiar 'everyday' Cyrillic orthography has been noted. This unusual example of orthography is characterised by the different function of some of the characters, compared to that in the 'standard' Cyrillic orthography of the same time. This situation can be considered an example of biorthographism, where both 'everyday' and 'standard' Cyrillic take up two different registers, one more formal and the other more informal. The last example to be mentioned here relates to biglyphism and refers to Russian Cyrillic of the eighteenth century. At the onset of the eighteenth century, Tsar Peter I established a 'civil' typeface, which caused a case of biglyphism between the new typeface and the older Cyrillic typefaces usually available in religious texts and much less frequently in secular texts.

Further Reading

Bunčić, D., S. L. Lippert & A. Rabus. 2016. *Biscriptality: A Sociolinguistic Typology*. Heidelberg: Winter.

Ambrosiani, P. 2020. 'Graphematic features in Glagolitic and Cyrillic orthographies: a contribution to the typological model of biscriptality'. In M. Condorelli (ed.), *Advances in Historical Orthography, c. 1500–1800*. Cambridge: Cambridge University Press, pp. 46–66.

Claridge, C. & M. Kytö (eds.). 2020. *Punctuation in Context: Past and Present Perspectives*. Bern: Peter Lang.

Dürscheid, C. [2002] 2016. *Einführung in die Schriftlinguistik*, 5th edn. Göttingen: Vandenhoeck & Ruprecht.

Mortara Garavelli, B. 2008. *Storia della Punteggiatura in Europa*. Rome; Bari: Laterza.

7   Representation and Interpretation

7.1   Orthography as a Historical Construct

7.1.1   *Regularity of Linguistic Representation*

Studying orthography requires, by definition, the acceptance of the fact that all writing systems operate following a set of – often unspoken – representational conventions. The way in which something will be written down and the meanings that will be assigned to different graphic units, as well as their arrangements and shapes, all depend on agreements shared by those involved in writing and reading orthography. Among the core analytical goals which preoccupy students of historical orthography is indeed that of identifying the conventions of linguistic representation underlying historical writing systems; understanding how specific spellings and graphic segments obtain their meanings and what specific aspects underlie and shape the establishment of these conventions. For anyone interested in analysing orthographic practices of the past, understanding or decoding the rules underlying orthographic principles across writing systems is important in order to be able to fully grasp the orthographic arrangements of a specific writing system at a given point in time. Those wishing to study historical orthography following the guide laid out so far would probably expect to be able to identify, in their working material, a collection of well-defined datasets from which to be able to put together the pieces needed for understanding a historical writing system. While there are analytical challenges that readers need to be made aware of, it is in fact possible to identify general principles of orthographic 'behaviour' across writing systems of the past, but these are often anything but well defined.

The task of identifying orthographic principles involves studying how different units of writing relate to each other and to units of speech and meaning. As a first point of discussion, readers should keep in mind that anything belonging to a historical writing system is, by definition, a historical construct and, as such, it bears all the complications and contradictions that result from the chronological journey of a given writing system. The reason why a dynamic investigative pursuit is required for understanding what would otherwise be a static classificatory exercise is diachrony. Studying orthography across time always involves a level of uncertainty, conditioned by the complex, arbitrary and, crucially, time-contingent relationships between writing and speech. The aim of this chapter is not only to show some of the potentially endless difficulties that one may encounter while analysing historical writing systems, but also to indicate some of the possible ways in which those working in orthography can recognise patterns in how writing systems function. The initial section of this chapter, in particular, seeks to illuminate some of the formal aspects of writing that more directly inform principles in orthography. In alphabetic writing systems, especially, the set of rules, conventions, regularities, patterns or preferences that govern spelling practices and/or their interpretation can be differentiated as two individual groups: phonemic and morphological (the latter also known as lexical). The discernment of these two very broad types of levels of regularity of orthographic representation presents an oversimplified picture of how graphic units map onto linguistic levels. However, they are based on the basic definitions of the grapheme identified in Chapter 4 and serve as a means to explain that it is precisely an interplay of *sound*-oriented and *meaning*-oriented graphic mappings that shapes alphabetic writing systems as a whole.

As seen in Chapter 4, the phonemic principle is at the core of more than one definition of the grapheme. This principle assumes one-to-one mapping between a graphic unit and a phoneme, but there are also some complications involved. For example, there is often a condition of *polyvalence*, a rather frequent phenomenon in alphabetic orthographies, where a graphic sign has more than one phonemic value. The multiplicity of graphic marking can occur both from grapheme to sound (one grapheme = many sounds, i.e. 'polyphony'), and from sound to grapheme (one sound = many graphemes, i.e. 'polygraphy'). The morphological principle, on the other hand, refers to the idea that graphic forms indicate morphemes in morphologically, i.e. etymologically and semantically, related words. Morphological spellings are meaning-based and, for this reason, they visually establish correlations between related words, regardless of the sound level; hence, as mentioned above, they are also called *lexical* spellings. In these examples of sixteenth-century morphological spellings from Early New High German, these correlations are rather obvious: see, e.g., *blatt*, 'leaf', corresponding to *blåtter, blattes*; *kålte*, 'coldness', as in *kalt*, 'cold'; and *kind*, 'child', as in *kinder, kindes* (from Voeste, 2007: 92; 2008: 15).

From a typological perspective, preferences for certain types of orthographic conventions over others are frequently language-specific. Haas (1970: 52) observed that different writing systems favour different types of divergencies: some, for example French, feature frequent polygraphy, others polyphony and yet others, like English, fall in between the two categories. Most recently, a number of common developmental trends across languages have been noticed in the literature, particularly between the sixteenth and the seventeenth centuries, and especially among those writing traditions that emerged with the rise of Latin Christianity (see Baddeley & Voeste, 2012a). A comparative view of the vernacular writing systems from the early modern period in Europe has suggested that there exist two distinct directions: some writing systems were more oriented towards incorporating and maintaining the Latinate elements of Latin orthography, and for this reason, they often detached themselves from direct sound-to-spelling correspondences; other writing systems, on the other hand, exhibited "greater independence from Latin" by adopting "phonographic systems of spelling" (Baddeley & Voeste, 2012a: 2).

The maintenance-oriented route can be seen mainly among the Romance languages, i.e. the French, Italian and Spanish writing systems, which were a natural product of the Latin writing tradition. For these languages, as Baddeley and Voeste put it, "there was initially no real break between the emergence of the vernaculars and the development of corresponding written systems" (2012a: 2). An interesting feature of the writing systems of Romance languages at their initial standardising stages is their inherently morphographic (as opposed to strictly phonographic) nature, in other words, their preference for meaning-based structures and not just form-based ones. Baddeley (2012) provided an interesting example of how orthographic features in fifteenth-century French manuscripts steered towards the morphographic principle. Since scribes would often write swiftly, several handwritten graphemes eventually grew in mutual resemblance; to resolve potential issues of ambiguity, scribes began to use mute consonants, which not only played a graphotactic role but were also useful for establishing a more explicit link with Latin.[1] A few abbreviations that could function as either Latin or French words were also used. All these morphographic features, Baddeley (2012: 99) suggested, indicate that manuscripts were not usually read out loud. The sixteenth century saw many attempts and initiatives aimed to reform French spelling in order to make it more sound-oriented, but the morphological principle was by far the most prevalent. Morphological orientation was in fact the main feature that distinguished the French orthographic development from Spanish or Italian, which gradually became established as more obviously sound-based orthographies. French orthography, however, never worked *purely* on the basis of the morphological principle, but rather it developed a mixed system, one that overlapped between phonemic and morphological.

The sound-oriented route for writing systems in Europe, instead, was adopted mainly by languages of the Germanic family, as well as some Central, Nordic and Eastern European vernaculars. The phonemic principle, much like the case

---

[1] The main rationale behind the graphocactic principle is the "combinability of letter segments within the graphic word and the interaction of these segments and their combinations" (translated from Voeste, 2008: 11). A working definition of the graphotactic principle is also given in Chapter 5, section 5.1.1.

of the morphological principle, was hardly ever followed strictly within each language and across all of these linguistic groups. While the starting point for these vernacular writing systems was primarily that of sound, the extent of their phonography varied diachronically: some writing systems, like that of German, English and Dutch, moved towards morphography, each following their own approach; while others, like the writing systems of Croatian, Swedish, Finnish and Czech, stayed "more or less" phonographic (Baddeley & Voeste, 2012a: 11). For German, Elmentaler (2003) investigated graphemic variation in texts from ten Duisburg town clerks, written between the fourteenth and the seventeenth century. Elmentaler's work, which explored issues like syllable differentiation, vowel class differentiation and umlaut marking, uncovered a non-linear diachronic development of orthography. More specifically, the orthographic choices of all of the individual scribes behind the texts analysed varied from those of the previous generations of scribes. Additionally, Elmentaler (2003: 291, 307) suggested that, according to his findings, there appear to be no uniform attempts to use either a narrowly phonemic or a morphological principle until the 1650s.

Voeste's work (2007, 2008, 2012, 2015) sheds more light on the processes of spelling "morphologisation" in Early New High German, which, she argued, had already begun to appear during the sixteenth century. There appear to have been two main factors behind the change from "segmental phonography" (i.e. phonemic spellings) to morphography: one was the changed perception of the written unit, which eventually led to distinguishing word units using "blanks" (Voeste, 2012: 168); the other factor was the introduction of Gothic cursive, which further facilitated word identification. Consequently, Voeste argued (2012: 169), written segments "began to be visualizations of semantic units, since written word-forms refer to the semantic level". Sixteenth-century German was therefore characterised by two individual orthographic principles operating concurrently: phonemic ("segmental phonography") and morphological ("word-bound logography", Voeste 2012: 169). Evidence of morphography may be found in the positional developments involving the graphemes <v> and <u> (compare the words *landuogt* vs. *landvogt*, 'baillif', as opposed to *vogt*) and <ſ> and <s> (for instance in the words *biſher* vs. *bisher*, 'until now', as opposed to *bis*, 'until'). Particularly interesting are compound words, since in this category of words the new word-internal placement of the letters <v> and <s> suggests, according to Voeste (2008: 109), an attempt to retain morphemic principles.

7.2   Making Sense of Diachronic Complexity

As discussed so far, historical writing systems generally operate on more than one linguistic level of representation. While graphemes map onto speech sounds, phonemic interpretations are supplemented, to a higher or smaller degree, by graphotactically encoded morphological and lexical information. In other words, orthographic conventions are often, to some degree, a reflection of the phonological structure of a language. Graphic words, however, are also created on the basis of rules regulating the ordering of individual orthographic units in a sentence, all of which usually respond to higher-level morphological or semantic principles regulating the language. Alphabetic writing systems, regardless of whether they feature simple phoneme–grapheme correspondences, are not mere transcriptions of speech. They are complex systems with their own structure, which needs to be uncovered in its systematicity, rather than being waived off as an insufficiently faithful representation of sounds. In some languages more than others, phoneme–grapheme correspondences are relatively complex. A number of historical writing systems, for example, feature graphic elements, sometimes known as *markers*, which do not have any phonemic value, for example <ъ> in Russian or the lengthening (*Dehnungs*) <h> in German. Some of these markers are occasionally used in so-called *syllabic spellings* in order to indicate specific structural, suprasegmental properties of the syllable, such as, for example, openness, closedness, length of the nucleus vowel and phonological contrasts. In Early New High German, spelling practice went from mainly phonemic to syllabic and morphemic; moreover, some initially phonemic spellings, such as the gemination of consonants, were gradually reanalysed as syllabic ones. Syllabic spellings may thus be found, in Early New High German, in the use of lengthening <h>, e.g. in *nehmen* 'to take', the doubling of vowel graphemes, e.g. in *eere* 'honor', and the gemination of consonants, e.g. in *kommen* 'to come' (Voeste 2007: 91, 2012: 180–1). These examples indicate that that some graphic units can function independently of the spoken forms and that writing is at least partially autonomous from speech.

Sound-related complications in the written language are, of course, something that many have been aware of for a long time. With reference to the English writing system, William Salesbury asserted back in 1547 that "You cannot fail to know that in English they do not read and pronounce every word literally and fully as it is written." As Horobin suggested (2013: 32–3), the reason for the complexities existing in English, just as for many other writing systems around the world, is that word spellings are the result of a meandering path of old and new conventions which somehow found their way to the present day. For English, the reason for the unconventional relationship between sound and spelling is often that, throughout its history, its vocabulary has been heavily influenced by other languages. The word *city*, for instance, is a French loanword and thus employs the French practice of using <c> to represent the sound /s/, while *ciabatta* is an Italian loanword which preserves the Italian use of <c> for /tʃ/. Thus, to put it more simply, the reason why multiple individual phonemes correspond to a given grapheme in English, in the examples given above, is that the loanwords retained their original grapheme–phoneme correspondences in the host language.

Another cause of disruption in English is sound change. One of the best ways to illustrate this is by making reference to present-day English spelling, in which a number of words contain graphemes that are not pronounced, like the <k> and <gh> in the word *knight*. These graphemes were once pronounced but have since ceased to be, so that present-day English spelling contains a number of 'silent' letters. On some other occasions, the correspondence between the graphic form of a word and its pronunciation, which may not have been direct in the past, was brought into alignment by the spelling. The introduction of 'etymological spellings', such as *adventure* for Middle English *aventure*, and *host* for Middle English *ost*, led to changes in the pronunciation of these words. Changes of this sort are also evidenced by the current pronunciation of the words *waistcoat* and *forehead*, which were originally pronounced as /wɛskət/ and /fɒrɪd/, but which, over time, developed to be pronounced more like they are spelled.

As the examples from English suggest, making sense of historical writing in its continuously evolving nature is not an easy task. Because of the complications that affect linguistic development over time, different guiding principles for different writing systems may apply at different moments in the history of development of a language. In other words, the relationship between the graphic unit and the principles regulating a writing system are dependent on the moment in history they are being analysed. The reason why time contingency is important is that different combinatorial restrictions in language-specific orthographies are often the result of changing types of medium (e.g. whether orthography appears in a manuscript or in a book) and even individual preferences of the scribe, the author or the printer. An example that Coulmas (2012: 101) gave about the influence of technological innovations is that of the form *ye* in English. This spelling form was invented by William Caxton (d. 1491), who introduced the printing technology to England from mainland Europe. The spelling *ye* was invented to replace the thorn *þ*, which was missing among the types available to him at the time. Orthographic changes in a writing system may also be constrained by external (e.g. social, political, cultural) factors inherent to cultural history. In the European continent, for example, the development of vernacular writing traditions is tightly connected with either Roman or Byzantine Christianity, and, as a result, Latin, Greek and Old Church Slavonic worked as the first and principal models of "scriptualization" (Voeste, 2012: 168). Thus, the linguistic functions of Latin and Greek graphic signs were transmitted to European vernacular writing systems as a whole, and, later on, they were shaped to include a way of graphically representing as many linguistic peculiarities of each vernacular writing system as possible.

Language-internal rules also change from time to time. Some of the combinations of graphic segments may be dependent on their character position within a word or a morpheme; other influential elements may include smaller surrounding graphic segments, their visual shapes and even their aesthetic properties. In several mediaeval and early modern European orthographies, as seen earlier on with the example of German, the graphemes <i>, <j> and <y>, <u> and <v>, as well as <s> and <ſ> were graphotactically conditioned by their character positions in a word, and by the neighbouring letters within the host words where the graphic units were found (see Scragg, 1974: 10–11; Baddeley, 2012: 99; Scholfield, 2016: 148, 153). Another example is that of Lithuanian texts of the so-called western variety, which, during the second quarter of the seventeenth century, featured two digraphs to indicate the sound /tʃ/, namely <cz> and <tz>. The use of these two digraphs was graphotactically conditioned, so that <cz> would appear in word-initial position, and <tz> everywhere else. Both graphic elements, therefore, worked as alternants, each with their own function (see Šinkūnas, 2014: 34).

Moving on from the language-specific examples of diachronic complexity provided so far, some additional statements can be made on the basis of other languages, at least within the remit of alphabetic orthographies. Over time, the gap between spelling and pronunciation is bound to widen in alphabetic orthographies, as spoken forms change and written forms are generally retained. Many of the so-called 'silent' letters in French can be explained in this way. According to Catach (1978: 65), more than 10 per cent of letters are silent in French, in the sense that they are present in the spelling but carry no phonemic information. In the past, a large number of these silent letters had a phonemic correspondence, but owing to sound change, their original sound values disappeared. For the Latin alphabet more broadly, it is possible to draw some generalisations on the complex relations between phonemes and graphemes. In particular, groups of similar sounds are identified as individual phonemes differently in different writing systems. Take, for example, the sounds /b/, /p/ and /ph/. In English, voiced /b/ as in *bill* is distinct from voiceless /p/ as in *pill*. The first grapheme in *pill* is pronounced with an aspiration, i.e. /ph/, but the same grapheme is pronounced without aspiration, i.e. /p/ in *spill*. Unlike the distinction between *bill* and *pill*, [p] and [ph] are allophones in English and, therefore, they are not distinct in spelling. In Mandarin, on the other hand, aspiration indicates a phonemic contrast, which is why *Beijing* has <b> in order to indicate a de-voiced /b/ in Pinyin, while <p> is for /ph/. Thus, the ways in which graphemes are interpreted with respect to phonemes change across languages.

The identification of groups of similar sounds as individual phonemes, and how this varies across languages, is certainly an important factor behind the correspondence between phonemes and graphemes, but not the only one. The history of individual writing systems is ripe with a number of relatively miscellaneous processes and events that introduce irregularities and disharmonies between orthography and pronunciation. To return to the examples of the European continent, a number of languages (and therefore, quite a few writing systems) feature uses of the grapheme <h> in a way that is not directly related to the spoken form of words. Spanish <h>, for example, was used in front of initial /we/ to exclude the phonetic interpretation /v/ before <u> and <v> were distinguished (e.g. in the word *huevo* /weβo/, 'egg', derived from Lating *ovum*). In other writing systems, <h> has a very different role. In French, for example, <h> usually works as a glottal onset barring the liaison of a final consonant with a following initial vowel (cf. the forms *les enfants* /lɛzɑ̃fɑ̃/ with *les halles* /lɛˈal/). In German, the grapheme <h> encodes the consonant /h/; in addition, the grapheme is used to indicate vowel length (e.g. in *mahnen* / mɑːnˈn/) and to indicate a syllable boundary before an unstressed vowel (e.g. in *drohen* /dRoˈn/). The grapheme <h> is often found in digraphs across many languages, for example English *th, sh, gh, ph, ch*. In addition to the case of <h> mentioned above, there is also the example of double consonant graphemes variously indicating consonant length, for example in Italian *addio* /addiːo/; vowel quality, for instance in German *Motte* /mɔtə/. Occasionally, consonant doubling may also take a logographic function, that is to say, the role of disambiguating words or morphemes that would otherwise have the same pronunciation and the same spelling (e.g. English *butt* vs. *but*). For digraphs and trigraphs, there are even more variable phonetic interpretations across writing systems than for individual consonant graphemes. The <th> spelling, which, in English, indicates /θ/ in *thought*, /ð/ in *booth* and /t/ in *Thames* has no equivalent in many other writing systems in Europe. The trigraph <ous> for /u/ is frequent in French, but non-existent in many other languages, if we exclude French loanwords. The digraph <oe> for /u/ is a characteristic of Dutch, while <sch> is found in German /ʃ/, <nh> for Portuguese /ɲ/, and <ld> for Norwegian /lː/. Examples like these testify to the fact that digraphs and trigraphs play an important role in making up for the scarce range of signary available in the Latin alphabet. Digraphs and trigraphs often made an appearance in writing systems either intentionally or as a spontaneous way to suit the needs of a given language.

7.3   Logographic Developments

7.3.1   *Chinese Script*

The previous section has provided some examples of complex relationships between sound and spelling in alphabetic orthographies. While the examples given may have been more or less straightforward for the reader, there are also difficulties inherent to studying logographic/morphographic systems. As morphographic scripts spread, they change, both in the way they look and in the way they are to be interpreted. Structural adaptations are a requirement every time that a logographic script is passed on to another language, a change occasionally accompanied by a change of type. This switch is exemplified by the case of Chinese characters and Japanese kana, which are the main topic in this section of the chapter. The scripts of East Asia represent a relatively complex area of analysis for the average Western student of historical orthography, and a brief overview is therefore important in order to prepare most readers for the foresaid difficulties. Consider, for example, the Chinese script, which is by far the most widespread across East Asia: how can the many thousands of Chinese characters be processed and classified for the purpose of, say, dictionary making? The answer to this question is not straightforward, because of the different ways in which Chinese characters are classified. Taking into account the script's diachronic development, Chinese characters fall into five (sometimes six) groups, following the principle of their composition. The first category is made of pictographic logograms, for instance those available from ancient oracle bones. Secondly, there is a category containing words with other visually logical logograms. For instance, the numbers one, two and three are represented respectively by one, two and three lines. In the third group, logograms express ideas, for instance the combination of the characters for 'sun' and 'moon' gives rise to the logogram indicating 'bright', as follows:

日   月   明
sun   moon   bright

Fourthly, logograms may involve some kind of rebus, for instance the character for elephant may also indicate an image, on the basis of a homophonous pronunciation of the words indicating 'elephant' and 'image'. Lastly, logograms may be the result of a blend between a character indicating the meaning of a word with a character indicating its pronunciation. The character for 'female person' is combined with a phonetic character in order to express the meaning of 'mother':

'female person' +   mǎ   =   'mā' (mother)

The numbers of characters in the five groups explained above have changed diachronically. The Shang dynasty – during the second millennium BC – saw a higher proportion of pictographic characters than any other time in the history of Chinese writing. Today, most of the characters in the Chinese alphabet have semantic-phonetic properties, but this is not the system used for compiling dictionaries: rather than using an alphabetical order, dictionaries follow schemes based on character shapes. Other dictionaries follow an order based on the number of strokes needed to draw a given character, on the basis of the way in which writing is taught to children. The first Chinese dictionary, produced in the second century AD, used the so-called *radical-stroke* system, which arranged its 9,353 characters under 540 semantic keys or radicals, for instance 'water', 'vegetation', 'insect'; later on, the number of keys was lowered down to 214. The radicals were in turn ordered according to the number of strokes – from 1 to 17 – with a fixed order imposed on radicals having the same number of strokes.

In order to make use of the dictionary, the reader had to establish combinations between the word that they were interested in and the possible relevant radicals. In the character for 'mother', the radical would likely be found under 'female person', but the matter was not always as straightforward. In fact, finding radicals was often so difficult that a "List of Characters Having Obscure Radicals" would sometimes make its appearance in dictionaries. Despite the difficulties, the radical-stroke system of 214 radicals became the norm until the mid twentieth century. From then onwards, simplified characters made dictionaries much easier to compile, as radicals were distributed between 186 to 250 categories at most, but still not as easy to consult. The variation of radical categories meant that each dictionary followed its own standard, clearly causing a lot of confusion. The sound element of Chinese characters was also used, sometimes, in order to classify radicals, following a roughly syllabic approach. This system seems to have been less popular among native Chinese speakers and more widespread across missionaries. Among the first foreign dictionary makers in the 1880s, William Soothill classified some 4,300 characters on the basis of 895 sound units.

The 'Soothill Syllabary' features columns headed by a sound unit, such as the one mentioned above for the word *mother*. The pronunciation of the characters in a column follows closely this sound-based component, but there are also differences across the columns in terms of character outlook, stroke number and meaning. If one selects a number of sound-related columns and then identifies whatever characters have a similar semantic element (radical) in common, they will have made a table with its columns classified by the same or a similar sound unit and its rows by a similar semantic unit. In the column under sound component 264, 'áo', the sound unit is a helpful tool for understanding the pronunciation of four characters, which consist of a blend between sound 264 and the semantic elements 9 ('person'), 64 ('hand'), 75 ('wood') and 85 ('water'): the four combined characters are pronounced 'áo' ('proud'), 'áo' ('shake'), 'āo' ('barge') and 'áo' ('stream'). If, however, one follows a row of the table, for example that for all characters with the semantic element 9 for 'person', the semantic element does not serve as a good tool for understanding meaning: semantic 9, combined with phonetics 264, 282, 391 and 597, gives four characters with no immediate link with 'person', namely 'proud', 'good', 'lucky' and 'help', each of which also has its own distinct pronunciation. Thus, the sound unit of a character gives a more reliable hint about its pronunciation than the semantic element does about meaning. This clearly indicates not only that the Chinese script is logographic but also that sound-related judgements play quite an important role. From the modern history of Chinese, both semantic and sound-related clues have been used as aids for reading characters. A clear example to illustrate this concept is that of the following characters, which have the same sound component 丁:

A 仃 'dīng' ('alone')

B 氵丁 'tīng' ('sandspit')

The sound component 丁 is pronounced *dīng*, and it is shared in good part by both character A and character B. The semantic element in both A and B is also relevant, though considerably less so than the sound component. In A, 亻 (semantic 9) indicates 'person' (cf. 'alone'), in B 氵 (semantic 85) indicates 'water' (cf. 'sandspit'). The sound-based or the semantic components would be helpful clues for beginning to guess the meaning and pronunciation of characters A and B. However, knowing the significance of the three components would be a requirement for a correct reading, since their shapes alone would give insufficient information. In other words, even for a native speaker, reading Chinese – and this applies to both historical and present-day writing – takes mnemonic and visual abilities, in order to identify interconnections.

Let us briefly take stock. Historical Chinese writing is nothing like as systematic as the language used by the Chinese telegraph clerks of the recent past, who translated each character into a standard four-digit code. Yet Chinese characters, since the first time they were used in history, have never been entirely random. Figure 7.1 gives an example of ancient Chinese calligraphy, where, more than a thousand years ago, each character already shows an impressive level of structural complexity.[2]

---

[2] Images in this chapter are reproduced by kind concession from Robinson (2009). Copyright permission has been obtained from Oxford University Press.

Figure 7.1 Ancient Chinese calligraphy rubbings, with more than a thousand years of history (Source: hudiemm/Contributor/Getty Images)

7.3.2 Japanese Script

Japanese writing is radically different from Chinese across a wide range of linguistic levels: phonologically, grammatically and syntactically. There is, however, one thing that the two have in common: Japanese based its writing system on Chinese characters, which they call *kanji*. While they borrowed the same characters as Chinese, the Japanese changed the Mandarin pronunciation of kanji in order to make it closer to the sounds of Japanese. By the first half of the first millennium AD, the system had been integrated with a reasonably small number of additional sound symbols named *kana*, stemming directly from the kanji. The purpose of these additional symbols was to express more clearly the sounds of Sino-Japanese kanji and to facilitate transcription of Japanese vocabulary. While it may have made sense to elevate the invented kana as the basis for the full Japanese writing system, Chinese characters were hugely prestigious and could not have been discarded. For Japanese culture, it would have been the equivalent of rejecting Latin as the basis for most European writing systems – a concept that would clearly have been perceived as culturally counter-intuitive and arrogant. It is probably for this reason that even the earliest works of Japanese literature, including *Kojiki*, an ancient history of Japan produced in AD 712, was written in kanji. In modern times, however, kanji is increasingly perceived as being more difficult to use than using the kana script in its entirety would have been, and it is not as suitable for computing. Inevitably, the difficulties that kanji brings with it have led to some decline in its status, compared to kana and the Roman alphabet. The booming of Japanese *manga*, especially throughout the second half of the twentieth century, is likely to be linked to the difficulties that most readers experienced with Chinese-based writing. In addition to the literary popularity of comics, kanji is also responsible for encouraging the rise of smaller Japanese kana, syllabic symbols marking the Japanese pronunciation of each kanji.

The kana is split in two different varieties, called respectively *hiragana* and *katakana*, each of which features about forty-six signs that can be combined together in order to represent more complex syllables and can also be supplemented with two diacritic marks. An interesting feature of hiragana is the abundant presence of curved lines, while katakana is characterised by more frequently occurring straight lines. The presence of two different scripts is due to the fact that hiragana was once employed in informal writing and katakana in more formal pieces like official documents, histories and lexical works. Today, hiragana is definitely more popular, while katakana is used for purposes that are similar to those of italics in present-day English. Thus, for example, foreign words and fresh word borrowings very often appear in katakana. Alternatively, *romaji* is sometimes used to indicate foreign words, which is basically a transliteration of the roman alphabet. From the 1980s onwards, with increasing globalisation, the Roman alphabet became very trendy in Japan, for example in adverts, and gradually replaced katakana in magazines, newspapers, on television and billboards. The decision of whether to use kana or kanji in a sentence depends on a lot of variables, and sometimes the two are almost equivalent in a range of functions. In very broad terms, though, kana can be used to represent inflectional affixes, grammatical particles, many adverbs and the vast majority of words of European origin, while kanji serves a wide range of nouns, both Japanese and Sino-Japanese ones, other than those of western origin, as well as a great number of verbs and adjectives.

In principle, kana can be used to write just about anything in Japanese, and one of the greatest pieces of Japanese literature, *The Tale of Genji of the Early 11th Century*, was written in hiragana. In the past, kana was used more frequently by women, while today it is used, for example, for Japanese Braille, without using any kanji. In everyday writing, a mixed kana-and-kanji script is used today, since spelling out the kanji phonetically would make sentences much longer. Moreover, using kana alone would create confusion between kana in adjacent words, because individual words in Japanese are not split by spaces. Additionally, a large number of Japanese words are homophonous, which means that they would be spelled the same in kana. Homophony, together with the prestige-induced factors established earlier on, is indeed the main practical reason why kana was historically never used on its own to write Japanese, thus guaranteeing a long life to the kanji script. One very inconvenient feature of kanji is that it does not allow one to spell out individual words, for example when a speaker is asked for their name and address. Describing each of some 2,000 symbols is an almost impossible task, not least because kanji shapes vary so widely from one another. Thus, in some restricted situations like face-to-face interactions, for example whenever a pen cannot be used for writing things down, spelling out words in kanji can be clumsy and has probably been so for a long time. It is not rare to see a Japanese person spell out their words in the air or on the palm of their hand, with the aid of the index finger of the other free hand.

Frequently, this very process leads to a lot of ambiguity, and a person must eventually resort to using an appropriate common word as a label for the kanji. For instance, of the many kanji units that can be read as *to*, only one can also indicate the noun *higashi* (meaning 'east'); this character is then readily labelled as *higashi to iu ji*, which means 'the character higashi'. When a kanji has only one reading, though, and one wants to describe that reading, the matter is not as straightforward. In order to identify the kanji that refers to the word *sato*, meaning 'sugar', one would probably say something along the lines of "It's the kanji used in the last syllable of the word for sugar." If this type of description does not help the listener to identify the character that one is suggesting, one must then refer back to the shape, following again a long-winded description ("It's the kanji with the 'rice' radical on the left and the tang of 'Tang dynasty' on the right"). While that provided above might sound like an amusing axiom, it is actually quite telling about how interesting Japanese writing, both in its present-day form and in its historical shape, can be as an object of empirical work. It provides some compelling material for psychological insights, among other fields, and has remained alive despite the difficulties that accompany it. A modern authority, James Marshall Unger, once affirmed that "Japanese culture has not flourished because of the complexities of its writing system, but it has undeniably flourished in spite of them."

7.4   Disappearance of Writing Systems

7.4.1   Deciphering Unknown Scripts

In the remainder of this chapter, we turn to the question of interpretation. The disappearance of writing systems adds an additional layer of difficulty to the already complex task of analysing typological principles of orthographic 'behaviour' across writing systems. Unknown scripts force us to take a step back in typological work and prepare for pursuing a more basic quest in studying historical orthography: interpreting an unknown script. Easier said than done, one might say. For one thing, there is no single theory that can explain successfully why scripts eventually disappear: each script has its own story and its own reasons for dying out. Commerce, culture, language, politics, prestige, religion and technology, each at different degrees for individual languages, are all participatory elements in the fate of individual historical scripts. The reasons why scripts disappear may be as telling as the reasons why they made an appearance at all in the first place. Thousands of years ago, for example, a radical change in the political and societal set-up of Egypt sanctioned the end of hieroglyphic and demotic scripts and opened the door to the rise of a new writing system. Nevertheless, the Egyptian scripts were not wiped out completely; instead, hieroglyphic was slowly marginalised by a number of competing agents of change, including politics, language, script and religion. At the other extreme, almost everyone agrees that the scripts of the Indus Valley civilisation and Easter Island (Rongorongo) are undeciphered. To date, no one has been able to establish an unambiguous way to read the inscriptions convincingly.

The examples above are an excellent way to suggest that lost and undeciphered scripts are an area where diachronic development gives rise to a wide range of complications, which in turn make the identification of well-defined levels of analysis more complicated. In the case of the Mayan glyphs, for instance, most scholars agree that the great majority of the inscriptions can be given some meaning, while at the same time there are quite a few individual glyphs that are equivocal or mysterious. Thus, there are no thresholds that one can use to decide whether a script has been deciphered or not – the diachrony of orthographic development makes the process of deciphering one that can be achieved in different degrees. The most useful way of measuring out whether a script has been deciphered in enough detail is when a proposed decipherment can produce consistent readings from new samples of the script, and when these readings are performed by different groups of people rather than the same individual, for the sake of objectivity. With this definition in mind, one can claim safely that, among the most famous and widely accepted scripts, the Egyptian hieroglyphs were deciphered in the 1820s, Babylonian cuneiform in the 1850s, Linear B in 1951–3, the Mayan glyphs in the 1950s and the Hittite (Luvian) hieroglyphs of Anatolia during the twentieth century. Along with the group of deciphered scripts, there are quite a few undeciphered ones – for convenience, these are listed in Figure 7.2, which is a reproduction of a table available in one of the most recent introductory books while deal with the subject (Robinson, 2009). In the figure, the asterisk, *, marks scripts for which there is no agreement about their nature and/or their underlying language.

There are generally three groups of undeciphered scripts in historical orthography: an unknown script writing a known language, a known script writing an unknown language and an unknown script writing an unknown language. The Mayan glyphs were, until the 1950s, an instance of the first category, because the Mayan languages are still spoken in Central America today. The Zapotec script may also be another example of an unknown script writing a known language, if the scholarly assumption that it refers to a language related to the modern Zapotec language family of Mexico is true. Rongorongo is a third example, if we assume that it writes a Polynesian language connected to the Polynesian language still spoken on Easter Island. With reference to the second group – a known script writing an unknown language – Etruscan writing could

Name of script	Where found	Earliest known	Script known?	Language known?
Proto-Elamite	Iran/Iraq	c. 3000 BC	Partially	No
Indus	Pakistan/N.W. India	c. 2500 BC	No	*
'Pseudo-hieroglyphic'	Byblos (Lebanon)	2nd mill. BC	No	No
Linear A	Crete	18th cent. BC	Partially	No
Phaistos Disc	Phaistos (Crete)	18th cent. BC	No	No
Etruscan	N. Italy	8th cent. BC	Yes	No
Olmec	Meso-America	c. 900 BC	Partially	No
Zapotec	Meso-America	c. 600 BC	Partially	Partially
Meroitic	Meroë (Sudan)	c. 200 BC	Yes	No
Isthmian	Meso-America	c. AD 150	*	*
Rongorongo	Easter Island	pre-19th cent. AD	No	Partially

Figure 7.2 Major undeciphered scripts (from Robinson, 2009: 54)

be mentioned as a good example. The script is very comparable to the Greek alphabet, yet Etruscan remains, to date, a mystery. For the third group, the Indus script is a perfect example, since both the graphic marks and the language that they refer to remain unknown. There is a chance, however, that the language of the Indus Valley civilisation that the script refers to is included in the family of Dravidian languages, for example Tamil and Brahui, used mainly in south India and across areas of Pakistan. Having established what constitutes an unde-ciphered language, and what groups of undeciphered languages exist in histor-ical orthography, it is now important, for the purposes of this chapter, to explain how the decipherment of an unknown script occurs in practical terms.

Typically, there are three relevant stages: (1) an initial, detailed study of the written marks, words and their graphic environment in all of the samples available, with a view to gleaning any possible detail useful for reconstructing the writing system and its meaning; (2) an attempt to assign sound values to the graphic marks detected in order to reconstruct potentially identifiable words and link those with a postulated language; and (3) double-checking of their reconstructions against some reliable primary evidence, to make sure that the results obtained are objectively true and did not occur just by coincidence. Admittedly, the three steps outlined above are hardly ever followed linearly; instead, researchers often go back and forth between the three, adding numer-ous layers of analysis that are here disregarded for the sake of simplicity. While these three steps often constitute the core of the analyses undertaken by scholars for decipherments, there are some conditions that need to be attained for these steps to become feasible. First of all, one should have extensive enough working material, and, for unreadable scripts without any bilingual people familiar with them or identifiable proper names, one should be dealing with a concealed language within the same family of a language already known. For these same reasons, and unless some major discoveries are made in the future, the Olmec and Isthmian scripts from Mexico, the Phaistos Disc from Crete and the Byblos script from Lebanon, all included in Figure 7.2, will remain unknown forever. An example of an apparently impossible enigma that was eventually solved is that of the Linear B script, a syllabic script that was used for writing Mycenaean Greek, the earliest attested form of Greek.

7.4.2   Cracking the Code

Among the elements that can be understood quite straightforwardly in an unknown script, there are two which involve some important properties of writing. First of all, *direction*: from left to right or from right to left, from top to bottom or from bottom to top. Clues that are often used in order to understand direction are the position of unfilled space in the text, the side towards which characters are pressed on the material, as well as the angle faced by the written signs (e.g. in Egyptian hieroglyphic). One complication, however, may lie in the fact that scripts exist which can be written in both directions – first from left to right and then from right to left, then again from left to right, and so on. A second clue that can be used for deciphering scripts is the *way of counting*. Numerals are usually visible and can be easily distinguished from the rest of the text; there are examples where numerals are used for counting items and are associated with words probably indicating the objects being counted. Examples of scripts where numerals are fairly obvious are Linear B and Mayan and, among the undeciphered scripts, the proto-Elamite script. Other examples include the Etruscan script, Linear A, and the Zapotec and Isthmian scripts, as well as, most likely, the Indus script; on the contrary, the Meroitic script, Rongorongo and the Phaistos Disc seem free from any trace of numerals.

While those above are useful clues, deciphering the sign system as a whole still remains one of the hardest tasks in historical orthography. In the scant evidence available, the letters are often joined up and there is likely a degree of individual writer variation, which makes it difficult to disentangle idiosyncrasies from identifiable standard usages. Since nobody can claim with absolute certainty, especially without much primary data in their hands, whether different-looking graphic signs are allographs of the same sign, the most difficult task for those attempting to decipher scripts is indeed that of distinguishing allographs among the signs that look different from the others. From the evidence that we have to date about deciphered scripts, it looks like undeciphered scripts may feature three or even four allographs of an individual sign, which clearly makes the task of deciphering any unknown script monumental. The only way for epigraphers to identify allographs with some level of certainty would be to analyse the occurrence of each sign and its context across a range of similar inscriptions. Failure to follow this analytical approach will make it impossible for researchers to classify the signs in a script correctly or to figure out how many of these there are in a given script. While classification is clearly a very important part for decipherment, the *number of signs* is also quite an important matter for decipherment. This piece of knowledge about an undeciphered script allows researchers to get an understanding of whether they are first of all dealing with an alphabetic, consonantal script, a syllabary, or a mixture between syllables and logograms – all of which can be established, in principle, even prior to any attempt to guess the sound values of the signs.

Naturally, there is a lot of variability in how many signs there are in a script, so understanding script sizes is in itself not always a straightforward task, but there are some average values that we can use on the basis of the scripts that we do know. Alphabets and consonantal scripts generally have 20 to 40 signs: Hebrew has 22 signs, English 26, Arabic 28 and Cyrillic 43. For syllabic scripts, where the signs indicate syllables rather than vowels and consonants, the average number of signs is between 40 and 90: Persian has 40 signs,

Japanese about 50 syllabic kana, while Linear B has 60 basic signs. In other more complex scripts where there is a mixture of syllables and logograms, as, for example, in Egyptian and Mayan hieroglyphics, as well as Babylonian cuneiform, the number of signs generally reaches the hundreds, sometimes even thousands, as is the case of Chinese (and the Japanese kanji borrowed from Chinese). Of course, there are exceptions to the rules established above: consonant-rich languages of the northern Caucasus, for example, do not fall within the categories established above for alphabetic scripts, because they feature more than 40 basic signs. However, it is a reliable enough system – sufficiently so to have been taken up by most modern and contemporary decipherers, since the system above was established in the 1870s. For example, those who worked on Ugaritic cuneiform were faced with a number of basic signs amounting to 30 – which meant that Ugaritic could not be a logosyllabic script like Babylonian cuneiform. Similarly, the first steps made towards the decipherment of Linear B consisted in the understanding that it was, first of all, a syllabic script, not an alphabet or a logosyllabic script. For some of the scripts which, to date, remain undeciphered, scholars have been following a similar route, and some of the milestone pieces of knowledge in this sense include the fact that Linear A has about 60 sound-based signs, while Rongorongo has something like 55, meaning that both Linear A and Rongorongo may be syllabaries.

If the signs of an undeciphered script are classified carefully, and the allographs are found, signs can then be assigned numbers and each piece of evidence where the script is attested can be translated to a series of numbers rather than graphic symbols. More sophisticated approaches to deciphering scripts nowadays also use computerised systems, which allow one to compile more complex catalogues of individual signs and connect the information gathered to whichever pieces of evidence exist where the individual signs are used. This system is not too different from the concordance tools used by scholars in philology, especially those interested in the uses of individual words in a study corpus. Whether manual or automatic, these types of analytical steps offer scholars the possibility of gleaning interesting insights into how and when the signs are used, drawing relative and absolute frequencies which can include a range of metadata, like dates of attestation, source of evidence, any presence of allographs and so on. Other interesting phenomena that can be analysed using concordance databases are whether an individual word – or more pre-cisely, what one thinks might be an individual word – occurs adjacently to other lexical items, and if so, in which contexts it is found most often.

Machine-assisted analyses have afforded scholars the ability to make huge steps forward in the understanding of scripts like the Linear A, Meroitic and Indus scripts; in general, however, they still remain at the margins of archaeological and linguistic decipherment. Computers can go only so far in helping us to decipher enigmatic scripts, and that is because the process of decipherment also involves a degree of logical and inventive thinking. In other words, successful decipherment requires that researchers use their own intuition, relying on as much linguistic, archaeological and cultural knowledge as possible, while also avoiding leaning naively towards the speculative. Computers struggle with recognising allographs, though future endeavours might provide a level of computational complexity that accounts for them. A third problem may be that there are not sufficiently extensive primary sources for computers to process in a way that is empirically meaningful. A fourth problem is that of the graphic complexity of scripts like the Mayan one, which is rather difficult to process numerically and systematically.

This point about the Mayan script leads to an interesting side note about Mayan: without a doubt, this is one of the most fascinating discoveries for those interested in historical linguistics more broadly. The 'alphabet' in Figure 7.3 is from the surviving copy of an original manuscript written in the sixteenth century by a Spanish priest, Diego de Landa, who worked among the Maya in the Yucatan. In the mid twentieth century, this manuscript was paramount for deciphering the phonetic Mayan glyphs. In the mid sixteenth century, Landa, later bishop of Yucatan, asked an elderly Maya man about his way of writing. Unfortunately, though, Landa spoke Spanish, and although he was using the aid of his gesture to refer to symbols in the script, he did not understand correctly some of the information received. Landa thought that Mayan worked like any other alphabetic system, and he did not realise that the Mayan phonetic signs were basically syllabic with a blend of pure vowels, though he had come to realise that certain signs, for example 'CA' and 'KU', indicated syllables. Another point that Landa missed was the fact that most Mayan glyphs were logograms, and not phonetic signs, and that the Mayan script in its entirety is, in fact, a logosyllabic script and not an alphabet. Eventually, when he casually uncovered some of the mysteries of the Mayan script, Landa destroyed a large number of Mayan manuscripts, as he thought that such a superstitious way of viewing the world could come only from the devil.

While the Mayan script definitely represents one of the most fascinating examples of decipherment, history teaches us that alphabets were not necessarily just lost, but sometimes ciphered and hidden. This was the case of the Enigma machine, a cipher device developed and used during the Second World War to protect commercial, diplomatic and military communication. The system was used extensively by Nazi Germany in particular, in all branches of the German military. The Germans thought, wrongly, that using the Enigma machine would allow them to communicate safely, in order to coordinate military decisions across all corners of Europe. The Enigma machine was

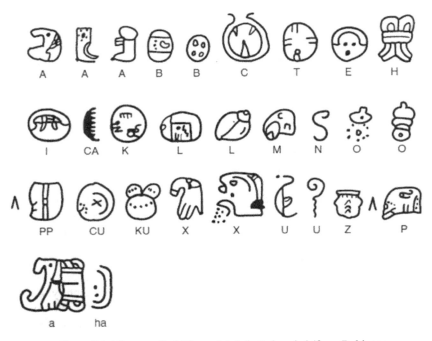

Figure 7.3 The so-called Mayan 'alphabet' decoded (from Robinson, 2009: 59)

believed to be so safe that even the most top-secret messages were enciphered via its electrical circuits.

Enigma worked using an electromechanical rotor mechanism, which scrambled the twenty-six letters of the German alphabet. In order to cipher messages, the sender entered his text on the Enigma's keyboard and another individual wrote down which of the twenty-six lights above the keyboard lit up after each key was pressed. When plain text was entered, the lit-up letters were the encoded ciphertext; when ciphertext was entered, the message was reverted to readable plain text. The rotor mechanism changed the electrical connections between the keys and the lights with each key press, so that the lights did not always correspond to the original place of the relative letter. The security of the system was dependent on a number of machine settings which were usually changed daily, based on secret key lists distributed in advance, and on other settings that were changed for each message. The receiving station had to know and use the exact settings used by the transmitting station in order to be able to decrypt the message. Over time, Nazi Germany introduced a number of improvements to Enigma, which slowed down the decryption efforts of many people, but it did not prevent Polish mathematicians from deciphering the system eventually – a fact that allowed the Allies to use Enigma-enciphered messages to their strategic advantage. Linguistically speaking, the example above is an interesting historical case not only of decipherment but also, paradoxically, of different 'orthographies' co-existing in the same script.

Further Reading

Baddeley, S. & A. Voeste. 2012a. 'Introduction. Orthographies in Early Modern Europe: a comparative view'. In S. Baddeley & A. Voeste (eds.), *Orthographies in Early Modern Europe*. Berlin: De Gruyter Mouton, pp. 1–13.

Baines, J., J. Bennet & S. Houston (eds.). 2008. *The Disappearance of Writing Systems: Perspectives on Literacy and Communication*. London: Equinox Publishing.

Coulmas, F. 2012. *Writing Systems: An Introduction to Their Linguistic Analysis*. Cambridge: Cambridge University Press (see especially pp. 94–108 on polyvalence and uncertainty).

Robinson, A. 2009. *Writing and Script: A Very Short Introduction*. Oxford: Oxford University Press (see especially Chapter 4 and Chapter 7 on Asian and undeciphered scripts).

Rutkowska, H. & P. Rössler. 2012. 'Orthographic variables'. In J. M. Hernández-Campoy & J. Camilo Conde-Silvestre (eds.), *The Handbook of Historical Sociolinguistics*. Chichester: John Wiley & Sons, pp. 213–36.

Part IV

Understanding Orthography

8   Orthography and Standardisation

8.1   Understanding Standardisation

This chapter opens up the fourth and final part of the book, devoted to understanding development and change in orthography. The goal of this chapter is that of providing a framework that readers can use as an example to contextualise orthographic developments, with special reference to the linguistic phenomenon of standardisation. Within the remit of this chapter, historical English holds a special place, for both practical and conceptual reasons. Research in the standardisation of English orthography, especially with reference to the early modern era, has, over the last few decades, gone a long way (full references to relevant publications are available in Condorelli, 2020d). The growing output of research work in English orthography means that there is enough material, to date, to inform a full chapter on standardisation in a coherent way. As will be evident in the chapter, some of the research work in English informs current theoretical knowledge in standardisation more broadly, which in turn means that English is excellent 'ground' for a discussion about orthography and standardisation. The attentive reader will also notice that Part IV is relatively richer in references to research work in the early modern era, with which I am most familiar. The intention behind the increased number of references is that of facilitating a more advanced understanding of historical orthography as we approach the final part of this book.

Now, let us begin with the basics – definitions. Standardisation is normally described as a process that involves several stages and follows some objectively identifiable steps, namely the *selection* of a norm, characterised by the minimisation of variation in form; the extension of the standard to a wide range of functions, also known as *elaboration* of function; the *codification* of the forms which emerge as minimally variant; the *maintenance* of the standard; and the *prescription* of the standard to the community (Haugen, 1966: 933; 1987: 59; Milroy & Milroy, 1999: 23; Agha, 2003: 231; 2006: 190; Nevalainen & Tieken-Boon van Ostade, 2006: 274–86). The foundational model of description above has been modified a few times so that the stages of standard development most commonly identified are not necessarily understood as successive, but rather they may overlap with each other or can even be cyclical (Leith, 1983: 32; Deumert & Vandenbussche, 2003: 4–7). Most recently, the understanding of standardisation outlined above was updated by Agha (2003: 231; 2006: 190), who saw the set of linguistic norms that emerge from the process of standardisation as a linguistic repertoire, which can be differentiated within the language as a socially recognised norm and linked with a framework of cultural and societal values.

All of the versions of the foundational model above have a shared, relatively straightforward and fundamental understanding of standardisation. For Haugen, a standard combines the two requirements of "minimal variation in form" and "maximal variation in function" (1966: 931). According to Milroy, "the process of standardisation works by promoting invariance or uniformity in language structure [and] consists of the imposition of uniformity upon a class of objects" (1992a: 129; 2001: 531). For Nevalainen & Tieken-Boon van Ostade, standardisation follows two fundamental processes, maximum application, i.e. *generality*, and minimum variation, i.e. *focusing* (2006: 310). These two conditions are best fulfilled in writing, but they are never likely to be met in full in any given standard. What, then, is a linguistic norm? As a model or pattern, a norm is more or less codified, more or less prestigious, and it is an abstraction that emerges in a community, one which may have been formed by an authority for special purposes (Locher & Strässler, 2008: 2). According to the *Oxford English Dictionary* (2021), a norm is "a value used as a reference standard for purposes of comparison", and, one may infer, *normalisation* refers to the imposition of a norm as a reference standard. If the concepts of standard and norm are so closely associated, it is because a norm forms a natural basis for a standard: a linguistic norm can be selected and held up as a reference standard. However, when a linguistic norm is selected as a standard and used as a yardstick, it becomes a prestige norm and is associated with values of correctness, appropriateness and social status.

The definitions above fit naturally with the understanding of standardisation as a set of norms which exist in incipient stages of development and then become less likely to vary, or redevelop to become less likely to vary and easier to predict. In this chapter, the said understanding of standardisation represents an inevitable assumption when talking about orthographic development, but it is not an inescapable requirement. In principle, being in possession of a standard written system with a clear set of rules to be followed is neither a necessary nor a sufficient condition for a language to exist if we look upon language simply as the property of a speech community with shared norms. However, if orthography is a core element in the ideological and symbolic production of societies and languages, there is one fundamental concept that runs through the history of every language. Standardisation is inseparably bound up with the written language, as it is in this channel that uniformity of structure is most functional and obvious. The process of standardisation, therefore, revolves especially around the act of improving on existing means of written expression, making them more uniform and complete, as well as more logically consistent and predictable.

Traditionally, the process of standardisation has been described as a unified, unidirectional narrative of linguistic development. The unidirectional perspective sees the emergence and dominance of a growing, centralised standard towards which all individual spellings gravitate (for English, see Fisher, 1996, especially pp. 36–83). The development of a growing standard spelling of English, for instance, was generally described as spreading irregularly over the course of two centuries (see, e.g., Scragg, 1974: 67; Salmon, 1999: 32; Nevalainen & Raumolin-Brunberg, 2005: 42; Nevalainen, 2012: 151). General evolutionary principles suggest that a complex trait like spelling may have evolved diachronically from simpler precursors. Among the English historical linguists that followed this statement, Hope (2000: 53) affirmed that standardisation often results in an unconscious trend towards more complex structures because of the sense of prestige linked with the differences between standardised conventions and non-standard ones. If this same concept also applied to orthography, then its diachronic development would follow something of a linear process, from simple to complex, and from chaotic to systematic.

The evolutionary linearity is imposed on history by a backward projection of a present-day standard on historical writing, and it can be seen as a legitimate attempt to create a history for standard orthography – to imagine a past for it and to determine a canon, in which normative forms are argued for and unorthodox forms rejected. In a way, historicising the language becomes a necessary condition for the concept of a standard to co-exist with that of a norm, intended as an elevated set of rules to be followed. The most inevitable consequence of concentrating on a unique history of orthographic standardisation is that a history of developments in individual graphemes or groups of graphemes, some of which may perhaps have been relatively autonomous from each other and apparently counter-intuitive, is made to appear as unidimensional. Such a view of the history of standardisation becomes, to use Lass's words (1976: xi), "a single-minded march" towards regularity. It is especially within the remit of this point of view that one can talk about spelling standardisation as a process of 'evolution' or 'forward-facing development'.

In contrast to the linear understanding of standardisation expressed above, a number of scholarly voices across generations have proposed a more complicated scenario, which sees a synthesis of competing forms and tendencies. According to said view, standardisation is a nodal process which undergoes stages of development and redevelopment through adaptation and under the pressure of socio-historical factors (see, e.g., Samuels, 1972: 165–70; Görlach, [1988] 1990: 18–24; Wright, 1994: 110–13). The advent of historical sociolinguistics has reinforced the idea above, not only uncovering and describing the existence of multiple competing sociolinguistic standards, but also developing a theoretical understanding of linguistic evolution as non-linear and non-prescriptive (see, e.g., Bakhtin, 1981; Bell, 2007; Nevalainen & Raumolin-Brunberg, 2012; Hernández-Campoy, 2015; Nevalainen, 2015). For historical sociolinguists, the standardisation of orthographies in individual languages would be the result of a convergence of multiple axes of linguistic change, each initially relatively autonomous from the other. The accumulation of multiple competing iterative processes would be in itself the essence of each axis in the process of historical development towards regularity and predictability. According to this framework, the standardisation of English spelling would therefore be best described as a multiple, rather than a unitary process, one that more faithfully describes "the hybrid linguistic nature of Standard English" (Hope, 2000: 49). The understanding of standardisation as a convergence of multiple axes of linguistic change does not need to reject all internal irregularities as erroneous but can accommodate them as "structured variation", markers of the process of linguistic selection between competing standards (Milroy, 2000: 20–2).

The development of structure in spelling, therefore, stems from the development of each individual spelling feature, which in turn comes out of a complex, dynamic and often unpredictable scenario. Among the linguistic elements which participated in defining orthography as we know it today, the development of English spelling in particular is perhaps one of the most convoluted and unpredictable in the history of standardisation; it is in fact the intriguingly complex patterns that characterise English spelling that make it a perfect subject for a chapter-long discussion about orthographic standardisation. The process of spelling standardisation in English is not something that we can usefully chart in a linear temporal continuum, if we are to avoid oversimplifications and distortions of language history; instead, we can only represent aspects of it, which can help us to glean insights into its continuous development. A more sophisticated way to understand the overall patterns of development in English would be to see orthographies within sections of the history of English as *Gleichzeitigkeit des Ungleichzeitigen* (a term used in Burkhard, 2002; Schlögl, 2013). This term translates to the 'simultaneity of the non-simultaneous' and refers to the idea that any historical moment represents a section through the historical continuum, which reveals different time layers featuring phenomena of a very different age and duration in continuous (re)development.

The view of spelling standardisation as a process that is never fully complete entails the idea that maximum application and minimum variation never reach a complete status but increase in the degree of *focusing*, a term used by sociolinguists (e.g. Trudgill, 1986: 86) to refer to a high level of agreement in a language community as to what does and what does not constitute 'the language' at a given time. When interpreting patterns of convergence as indicators of standardisation in spelling, therefore, standardisation itself would be best intended as a matrix of focus rather than of fixity. In other words, individual historical spellers tended to a greater or lesser extent to conform to an idea of a standard, but none of the individual texts surviving, or even a specific range of years within the sixteenth and the seventeenth centuries, can ever be said to demonstrate every characteristic of a standard. Thus, developments towards new graphemic arrangements do not contribute to making a clear-cut set of fixed shibboleths. Instead, they give form to what the nineteenth-century scholar Alexander J. Ellis, who first described it, called a "sort of mean", a kind of fixed magnet of spelling forms towards which printed English tended (Smith, 1996: 50). The sort of mean continues to be regionally and chronologically interfered by the "pluricentric" nature of the English language, "one whose norms are focused in different local centres, capitals, centres of economy, publishing, education and political power" (Romaine, 1998: 27). If we want to look upon spelling standardisation in English from a large-scale point of view, the term *supralocalisation* may come in particularly handy for addressing the conceptual difficulties that stem from a pluricentric language. Supralocalisation refers to the geographical diffusion of linguistic features beyond their region of origin, and, in this respect, it achieves the chief goal of standardisation, to reduce the amount of permissible variation while increasing the degree of focus (Nevalainen & Tieken-Boon van Ostade, 2006: 288; more about supralocalisation is discussed in Chapter 9).

If supralocalisation works well as a defining term to describe the spectrum of spelling developments from a large-scale perspective, however, it alone cannot capture the full essence of *spelling standardisation*, which stems from the complex range of definitions and nuances expressed in the chapter so far as a whole. Spelling developments in historical English, in particular, developed in a way that blurs many of the distinctions between *focusing, supralocalisation* and *standardisation* and were never a fixed point of reference. For this reason, it would be safer, I suggest, to describe orthography as a *standardising* process. The theoretical challenges existing to date certainly reflect the complexity of the relation between standardisation and spelling, but there is more to it than just that. The challenges are also caused by our lack of knowledge about the complex dynamics behind orthographic standardisation from a cross-linguistic perspective, which in turn are due to the paucity of sufficiently large-scale studies across languages. Empirical work in orthographic standardisation is paramount for scholars and students alike to fully understand standardisation in its complex facets, and it is for this reason that the remainder of this chapter focuses on knowledge collected to date on the specific case of English. The following sections provide an overview of what we know to date about the dynamics of English spelling immediately prior to and during the early modern era, drawing on some of the most relevant work in the field.

8.2   A Standardising Variety of English

8.2.1   The Linguistic Pool of London

The process of standardisation of English was a long and complex one, and saw some fundamental developments before the introduction of printing in England in 1476. In general, the origins of a standardised form of written English have been associated with four varieties of English, identified as Types I–IV, with characteristically focused spelling conventions, three of which were connected with the London area. Type I was the language of the Wycliffite manuscripts, some features of which appeared in vernacular medical writings from the Central Midlands in the fifteenth century. Type II was the language of the documents from the Greater London area produced before 1370, including, for instance, the *Auchinleck* manuscript, and is "Essex in basis with accretions from Norfolk and Suffolk" (Samuels, 1981: 49). Type III was the language of literary manuscripts, e.g. the earliest manuscripts of Geoffrey Chaucer's *Canterbury Tales*, Thomas Hoccleve's manuscripts and William Langland's *Piers Plowman*, as well as London guild account records. Type IV departed "from a combination of spoken London English and certain Central Midland elements" (Samuels, 1969 [1963]: 413–14) to become the language of the Chancery, adopted for writing royal and government documents in 1430. Type IV appeared at least two generations after Type III and was a mixture of features from Type III, with elements from the Central Midlands.

Numerous scholars see the origin of a standardising form of written English in the Chancery writings stemming from Type IV (Samuels, [1963] 1969: 411; Scragg, 1974: 52; Richardson, 1980: 728–9, 737, 740; Heikkonen, 1996: 115–16; Corrie, 2006: 111–12; Nevalainen & Tieken-Boon van Ostade, 2006: 274–5; Nevalainen, 2012: 133, 136) and suggest that the Chancery 'standard' was derived from the variety selected by Henry V's Signet Office, then accepted as the Chancery norm. This, presumably, later developed to become the suprar-egional standard adopted by printers and the language community at large, possibly due to the authority of the Chancery and of institutional endorsement. Some of the conventions derived from the Chancery documents include the spellings of the words *not, but, such(e)*, <gh> as a velar sound in *light* and *knight*, <ig> in the word *reign*, and the preference for <d> (rather than <t>) in the past tense and past participle forms of weak verbs. The written code adopted by the Chancery spread far and wide thanks not only to the circulation of documents, but also to the frequent migrations of the clerks who had served their apprenticeships at the Chancery. While the above seems to be a widely shared traditional agreement, there are also more recent voices that reject the claim that a single variety may have formed the basis of a standardised written form of English (see Hope, 2000: 50; Benskin, 2004: 1–40). Instead, they suggest that an inconveniently wide range of dialects contributed to the modern standard, and that the Chancery standard features a great deal more variation than is generally admitted. Laura Wright's edited volume (2020), in particular, has challenged the rather simplified development proposed by the orthodox explanations and pointed instead to a rather complex scenario where not only was English standardisation geographically fragmented, but it was also shaped by non-linear interactions between dialects, peoples and even foreign languages (e.g. Latin and French).

In the midst of these complex processes of development involving non-linear linguistic and socio-cultural interactions, one fact remains certain: London was a linguistic pool from which a standard was emerging between the sixteenth and the seventeenth centuries. The English printing industry, then, echoed the southern variety of English that had emerged by the late fifteenth century in the city, simply because it was there that the printing industry developed the most. Through wide-ranging trilingualism of the literate social ranks and extensive lexical borrowing, Latin and French spelling conventions also left their mark on the emerging standardised form of English that was being used in London. In systemic terms, the basic phonemic fit between English spelling and pronunciation, for example, was weakened by the adoption of new digraphs and grapheme–phoneme correspondences. Some other conventions that had been adopted from the Middle English period include <ou> corresponding to Middle English /u:/ and replacing the previous <u> in word spellings like *house*, <qu> for Old English <cw> in *queen* and <o> for Old English <u> in *love*. In the fifteenth century, <ie> had been taken over from French to represent Middle English /e:/ and, especially at the beginning, it had appeared most frequently in words of French origin. From the introduction of printing, London drew artisans and printing-house staff from various parts of the country and from abroad so that the London book business quickly became a melting pot of dialects and foreign languages. Contact influence inevitably played a role in shaping the emerging modern standard that was echoed by the introduction of printing and increased the overall complexity of the variety of spellings used in print.

Among the more recent commentators, Salmon (1999), Nevalainen (2012) and Rutkowska (2013a) showed evidence of interesting developments in the southern variety of English used in and around London. From the range of examples made available in their work, an increased level of focusing appears to have been in place already from the end of the sixteenth century, when attempts to systematise irregular features such as vowel length and, in some cases, vowel quality, are apparent. Vowels could be doubled to mark length, and digraphs began to be used to indicate quality: for example, <ee> was used for /eː/, <oo> for /oː/ and <ea> for /ɛː/, as in *seen*, *soon* and *sea*. Word-final <e> could similarly indicate the length of the preceding vowel (*made*, *side*, *tune*), and consonant doubling a short vowel (*hill*). During the sixteenth century, an effort went into keeping homophones apart, and spelling words like *all* and *awl* and *made* and *maid* differently. A third improvement was to regularise the orthography borrowed from mediaeval French by altering the spellings so as to reflect their supposed Latin roots. Respellings such as *debt* (< Middle English *dette*; L *dēbitum*), *doubt* (< Middle English *doute(n)*; L *dubitāre*) and *victuals* (< Middle English *vitailes*; L *victuālia*), for example, would have represented more preferable forms for those who knew Latin. Some of the most typical and widely known spelling changes that occurred over the seventeenth century, instead, are the distinction between vowels (<i> and <u>) and consonants (<j> and <v>), and the replacement of word-final <ie> with <y>.

Most recently, a couple of studies have expanded on the overview provided so far, providing interesting insights into spelling developments in English from a quantitative, large-scale point of view. Berg and Aronoff (2017), for example, conducted a diachronic investigation of spelling developments in four derivational suffixes, -OUS, -IC, -AL and -Y, drawing on material available in the *Helsinki Corpus of English Texts* (Rissanen et al., 1991). The authors argued that English spelling signals morphological information and avoids homography in suffixes and the final parts of words homophonous with them. This morphology-related information appears to be evident, the authors argued, specifically in spelling, with no equivalents in phonology. Additionally, the authors suggested, the standardisation of English spelling appears to have occurred predominantly as a relatively spontaneous, self-organising process. In particular, English spelling may be seen as a system which "gradually became more consistent over a period of several hundred years, starting before the advent of printers, orthoepists, or dictionary makers, presumably through the simple interaction of the members of the community of spellers, a sort of self-organizing social network" (Berg & Aronoff, 2017: 37–8). While Berg and Aronoff's claims are interesting, there is another piece of research that has provided, in my view, more compelling details for the large-scale development of Early Modern English spelling. Basu's work (2016) goes beyond the specific case of suffixes, it uses some more reliable corpus material and makes less unorthodox claims about the process of standardisation in English spelling.

8.3   Developments towards Standardisation

Basu's quantitative investigation was conducted using an early version of *Early English Books Online, Text Transcription Partnership* (EEBO-TCP, 2015–)

and identified two major waves of spelling standardisation in the Early Modern English era, one running over most of the sixteenth century and another one occurring in the seventeenth century. The work analysed the cumulative transition periods of individual word tokens to find out whether there was a general time pattern to linguistic change, and showed all new word forms that gained wide acceptance during the two centuries. The results indicated some radical differences between the two waves of development within the first two centuries of English printing, interrupted by periods of relative lull in the rate of orthographic change (Fig. 8.1). The first wave of standardisation, which occurred around the mid-to-late sixteenth century, appeared to be larger than the second wave and was correlated with the period where the process of printing matured in England. The rate of words becoming established as standard detected for the end of the sixteenth century was found to be not only higher, i.e. featuring a greater number of words, but also broader than the seventeenth-century wave. This pattern was interpreted to indicate that the words which shifted before and around the mid-sixteenth century were not aberrations, but, according to Basu, part of a broad, expanding set of

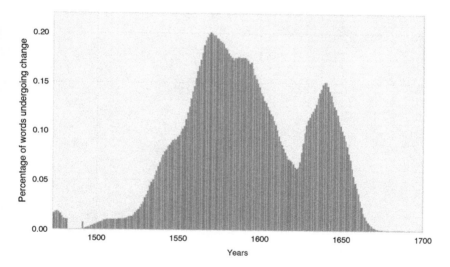

Figure 8.1 Percentage of orthographic forms per year coming into widespread use (from Anupam Basu, '"Ill shapen sounds and false orthography"': a computational approach to early English orthographic variation'; in L. Estill, D. K. Jakacki and M. Ullyot (eds.), *Early Modern Studies after the Digital Turn*, Tempe: Iter Press and ACMRS (Arizona Center for Medieval and Renaissance Studies), 2016, p. 194)

innovations. The second wave, which occurred around the time of the Civil War, on the other hand, was seen as fitting a traditional expectation of spelling standardisation in English, because it appeared as well defined and easily identifiable. The relative broadness of the two frequency waves of standardisation also showed that a degree of variation remained over the course of the early modern era. The norms that were codified as standard resulted from supralocal developments which converged to become standard usages, and formed well-defined waves of development which tended towards standardisation as a fluctuating development.

A corresponding bar chart drawn as part of the exploratory work in the same study (Fig. 8.2), visualised the number of words undergoing a downward transition in a given year – that is to say, it plotted the rates at which orthographic forms fell out of usage. A comparison of the two charts revealed interesting patterns of development, and showed that the rate of decline for these forms lagged slightly behind the rate of acceptance for new forms. Older spellings continued to occur in relatively low numbers, even after the new forms established themselves. The spike visible for the mid-seventeenth

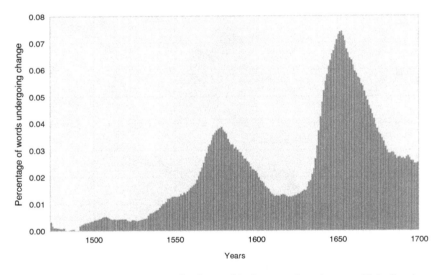

Figure 8.2 Percentage of orthographic forms undergoing a rapid decline in usage per year (from Basu, '"Ill shapen sounds and false orthography": a computational approach to early English orthographic variation'; in Estill et al. (eds.), *Early Modern Studies after the Digital Turn*, Tempe: Iter Press and ACMRS (Arizona Center for Medieval and Renaissance Studies), 2016, p. 194)

century revealed, instead, the presence of a process where a relatively large number of remaining variant forms were finally made redundant. This outcome was, Basu argued, the end result of the growing demands for efficiency in the process of printing made by the exploding volume of printed material during the Civil War. Even more so than the seventeenth century, the sixteenth-century wave was interpreted by Basu as a very significant phase of standardisation in the middle of the early modern era, one that has been almost completely overlooked by previous generations of scholars. The most significant observation about the first wave of standardisation is the fact that its onset predates most of the prescriptive comments from early modern grammarians on the standardisation of spelling. What is more, the years between the 1570s and the 1620s, during which most theoreticians published their ideas on spelling in Early Modern English, turned out to be much less unstable in terms of orthography than previously assumed. Unlike for Berg and Aronoff (2017), Basu's findings appear to be more in line with previous statements made on Early Modern English spelling as a whole. For Howard-Hill (2006: 16), printing was the cradle of change and development towards standardisation. Printers manipulated spelling and were driven by typographic pressures to serve their own business, responding to the changes which affected the printing industry between the sixteenth and the seventeenth centuries. According to Smith, the introduction of printing in particular was a key "external event" that accelerated the process of standardisation and encouraged a debate around linguistic reform (Smith, 2012: 174). For Rutkowska (2013a: 62, 167, 252), combined influences from two main sources, theoreticians on the one hand and printers on the other hand, were responsible for pushing Early Modern English spelling in a modern direction and for influencing its speed of development. According to Tyrkkö (2013: 151), it has been "commonplace" to attribute the gradual standardisation of English spelling in the Early Modern English period to the impact of printing technology.

To return to the model of standardisation introduced at the start of this chapter, the two waves of development uncovered by Basu alert us to some important qualities of Early Modern English spelling and its process of standardisation. First of all, the sixteenth and the seventeenth centuries were already beyond the selection stage: by the end of the early modern era, a standardising form of English had already been largely selected and accepted (perhaps by those who used the Chancery standard), but codification, unlike for other European languages (for French, see, e.g., Ayres-Bennett, 1994: 53), was still in its infancy. The two centuries over which the Early Modern English era stretches, therefore, can be seen as a continuation of the time of elaboration which had begun in the Middle English period and had departed from the London 'standard'. While it is generally agreed that elaboration is primarily a lexical process (e.g. by Milroy & Milroy, 1999: 31), it also affected orthography, as spelling was developing to become more predictable and more functional. Despite their tendency to achieve predictability and functionality, however, variant forms are expected to continue to persist as idiosyncrasies. When taken together, both of the individual waves of spelling developments describe a process of standardisation in continuous tension, regulated by forces of supralocalisation. The process of standardisation in Early Modern English, therefore, certainly does not fix all irregularities but instead allows for some variation in the spelling of English even when one particular orthographic form rises to become, in practical terms, a 'standard'.

A second interesting finding that stems from the results summarised from Basu relates to the overall conceptual understanding of standardisation in Early Modern English spelling. The process of orthographic change was phased and discrete, rather than uniform and gradual, and proceeded not from chaos to order, but from coherence to coherence, through reiterative and individual changes. Moreover, standardisation was an ongoing, slow development, which was never fully completed by the end of the seventeenth century. For this reason, as mentioned earlier on, diachronic spelling developments in Early Modern English, which tend to become a more focused set of norms, should be seen as elements of an *incipient* and *ongoing* process of standardisation, rather than complete, stand-alone elements of a standard. In light of the quantitative overview given in recent research, a distinction between *regularisation*, seen as a univocal and unidirectional development towards standardisation, and *standardisation*, seen more as an umbrella term for encompassing multiple stages of regularisation, should be retained in large-scale work on diachronic spelling development. Without a doubt, the findings made available by Basu from recent preliminary work on large-scale developments in Early Modern English spelling represent a useful and inspirational point of departure for future work in the field. At the same time, however, much as for Berg and Aronoff's (2017) study, there are elements from Basu's work that need to be taken with caution.

In particular, some statements more than others, not least the bold claims about the wholesale influence of the printing press on large-scale spelling developments, need to be corroborated with more substantial linguistic evidence than what was made available in Basu's chapter-long work. Previous statements in Basu's study (2016: 183–4), for example, suggest that graphemes form the basic units for the process of standardisation in Early Modern English, which means that a more extensive quantitative focus on graphemes is a desideratum in order to glean an understanding of the dynamics involved in the standardisation of English spelling. Moreover, the influence of theoreticians, schoolmasters, authors and readers, as well as printers, on the development of English spelling remains, to date, a widely debated, unsettled topic (see Scragg, 1974: 52–87; Salmon, 1999: 32; Nevalainen & Tieken-Boon van Ostade, 2006: 290; Percy,

2012: 1008). For Rutkowska (2016: 187), "the question of the extent to which theoreticians, on the one hand, and printers, on the other, have impacted on the regularization of Early Modern English spelling is likely to remain a chicken-and-egg problem for quite a long time". In my opinion, this is because systematic, large-scale studies are necessary to give more meaningful answers to big questions like the one posed above. Efforts to fill the gap outlined above in an informed way continue to multiply, and it is hoped that interest in the topic will not cease until sufficiently complex knowledge is built in order to inform our insights into orthographic standardisation. Among the other studies that could be mentioned here, in addition to those discussed so far for printing, there is, for example, that by Tyrkkö (2013). The author conducted a quantitative study of the use of abbreviations in 124 printed books – mostly specialised, surgical and remedy texts. The books, produced by 88 printers, were collected from the *Early Modern English Medical Texts* corpus – a collection that covers two centuries, between 1500 and 1700 (Taavitsainen et al. 2010). The quantitative study showed the presence of a very high level of conformity in the orthographic practices of the texts under investigation, noticeable, for example, in the abrupt abandonment of brevigraphs (scribal abbreviations) in the last quarter of the sixteenth century.

In my recent work (Condorelli, 2022), instead, I proposed a new model for the analysis of large-scale graphemic developments from a diachronic perspective, and a resulting new empirical method geared specifically for studying spelling standardisation between the sixteenth and the seventeenth centuries. My research put the newly developed method to use in four interconnected case studies, exploring and discussing the role and relevance of the printing press on the large-scale standardisation of Early Modern English spelling. The case studies conducted in my piece of research (see also Condorelli, 2020b, 2020c, forthcoming) focus on the standardisation of positional spellings, the standardisation of *i* and *y*, the standardisation of etymological spelling and the standardisation of vowel diacritic spelling. The discussion reflects on the relative influence of theoreticians, schoolmasters, authors, patrons and readers, in this order, and their relationship with printers, on Early Modern English spelling standardisation. In what follows, as a way of informing readers, an overview of each of these categories is given, discussing how they interacted and their role in the Early Modern English book market.

8.4   Agents of Standardisation

8.4.1   Language Theoreticians

Prescriptivism in the English language is a practice almost as old as the Early Modern English era itself. The first comments concerning the need for a spelling reform in English appeared around the middle of the sixteenth century, as a response to John Cheke's (1514–57) and Thomas Smith's (1513–77) interest in the pronunciation of Ancient Greek. While Cheke did not explicitly formulate any reform proposals, his translation of fragments of the Gospel of Saint Matthew was as an implicit statement in this sense (Dobson, 1957, I: 43). The most remarkable examples of spellings used by Cheke include the doubling of vocalic spelling and the use of word-final <e> to indicate vowel length (both as separate and as combined features). The occasional doubling of consonants to indicate shortness of the preceding vowel also constituted a relatively regular feature in Cheke's translation (e.g. *Godd,* see Dobson, 1957, I: 44). One of the first explicit improvements proposed for English spelling, instead, was occasioned by Thomas Smith, in his Latin treatise published in 1568. Smith's thoughts were echoed in English by John Hart (d. 1574), who was among the most innovative and productive advocates of a new spelling system based on pronunciation. Hart maintained that it would be "much more easie and readie . . . for the writer and printer" ([1569] 1955, fol. 4) to spell English if his suggestions were followed. Hart pointed out that "we should not neede to vse aboue the two thirds or three quarters at most, of the letters which we are nowe constreyned to vse, and to saue the one third, or at least the one quarter, of the paper, ynke, and time which we now spend superfluously in writing and printing" (fol. 5).

Among those that followed Hart, George Puttenham ([1589] 1968: 120–1) actively promulgated rules and patterns for spelling the English language and warned his audience against adopting the speech and spelling habits of lower-class, uneducated people and countrymen. Even more so than Puttenham, William Bullokar was bitterly critical of contemporary usage among the linguistic philosophers. For Bullokar, spelling conventions had become unpredictable because of the absence of rigorous norms which could maintain correct spelling forms. "For lack of true orthography," he said, "our writing in Inglish hath altered in euery age, yea since printing began" (Bullokar, [1580] 1968: 2). Unlike his predecessors and some of his contemporaries, Bullokar heralded a line of language theoreticians who were active between the mid sixteenth century and the early seventeenth century and who were opposed to a radical change to English spelling. Bullokar's approach reflected the growing need for control over orthography to allow for intercommunication, in a way that would not override the limitations of technology and would avoid the need to completely subvert the inherited English spelling system.

The complexity of the inconsistencies and variations in English spelling encouraged even further attempts at spelling reform, which were fuelled by a strong interest in the classical languages and an appreciation of their structure, literature as well as fixed orthography. Admittedly, even the earliest linguistic theoreticians had acknowledged the power and tenacity of custom as relevant to influencing English spelling. Hart had described custom as "any peoples maner of doings" and had affirmed that he was writing for the "good perswasion of a common commoditie" to those not "obstinate in their custome" (Hart, [1569] 1955: 3–4). It was Richard Mulcaster, however, who was most receptive to the power and importance of custom, with all its imperfections, as a basis for shaping English spelling: "The vse & custom of our cuntrie, hath alredie chosen a kinde of penning, wherein she hath set down hir relligion, hir lawes, hir priuat and publik dealings" (1582: N1v). Mulcaster tended to juxtapose "custom" and "reason" to argue that any prescriptive or reasoned philosophical argument on spelling had to take prevalent scribal and printing practices into account, although he did emphasise writing as the true measure of "custom" compared to the often error-strewn process of printing.

As well as a language theorist, Mulcaster was an experienced schoolmaster, with an interest in designing, codifying and promulgating a system of spelling rules for the use of teachers and, perhaps indirectly, even pupils. As evidenced by Mulcaster's example, the relationship between theoreticians and school-masters at the end of the sixteenth century was probably a close one. From Mulcaster's time onwards, spelling-books, grammars and dictionaries became quiet common in the Early Modern English world, to such an extent that, according to some scholars, their prescriptivist attitude also affected the work of printers. According to Brengelman (1980: 333–4), schoolmasters sought and followed recommendations from early theoreticians, and most of the spelling principles that we use nowadays are in fact the result of a collaboration between the two. A similar idea resonates in Salmon (1999: 32, 34), who maintained that schoolbooks, and especially Mulcaster's *Elementarie*, most likely affected printers, presumably through schooling. Examples of late sixteenth-century and early seventeenth-century schoolbooks which may also have been influen-tial include, for example, those by Clement (1587), Coote (1596), Hume (1617), Evans (1621), Brooksbank (1651) and Hodges (1653). For Rutkowska (2013a: 164), instead, lexicographers' practice may have gradually had a role in crystallising some spelling principles. Key titles for dictionaries and word lists include, for example, the work of Richard Huloet as early as 1552, later republished by Huloet & Higgins (1572). The earliest specialist English dictionary, instead, was written by Robert Cawdrey (1604) and was later used as a basis for other work (see Butler,1633; Hodges, 1644, 1649, 1653; and Wharton, 1654).

8.4.2   The Author, the Patron and the Reader

If prescriptivism was a growing force, the figure of the author occupied a seemingly restricted, but nonetheless still important place in the thriving culture of the Early Modern English era. Especially at the dawn of the sixteenth century, authors were not always primarily responsible for all of the books of their time. Many of the early texts that were handled by printers on a daily basis, for example, would have begun in oral or written form; there would have been drafts, notes jotted down on separate sheets of paper, or in margins and notebooks; revisions would have involved both new changes and revisiting earlier ideas; fair copies would sometimes not have been autograph manuscripts, but corrected by the author; and complete versions may have existed in different states, with texts adapted to specific circumstances. Some texts were copied without formal attribution, and we do not know who was responsible for their creation, and for putting them into circulation. Sometimes, a person would have preserved the words of another, for example the comments made by Jonson to Drummond (see Bland, 2005: 145–86).

During the later sixteenth and the seventeenth centuries, the author gradually joined the printer as a player in the story of the printing world, and was perceived as an important component within a broader system that created and distributed writing. The relationship between the author and the printer, and their involvement in the in-house stages of book production, however, is nothing less than a controversial matter in the scholarly tradition. For Simpson (1935: 1), the role of printers and correctors in determining the final form of printed matter in proofreading has been greatly exaggerated, and he considers it a "mischievous" error to suppose that authors did not normally proofread their own work. Proofreading, Brengelman continued (1980: 333, 336), was not generally carried out by printers but rather by authors themselves, who were mainly responsible for passing directly over to us a great many of the spellings that we know today. According to Brengelman, the more responsible presses submitted proof copy to the authors and followed the authors' preferences in matters of spelling. Admittedly, he continued, less responsible presses ignored their authors' wishes but could hardly have contributed towards the development of a standard spelling (Brengelman, 1980: 343).

For Howard-Hill (2006: 16), instead, Early Modern English printers did not attempt to follow the spelling of the original authors at all, and used the authors' original writing only as a starting point to introduce their own in-house set of rules. The author's manuscript would often undergo a level of processing from the master-printer or the corrector, and the actual process of composing also involved steps which were likely to alter the author's original text. For example, while there were printers who employed experienced proofreaders and correctors among the most learned authors, these would often have a preference for Latin forms regardless of the author's original spelling choices (Tyrkkö, 2013: 151–2). According to Malone (2006: 404–5), authors were generally present in the printing house when their books were in press, but there were also numerous references by authors to excuses for their failure to proofread their own work.

Regardless of the extent to which they were actually influential in the process of book production, authors were hardly ever major players in the economic game of the printers. During much of the Early Modern English era, the author had little hope of making an independent living out of his writing efforts, and therefore books were often presented to readers with some remarkable monetary assistance from patrons. After the collapse of most of the major monasteries and the turbulent situation that shook the Church of England in the 1530s because of Henry VIII's split with the Pope, the patronage of writers was to become fully secular; in essence, the monarch and the nobility embraced the fact that part of their role and authority consisted in preserving and protecting knowledge. Authors and printers were aware of the fact that a book could not be sold abroad if some rich and powerful patron was not behind the publication and could therefore guarantee its suitability for exportation. The system of patronage in England was, for a long time, unsystematic and somewhat irregular, and those who benefited from it did not have many expectations. Sometimes, the presence of a protective name at the head of a publication was still not enough for the average writer, and in fact most authors did not receive much financial support outside of the book production costs. Most authors, in any case, already had some other job or some kind of intellectual recognition, so they were not pursuing money with their books. Their dedications were usually acknowledgements of loyalty and gratitude rather than attempts to attract future sponsorship. Over time, when writers proliferated and became more established figures in English society, and when writing became a recognised profession – which only happened towards the end of the Early Modern English era, if not beyond it – patronage became of greater monetary and career advancement value.

The importance of having a powerful person to dedicate the title to was, in the book market of the time, not only monetary. In a time where aristocrats ruled society, a noble name was a guarantee that the contents were worth publishing, in the sense that the work did not contain any material that could put the aristocrats in danger – something like an implicit censorship-safe guarantee. Clearly, during most of the early modern era, buying and storing a book could become, depending on the title, quite a risky business, so it was important for readers to be assured of their borrowing or purchase. Whether this attitude reflected vestigial feelings about the power and value of books on the whole is uncertain; there may have also been the practical idea that owning some books could be compromising for individuals living in the ever-changing and unpredictably threatening Early Modern English society. An interesting feature of patronised publication is the widely shared belief that the patron would protect the author against 'malicious tongues', 'backbiting', 'detraction' and 'serpents'; to some extent, patronage even had something of a thaumaturgic purpose in protecting against bad luck. The most widespread sentiment among readers, frequently expressed in the form of complaints, was that there were actually genuine reasons for worrying about their own safety when purchasing books. It would be understandable if this fear were expressed mainly in connection with religious books, which were often objects of contention, but concern among people actually also related to the publication of books of medicine, law, history, philosophy and poetry, to name a few.

It is thus likely that publishing a book exposed the author to a great deal of bitterness and condemnation from the literate, which could then reverberate on society's perception of the writer. The resentment against authors was nurtured, in particular, by envy, factionalism, small-mindedness, anti-intellectualism, cultural hostility – all of which could make the life of an Early Modern English author quite miserable. An interesting piece of evidence that shows how important patronage was for moral defence rather than monetary sponsorship was the fact that playwrights, who produced some of the best-paid pieces of writing, also dedicated their plays to patrons. Within the remit of playwriting, the figure of the patron was necessary in order to stop the local authorities from hindering the theatre owner's jobs and to prevent officials from interfering with actors or performances by means of censorship. Noblemen enjoyed the work of actors simply for their entertainment, and it was therefore in their best interest to protect their work by acting as patrons. Literary patronage became so important that a number of companies in England bore a lord's name: Leicester, Worcester, Oxford, Sussex, Essex, Derby, Shrewsbury are only some of the most notable examples.

For quite some time, the relationship between patrons and authors seemed to be something of mutual advantage that could potentially be sustained long term. Unfortunately, however, this was not so. While there were quite a few noblemen in the country who were ready to act as literary patrons for authors of literary, scholarly and religious works, the turn of the seventeenth century saw the number of authors gradually overcoming the capacity of patrons to provide support. The increased production of printed books, the expansion of the book trade and the rapidly increasing number of university graduates who tried to live by writing all contributed to the increasing isolation of the figure of the author. Professional writers therefore often ended up being stuck between the lack of a patron and their inability to convince a publisher to support them economically in an adequate way. While monetary relationships between authors and publishers really differed from case to case, it was not rare for publishers in the sixteenth and seventeenth centuries to pay authors only once – often a small sum given upon receipt of the finished manuscript. To put it quite bluntly, books were rarely ever sold for the financial benefit of the author, but for the stationer who bore all the expenses of publication.

As evidenced from the discussion about patrons, who acted to protect authors from the 'evil' reader, the emerging figure of the professional author in Early Modern English is inevitably bound up with that of both printer and reader. Since the late Middle English period, writers imagined readers as possessing the authority to change the text, turn a page or move away from a text, and often established a discourse that emphasised these and other modes of reader participation. Along with recognising readers' capabilities, authors also acknowledged both the potential and the threat offered by this participation to support or undermine an author's own power. In other words, the attention paid to writerly authority is incomplete without attending to its complement, readerly authority. One cannot understand Early Modern English authors without also taking into account Early Modern English readers, their relations to each other, and the meaningful roles played by each party – both through the ways in which authors anticipated readers' participation, and as readers effected it. In practical terms, readers presented the potential for productive partnership with authors through their participatory engagement with texts, even as they concurrently threatened the possibility of disruptive work. Accordingly, authors in Early Modern England focused on how readers could help or hinder through participatory reading practices, in order to maintain and develop their own status and engage readers in their projects. Authors were deeply interested in shaping the practice of readers' corrections, seeking to guide how and what readers responded to before readers ever set pen to parchment. In a way, authors explored what readers might become to them by anticipating readers' enthusiasm for textual participation, and viewed readers as possessing a growing power to contribute in sophisticated ways to the literary language. Readers could, in turn, support or disrupt authors' plans for their texts and, by extension, also those of printers. Additionally, readers could read in ways that supported beneficial interpretations of a text, or not read in a productive way at all, hampering the success of a book. Thus, readers were, in their actions, figures whose status provoked the ongoing interest and concern of authors and printers.

Both readers and authors in the Early Modern English era, then, were in turn subjected to what Milroy and Milroy (1999: vii) call "the complaint tradition", a culture of tension towards the maintenance of a standardised written language. The surge of prescriptive influences between the sixteenth and the seventeenth centuries was only a prelude to the massive legislation and prescription which occurred during the second half of the eighteenth century. What Blank (1996: 9) terms "prescriptivism" in the early modern era was "diagnostic in its methods and its aims" and hence, in terms of the framework provided by Haugen (1966), it can be located before the codification phase. The complaints about English that emerged from the very onset of printing in England often focused on the inadequacy of the vernacular and did not establish a model to follow. Nevertheless, they still put pressure and expectations on individual authors and readers respectively, a matter which takes us back, in a circular way, to the influence of theoreticians and schoolmasters.

Clearly, the context in which Early Modern English spelling became standardised was one of synergy and contrast between "competing magnets of prestige" (Smith, 1996: 65). On the one hand, these parties (readers and authors, patrons and printers) most likely worked in conjunction with the natural, language-internal processes of competition and self-organisation, and operated in synchrony by shaping the hybrid features of a more focused variety of English. On the other hand, if taken individually, each of the external parties identified above acted as constraining factors in the process of standardisation. Each of the parties may in principle have hindered, weakened, slowed down or, on the contrary, reinforced, accelerated or even helped standardisation, for reasons existing within the nature of orthography itself. Orthography is a practice which is bound up with other practices to do with literacy, which are themselves embedded in the social, economic, cultural and technological layers of the society where the spelling has grown. For Sebba "any explanatory account of orthography-as-practice must be sociocultural in nature" (2007: 14) and "the practices involving literacy in which a community engages are inevitably related to the type of orthography which will emerge as one of the technologies underpinning those practices" (pp. 23–4). These statements somewhat echo those made by scholars like Terttu Nevalainen, who claimed that the standardisation of English spelling was in fact "a multi-party affair" between language theoreticians, schoolmasters, authors, readers and printers (2012: 156).

Interactions among these parties generally occurred in a world where the advent of printing had not made handwritten book production immediately obsolete. The manuscript industry stayed alive alongside the emerging printing industry well into the sixteenth century. Printing and handwriting did not end up becoming competing technologies until later in the Early Modern English era. Scriveners still engaged in jobs like producing copies of such things as legal texts, literary works, letters and other documents of note, and were still regarded as an effective publication route. Most of the incunabula produced at the intersection between the age of manuscript and that of print consciously imitated the layout and conventions of printed texts whilst every printed book was first a manuscript; even when a book had been printed, it might well be marked up and corrected for a later edition by hand. Readers might annotate or emend, making a book into a composite document and leave their traces, like the inky thumbprint of a pressman, in the margin. For many, the difference between print as a mechanised form of mass manuscript production, and print as a technology with other aesthetic, technical and socio-economic concerns, was not self-evident. One of the most immediate examples of the way in which the world of print and that of manuscripts co-existed consists in the fact that many early modern readers were keen to personalise the volumes that they owned, not just with marginal annotations, but by creating *Sammelbände*. These were collections where multiple texts were bound together as one, creating personal books which contained both printed and handwritten texts. These and other examples demonstrating the overlap between the world of printing and handwriting are certainly interesting and deserve more attention from researchers in the future.

Further Reading

Howard-Hill, T. 2006. 'Early modern printers and the standardization of English spelling'. *The Modern Language Review*, 101, pp. 16–29.

McKenzie, D. F. 2002. 'Printing and publishing 1557–1700: constraints on the London book trades'. In J. Barnard & D. F. McKenzie (eds.), *The Cambridge History of the Book in Britain*, vol. IV: *1557–1695*. Cambridge: Cambridge University Press, pp. 553–67.

Milroy, J. & J. Milroy. 1985a. *Authority in Language: Investigating Language Prescription and Standardisation*. London: Routledge & Kegan Paul.

Nevalainen T. & I. Tieken-Boon van Ostade. 2006. 'Standardisation'. In R. Hogg & D. Denison (eds.), *A History of the English Language*. Cambridge: Cambridge University Press, pp. 271–311.

Wright, L. (ed.). 2020. *The Multilingual Origins of Standard English*. Berlin; Boston: Mouton de Gruyter.

9 Orthography and Language Change

9.1 Inevitability of Change

The previous chapter has provided a quick overview of some of the complex relationships between theoreticians, schoolmasters, patrons, authors and readers in the burgeoning world of the early printed book. The discussion has made reference to orthographic developments during the Early Modern English era, and how standardisation was subject to ongoing pressures and contrasts. While the information provided in the discussion is as exhaustive as possible, it remains difficult to convey faithfully the complexities underlying the overall process of orthographic standardisation. One important message that needs to be added to what has been said so far, for example, is that exogenous determinants, i.e. external socio-cultural, political and economic ones, are often not exclusive agents in the process of orthographic standard-isation. Many of these factors frequently occur in close interaction with endogenous determinants, i.e. internal systemic agents. Their role as impulses or as limiting factors for standardisation is so intertwined with that of the exogenous determinants that it is often difficult to discern which reasons were most responsible for encouraging standardisation as a whole. Endogenous factors can hinder, weaken, slow down, or, on the contrary, reinforce, accel-erate or even help uncovering the effects of exogenous factors. With that said, what, if anything is an endogenous factor, with specific reference to ortho-graphic development?

An immediately relevant example would be that of self-organisation, which is the result of a process of internal competition across orthographic units for a given position or function within a given writing system (for a broad over-view unrelated to orthography, see Rocha, 1998: 3). According to de Boer (2011: 612), self-organisation is the product of the interaction of two different linguistic perspectives. It can be considered as behaviour and knowledge of an individual, and it can also be seen as a system of conventions in a language community. In fact, these two points of view can be seen as components of two levels at which orthography as a whole can be studied. One is the individual level, where detailed individual behaviour is analysed; the other is the population level, where individual behaviour is averaged and abstracted, and more general trends and processes are investigated. In most cases, both the individual and the population levels are intertwined and interdependent: individuals' behaviour is determined by conventions in the group, and concurrently, group conventions are created and maintained through individual behaviour.

Broadly speaking, self-organisation involves repeated interaction between elements on a microscopic scale that results in organisation on a macroscopic scale. Going back to the two linguistic perspectives described in the previous paragraph, the individual level corresponds to the microscopic scale, while the population level corresponds to the macroscopic scale. The macroscopic scale can be described with far fewer parameters than would be necessary to describe the behaviour on the microscopic scale. Both the microscopic and the macroscopic scales interact in a way that makes the writing system efficient from a communicative point of view. The internal organisation of all writing systems is undeniably functional – if there was no need to communicate effectively, none of the orthographic developments that most languages underwent during the process of standardisation would have arisen. This means that the language-internal factors discussed by some scholars for the development of diachronic orthography, for example suffix spellings (Berg & Aronoff, 2017, briefly discussed in Chapter 8 with reference to Early Modern English), albeit being somewhat unorthodox, may not necessarily be in contrast with the influence of exogenous determinants. Instead, self-organisation might have worked as a principle underlying the imposition of pragmatic agreements derived from exogenous factors, such as those discussed in the previous chapter on standardisation.

In theoretical terms, the interplay between exogenous and endogenous determinants in the development of standardised orthographies results in something peculiar to orthographic standardisation. Underneath the umbrella of standardisation, there are multiple processes of regularisation, both at the individual and at the population levels, which in turn are the 'fabric' of orthographic standardisation itself. As shown by some of the many studies existing in the diachronic orthography of individual languages, the history of orthography is often not just part of a history of standard orthography, but also, perhaps even especially, a history of individual spellings. The emergence of systematicity in English spelling, for example, is a product of multiple, individual pathways at graphemic level, which were initiated and fostered by a multitude of exogenous and endogenous pressures (see Condorelli, 2020b, 2020c, forthcoming). The individual pathways which formed the process of standardisation in English spelling were, in turn, facilitated by the prior development of agreed norms in selected areas of the spelling system, which arose from the manuscript tradition; in other words, spelling standardisation was superimposed upon suitable pre-existing convergent stages of spelling regularity (Milroy, 1994: 20). In most cases, present-day orthography is the result of bricolage and alteration, strongly influenced by historical, sociological and pragmatic changes.

As the example of Early Modern English has shown in the previous chapter, the gradual emergence of the vernacular as a national language during the course of the sixteenth and seventeenth centuries, celebrated by Jones (1953) as "the triumph of English", was a more complex process than the title suggests. The process of standardisation is often one in continuous tension; it certainly does not fix all irregularities, but instead it allows for a degree of variation to exist even when one particular orthographic form gradually becomes, de facto, a 'standard'. The element of variability and incompleteness in any process of standardisation is direct evidence of a universally accepted axiom within all fields of linguistics: languages constantly change, and although it is sometimes possible to slow down change in progress through external interventions (normative ones, for instance), it is impossible to stop it altogether (see Trudgill, 2001 for a sociolinguistic approach to language change). Orthography is an expression of the ever-changing nature of language: it bends from the impact of interaction with other writing systems, and it develops through the need or desire for more systematicity. Sometimes, writing systems flourish and become standards, while at other times they are partially or wholly engulfed by other writing systems. No writing system is just one writing system, and neither is it just letters – rather, it is an agglomerate of interactions with other writing systems and, therefore, other letters. Orthographic changes have been documented for centuries, and they represent the cultural and communicative necessities of a society. It would be unrealistic, therefore, to expect that new technological advances and the need to communicate using new technology would generate different orthographic developments today.

While all change is inevitable, some of it is, of course, unfortunate. Of the world's approximately 6,000 languages, every two weeks one of these languages, and any related orthography, disappears. At this speed, some of the world's writing systems face an even greater risk of extinction than any currently endangered animals. The extinction of writing systems is a big loss; when a writing system is no longer used, the cultural and linguistic knowledge encoded in it are gone forever. Interestingly, although many of the concerns about orthographic maintenance and death are about some of the most standardised and codified writing systems in the world (e.g. French, Spanish and English), it is often because of these more widespread orthographies that many endangered writing systems or scripts are lost. The disappearance of writing systems is like sand between our fingers and appears to occur so abruptly because it is difficult to observe change. According to Labov (1994: 25), who speaks of "synchronic study of linguistic change in progress", it is generally possible to see change both in variation across time (*real time*), and in variation across generations (*apparent time*). In order to "extract evidence for change in progress", Labov (1994: 26) continued, "we must separate the variation due to change from the variation due to social factors like sex, social class, social networks, and ethnicity, and from the variation due to internal factors like sentence stress, segmental environment, word order and phrase structure". With orthography, separating variation due to change from variation due to social factors is not always easy, since "the evolution of orthography can be understood only when the dynamic interaction between extra- and intra-linguistic processes and pressures is brought into consideration" (Smith, 1996: 78).

Within the remits of orthography, the key object of such dynamic interaction is what historical sociolinguists normally call an *orthographic variable*, that is to say

a feature of an orthographic system of a given language, related to the phonological, morphological, or lexical levels of that language system, and realised by different variants under specific extra-linguistic circumstances. Like the more general term linguistic variable, it can be considered to denote an abstract entity realized by two or more variants, which are not always predictable by phonological, morphological, or any other kind of linguistic conditioning (Rutkowska & Rössler, 2012: 219).

The topic discussed in this chapter, language change and its far-reaching effects, is founded on the concept of variation explained above, as this can lead to permanent and/or widespread change in orthographic behaviour. In historical writing, variation represents the norm rather than the exception. Queen Elizabeth I, for instance, who produced a large number of autograph letters, used a single spelling for only half of the words that she used in the documents that have survived to date (707 out of 1,389), although her writing was of course not completely chaotic (523 of the remaining 682 words feature only two variants; see Evans, 2013).

Much like for the previous chapter, the discussion draws on a number of examples from previous research work in the early modern era, and while there are some differences in how extensively this specific chapter can be informed compared to a chapter on standardisation, some sufficiently solid definitions can still be used as a basis for discussion. So far, several studies have looked at prescriptive literature and metalinguistic comments on the development of orthographic systems, reflecting on the processes of standardisation at various stages (see, e.g., Vandenbussche, 2002; Nevalainen, 2012). However, fewer studies have traditionally been carried out on orthographic practices as variable usages of language, in the same way that a variable usage of morphological or phonological variants might inform us about the internal grammar of the speaker. In some of the most recent work, especially that falling under the umbrella of historical sociolinguistics (see Hernández-Campoy & Conde-Silvestre, 2012), the binary nature of the difference between vernacular and standard languages has, luckily, almost completely disappeared so that variation is not eliminated a priori from the overall appreciation of a given writing system. An approach in terms of a register continuum is now preferred, and historical sociolinguists always carefully describe the type of data that they are studying so that one can situate it on the developing continuum (see Watts, 2015: 5–6).[1]

9.2   Types of Linguistic Change

Among the models of language change most frequently used to study the continuum of chronological development, 'transmission' and 'diffusion' were extensively discussed by Labov (2007). *Transmission* involves native-language learning by children and guarantees continuity across generations. Children are seen as able to imitate perfectly the language of their parents' generation, simply by a process of copying. Transmission accounts for change, but it does so only as a process that goes following the same wave over time, for instance, by generalisation of one specific innovation to more linguistic scenarios. This process leads to change from within the structure of a language, and is known as 'change from below'. Specific changes in the system are passed on to new generations, who will then apply these changes to their language and distribute them more broadly than ever before. Transmission as a change-from-below process assumes the existence of a society which is almost completely static. Transmission is often associated with *incrementation*, a term which refers to the generalisation of an innovation to more contexts than before. Incrementation does not mean that developments do not occur, though when they do, they often occur, as mentioned above, in the same direction across the generations.

Diffusion, instead, involves change happening by contact, from one community to the other. As we know, social changes brought about by socio-historical events may have an impact on the stability of individual communities and may create more heterogeneity, increasing the potential of contact across peoples. The process of diffusion sometimes consists in the introduction of forms from other systems, and in this case change happens

---

[1] Oral and written languages may also be considered to fall on a continuum with respect to each other, rather than being in binary opposition – of course, when language is written down (by hand, on a typewriter, a press or a computer), it is no longer oral, so this aspect is binary. However, researchers, and historical sociolinguists in particular, have described types of non-standard written data that is often closer to vernacular language than to the standard one, and which can contain features of a typically oral language, like traces of pronunciation in the spelling (for a detailed discussion on different types of such data, see, among others, Elspaß, 2012; Martineau, 2013).

'from above'. Typically, a change from above occurs when an adult learns a new feature, and it is a process which is often prone to error. Thus, specific orthographic features may be taken, but the complex writing system of the lending language will remain unknown to the adult speakers. Complexities are usually integrated more easily into the host system by children so that only a selected few features spread out across the host language. Unlike transmission within communities, diffusion across communities has a correlation with the wave model normally used in diachronic linguistics.

The core definitions of transmission and diffusion established so far have been subsequently discussed and improved by numerous scholars (e.g. by Cheshire et al., 2011; Stanford & Kenny, 2013; Tagliamonte & Denis, 2014). Among the most recent commentators, Cheshire et al. (2011: 156) suggested that viewing language change as a process of development from below and from above represents a useful framework for approaching linguistic features diachronically. Labov's models, however, are not always easy to apply to orthography, as they have so far almost exclusively referred to sound change. In principle, sound change seems a much more suited subject with which to explore the two models of language change than diachronic orthography. In particular, orthography – and, more broadly, writing – is a less spontaneous linguistic area than speech; technically, writing is not an element belonging to the natural process of language learning but rather it is acquired gradually, growing up, usually at school.

Depending on the stance that one takes for explaining diachronic orthographic development, it may become natural to consider the difference between internal changes from below and changes from above not valid for orthography. If orthography was to be seen as something that comes entirely from above, as some believe, then the idea of diffusion would not apply to it. However, as the history of writing in the European continent shows us, orthographies are not necessarily always tailored for their respective societal groups. Several unrelated peoples in Europe began to use the Latin alphabet and the Latin-based letter-sound correlations, even when the phonological system required some substantial modifications to the Latin base for it to work efficiently on the sound repertoire of a foreign language. Thus, orthography can in this case be viewed as an enormous contact event, a feature that has made its way from another system by means of a process of diffusion. That being said, it is still logically possible to suggest that orthographic development can frequently be viewed in a similar way to changes in speech. For example, orthographic change, much like speech development, often creates an S-curve and is the object of a number of individual-dependent mechanisms and functions. Orthographic features can also be absorbed during reading in a more subconscious way. All of these elements are useful points of departure in order for one to approach orthography as a linguistic phenomenon bound to exactly the same principles as other levels of linguistic analysis.

Even if we see orthography as a normal language event similar to other linguistic levels, though, Labov's models do not come without at least one important problem. The difference between transmission and diffusion is based on the ability to identify tangible and specific language groups, that is to say, groups of language users with shared linguistic agreements. Transmission occurs inside these language groups, while diffusion is a process which requires in its definition the idea of overcoming the boundaries of communities. Both transmission and diffusion can be identified especially in comparative studies of easily identifiable communities with separate migration and settlement backgrounds. Each community, however, can also have multilingual traits, which means that language contact may also occur internally within an individual group. Unfortunately, identifying specific linguistic groups is difficult when we do not have enough contextual details. Consider, for example, the European population from the sixteenth century to the end of the nineteenth century: it was heavily affected by immigration in the north-west and was eventually depleted by a series of crises. These unfortunate events forced people to move in large numbers to other areas of Europe, thus creating a remarkable amalgamation of cultures and languages. For these and other similar reasons, identifying language communities in history is not always an easy task, and most of the time there is not enough background information for one to be able to reconstruct community profiles.

Because of the complexities inherent in the historical realm of orthographic change, it is difficult to gauge the degree to which the current sociolinguistic theories on contact-induced phenomena are applicable to historical communities. Labov himself (2007: 348) admitted that the idea that he put forward about the linguistic community may depend exclusively on the present-day North American model from which he gathered his data. He indicated that European dialectology usually describes the diffusion of features from one area to the next, more than anything else related to transmission (Labov, 2007: 348). Milroy's dialectological framework (2007) seems to address some of the deficiencies outlined above for Labov's models, because it reworks the idea of *contact*. According to Milroy (2007), diffusion may be seen as equivalent to supralocal changes, which are in continuous development, as they appear to shift swiftly from group to group, across large regions. They are absorbed by language users across the linguistic regions, and across different corners of the world – which in turns entails that close-knit contact is not a requirement for the changes to occur. While these types of changes definitely need more research from a socio-historical point of view, examples from present-day sociolinguistics include well known forms used on social media (see, for example, *be like*).

Transmission, instead, happens in the context of small and local networks and communities, in which close interaction and contact encourages users to imitate the specific rules underlying a given linguistic system. In such local, close-contact situations, maintenance is seen as a highly important process – one that is applicable also to orthography (on maintenance, see Milroy & Milroy, 1985b). Local changes happen as soon as the network or community structure becomes subjected to change, whether this is by interaction with other societal groups via people on the edge of the circle or wholly internally. Milroy's (2007) view has implications for learnability, but maintenance is not the core mechanism as with Labov (2007). Maintenance within networks is a process relevant to all generations involved, which means that this view does not expect the application of individual change models to different age categories.

Stanford and Kenny (2013) suggested that intensity of interaction is enough to create a computational take on Labov's (2007) findings, and that it is possible to account for the effects of transmission and diffusion even when potential language learning discrepancies between generations are not considered. A motive why one could argue that there is no distinction between children and adults may be found in a property specifically belonging to orthography – the fact that it does not always work as a real-time event. Individuals who learn the sound values behind graphemic conventions in a given set of letters may go back to their writings and correct whichever mistakes they find, according to the newly learned rules. Orthographic conventions can be learned and adopted at any point in anyone's life, and the time of acquisition will, of course, interact with all the other variables involved in learning orthography.

In the remaining part of this section, transmission and diffusion are discussed, departing from the idea of writing traditions, especially from orthographic conventions specific to individual areas in Europe. One of the most compelling linguistic events that occurred in Europe between the Middle Ages and the present day is the process of *supralocalisation*, immediately followed by standardisation. As briefly seen in Chapter 8, supralocalisation refers to the geographical diffusion of linguistic features beyond their region of origin, and, in this sense, it acts as an antecedent to standardisation by gradually minimising the degree of variation and maximising the amount of focusing. While supralocalisation is an essential prerequisite for later developments to occur, and therefore it is, chronologically, of primary importance within the linear development of standardisation, it cannot be equated to standardisation itself. The present chapter focuses on supralocalisation as a specific aspect of the broader discursive umbrella of standardisation, which has been the main object of discussion in Chapter 8. It is for this reason that, although supralocalisation generally occurs before standardisation in chronological terms, it is discussed in a chapter that immediately follows an overview of standardisation more broadly.

In the following sections, transmission and diffusion are generally discussed with reference to research work in English, German and Dutch, which has contributed a great deal to informing our current knowledge on the topics. In line with the European research tradition, *diffusion* is understood, with reference to orthography, as the principal mechanism of orthographic development, broadly consisting in the expansion of new features through a given linguistic region driven by close interaction. The concept of *transmission*, which admittedly depends on the questionable idea of uniform social groups, may also be a useful idea in some socio-historical scenarios in orthography. Relevant examples are explicit school education activities, given in different ways, for instance materials where orthographic rules are explicitly codified for the benefit of the youth, as well as in narrow circles of adults. This phenomenon may still be labelled as transmission, and not maintenance, because it frequently entails educational scenarios. Overall, diffusion and transmission most likely worked in conjunction with natural, language-internal processes of competition and self-organisation, and operated in synchrony towards shaping the hybrid features of more focused writing systems over time.

9.3   Transmission

9.3.1   Instruction and Metalinguistic Practices

Writing is a linguistic ability that is essentially learned. While there are of course people who learn how to read and write without the need for formal instruction, the process of schooling is the basis for the majority of people. The core idea in schooling is the transmission of rules, without which it would be impossible to conceive anything close to the passing of conventions. Writing was a learned ability also in the past, albeit the concept of 'school' was a great deal different from our own. In mediaeval and early modern Europe, transmission of writing rules was a job for monasteries first, and then private and public schools. Schooling at the time also consisted in home-based learning, though this was conducted at different levels of quality depending on the means available to the family. The fact that instruction may have been a key motor behind the process of transmission is also evidenced by the many grammatical traditions across Europe inherited from the classical authors. The Western European prescriptive practices in particular heralded the interest in establishing fixed writing conventions which could be passed on across generations by means of a public or family-based schooling system. The process of transmission via the schooling system, however, is quite problematic to investigate empirically for some historical periods of time more than others. Some linguistic scenarios for relatively focused periods of time show such a fragmented approach to establishing transmission rules that one is sometimes left wondering how feasible it is to provide evidence for any process of continuity between instruction and orthography at all.

Prescriptive activities, like the publication of grammars and spelling books, as discussed in Chapter 8, also provide some useful material with reference to studies in transmission. In general, however, not all attempts to establish a relatively solid form of instruction were equally efficient in their goal of fixing orthographic conventions. The general problem with analysing transmission in this way is similar to the problem connected to public or home schooling. It is in principle possible that metalinguistic publications played some role in the transmission of writing conventions. For Rutkowska (2013a: 164), for example, early lexicographers' practice may have gradually had a role in crystallising some early-print spelling principles in English. In general, however, we do not have clear data about the rules which were passed on to new groups of languages users. The specific case of early prescriptive textual practices in English falls in line with broader cross-linguistic research on the early modern era, which shows a general state of reluctance to accept the direct influence of early language theoreticians on patterns of language use.

In any case, while the effectiveness of prescriptive practices is dubious, metalinguistic practices provide some precious evidence for the existence of a conscious need for passing on orthographic rules in history, as well as a means of measuring out orthographic transmission over time. As a whole, the history of grammar production and language description and prescription in historical linguistics will probably have had some importance in the shaping of orthography as we know it today. If this had not been the case, we would simply not have such abundant collections of metalinguistic resources from so many centuries and so many corners of the world. However, it is almost impossible to pin down how a given orthographic rule may find its way from a group of people to a book and then from a book to a new set of individuals. Likewise, questions that are difficult to answer are which areas of the language were affected first by the alleged metalinguistic influences and at which moments in time for which groups of people. In other words, we will not always know whether extant metalinguistic texts were actually used in the historical classroom, and if so, which texts exactly, and to what extent and how the teacher made use of them.

The fact that orthographic conventions can be recorded and cross-matched from across different moments in history is in itself indirect proof of transmission. However, to give a hypothetical, simplified example, the suggestion that <t> and <p> were used as aspirated plosives in word-initial position in English in connection with the appearance of some metalinguistic comments on the subject does not provide a great deal of information on the mechanics of transmission for the two graphemes. Admittedly, whenever some well-established conventions become disrupted or drop out of use altogether, there could be some concrete reasons to argue, albeit indirectly, for the potential influence of metalinguistic practices. The inconsistent use of <h> in Middle English, for instance, including both the dropping of <h> and the addition of an unexpected <h> at the beginning of vowels, represents some fairly solid evidence. In particular, those who did not have the sound /h/ in their own phonetic system were often likely instructed to use <h> or they were repeating patterns seen in other words which they would not usually utter with a /h/. Milroy (1992b: 199) gave a good few thirteenth-century examples from East Anglia including spellings of the verb *have* like *adde*, *adden*, *aue*, and also *ate* for *hate*, *is* for *his*, *om* for *home* and several others, together with the appearance of *h* in forms like *ham* for *am*, *his* for *is* and *hure* for *our*.

The contrast between the need to represent pronunciation in writing and that of passing on orthographic conventions is much of a recurrent theme in history. Comparable examples of *h*-dropping and *h*-epenthesis can be identified in Middle Dutch, particularly in sources from the south-west of the Dutch language region known as the Flanders, and carried on until at least the eighteenth century. Rutten and van der Wal (2014: 24–5) discussed a number of changing patterns available in seventeenth-century private letters from the Zeeland area in the south-west of what we now call the Netherlands. Examples include the dropping of <h>, for example in *andt* for *handt* 'hand', and its insertion in *hacht* for *acht* 'eight'. Other examples cited in their study include some additional and related consequences of the fact that <h> had been imposed, through teaching, to language users who did not have /h/ in their speech. One of the historical Dutch renderings of the letter <h> is /ha:/, changed to /a:/ by speakers without a /h/. The letter <a> is, though, also pronounced as /a:/. This indicates that for h-less language users, the alphabet featured two letters with the same sound signification. These confusing grapheme–phoneme correspondences encouraged seventeenth-century individuals from Zeeland to swap <a> for <h> as in *aebben* (instead of *hebben* 'have') and to write <h> for <a> as in *hpril* (instead of *april* 'April'). The cases from English and Dutch show a detachment from norms that may have potentially been passed on via the schooling system or by metalinguistic comments (or indeed both concurrently).

In addition to these examples, there are other historical-sociolinguistic examples where transmission and its consequences on linguistic development can be studied more precisely. The requirements for these situations to be found and analysed are, first of all, the existence of proof of real teaching activities, and, secondly, a clearly identifiable linguistic community. An important element which is likely to increase our chances of fulfilling the two requirements above is the existence of a reasonably well put-together collection of primary material. The first goal is quite difficult to achieve, but studies like that by Van der Feest Viðarsson (2017) provide some excellent examples of archival material which achieves it. The author overviewed some Icelandic student essays from the nineteenth century and showed how these were written within an identifiable schooling group framework. The essays were also marked by the teachers, which means that the material provides direct evidence for teaching and learning approaches in the community. Another interesting example of orthographic transmission through education is offered by the new Dutch linguistic norms established from around the nineteenth century as part of the process of nation-state formation, which brought about a new wave of official conventions for the orthography and structure of Dutch (as discussed in Rutten, 2019). During the first few years of the nineteenth century, nationalist sentiment had begun to supplant traditional regional identities and was drawn upon by politicians as a basis for a new nation-building mission. The establishment of a nationalised set of linguistic rules was connected to the concurrent restructuring of the schooling system, which in turn brought about a national framework of instruction regulation.

This type of regulation at the time was a conscious attempt to instil normative language rules among teachers and school inspectors. By the early nineteenth century, several schoolteachers were fully committed in their mission to pass on the recently established rules to their students. In a short time, grammars were rewritten to cater for the new orthographic rules – an event which shows good sensitivity on the authors' part to the recent conventions. As argued in Schoemaker and Rutten (2019), the creation of new and revised schoolbook editions also suggests subjection on the part of the authors to the new orthography. Archival research on private letters, diaries and regional newspapers produced prior to and following the new conventions demonstrate the widespread diffusion of the new orthographic rules across individuals and their writing of any type, including personal (see Krogull, 2018). It is possible that faithfulness to the new rules was encouraged by a wish to boast knowledge and intellectual authority, which in turn caused a decisive, conscious shift from old to new orthographic conventions. Overall, the Dutch example of the early nineteenth century suggests that the transmission of writing conventions can be studied productively if primary texts are available, as these show proof of norm transmission and reception. The ideological background is the attempt to build, via the schooling framework, a more even group of people of the Dutch nation.

9.3.2   Networks and Communities

While child-language acquisition represents the primary means by which transmission in orthography may occur, some adult contact scenarios outside of the traditional schooling system may also contribute to orthographic transmission. Small social groups are a potential socio-historical scenario where orthographic conventions are passed over from one individual to the next, as examples of orthographic maintenance or change. Without formal education, however, one must find in empirical material some evidence of norm implementation. To this end, Nevalainen and Raumolin-Brunberg (2016: 220–1) provided an interesting study of language variation and change in sixteenth-century English letters, focusing on the Johnson merchant family. Their study indicated that the linguistic features of some people within this family showed similar features with reference to six morphosyntactic developing features (unfortunately, without addressing orthography directly). Notably, though, the similarities identified among their linguistic patterns also showed the existence of a social framework of master–apprentice connections. The identity of the southern merchant, John Johnson, was closely comparable with that of his apprentice from Calais, Henry Southwick. Similarly, the profile of Johnson's relative Anthony Cave broadly matched with that of his apprentices Richard Johnson and Ambrose Saunders. These patterns are a fairly clear indication that transmission occurs not only from parents to children, but also among colleagues.

Another interesting piece of work on the English language is that recently conducted by Sairio (2009: 226–92), who investigated orthographic patterns in the eighteenth-century Bluestocking community surrounding Elizabeth Montagu. Her study indicates that connections between network tightness and spelling choices are loose, while different variables like social position, gender and the type of relationship between writing parties are more influential. Conde-Silvestre (2019), instead, studied a corpus of English letters which revolve around Sir Thomas Stoner II. The author suggested that the authors of the letters were part of a community of practice, because they were all absorbed by a similar effort to retain the so-called *enfeoffment*, i.e. the feudal organisation. The analysis consisted in matching the spelling patterns of the corpus with those of a series of cognate letters belonging to the same collection, but authored by individuals other than those tied to the framework of *enfeoffment*. Making reference to a few orthographic features in particular, Conde-Silvestre indicated that the community of practice becomes linguistically more focused, which entails a decrease of variability, possibly indicating the implementation of writing rules from above.

Professional groups are additional frameworks for the implementation of orthographic transmission. It is commonplace to suggest that the process of standardisation was owed to efforts made in monasteries and printing workshops (detailed references available in Chapter 8). These attempts to achieve a standard may be seen as efforts, on the part of scribes and printers, to abide by rules existing within communities of practice. Among some of the most notable examples of studies which investigated these issues, that by Tyrkkö (2013), as briefly mentioned in Chapter 8, observed an appreciable increase in the degree of spelling standardisation. Rogos (2013), on the other hand, studied fifteenth-century Geoffrey Chaucer's *Canterbury Tales* and the scribal behaviours involved in copying it (Rogos, 2013: 118). Rutkowska (2013b) provided similar indications about the practices of sixteenth-century printers across editions of the same text. The author suggested that an increased level of standardisation can be justified by contextualising the orthographic features within communities of practice working on three levels. The narrowest level consisted in the working environment inside printing workshops; the second level consisted in the fact that multiple printers ran their business concurrently, and often belonged to one guild, keeping their shops physically very close to each other; and the third and last level consisted in the fact that, within these communities, rules for producing texts were passed on to younger individuals.

A useful approach to investigating tramission of the type explained so far is by looking at features which did not occur when they were spelled out in normative publications. McLelland (2014: 266) discussed the fact that the German seventeenth-century grammarian Justus Georgius Schottelius prescribed the use of *kk* in forms like *wekken* 'to wake'. For roughly thirty years, a number of language theoreticians and learned writers submitted to this convention, but by the end of the seventeenth century, <kk> had fallen out of use for good. Flemish theoreticians of around the same time show a similar situation, with reference to their prescription of a range of diacritics to indicate etymologically distinct *e*- and *o*-phonemes (Vosters et al., 2012; Vosters & Rutten, 2015). Unfortunately, again, their suggestions did not come a long way, and they were adopted only by a select few. All of these examples are indications of transmission occurring in social work environments.

9.4   Diffusion

9.4.1   *Regional Diffusion*

Let us now move on to the process of diffusion, with special emphasis on three individual types – diffusion across regions, across social groups, and across genres and contexts. An important goal for studying the regional and social diffusion of historical writing systems is to obtain large enough collections of historical material in order to appreciate the degree of variation across a variety of parameters. Ideally, these should be evenly representative of different social variables, including region, social class and gender, where possible. Diachronic comparative work that seeks to analyse orthographic features against similar genres and registers, drawing on material from comparable contexts and purposes, affords an understanding of the extent to which different writing systems were shaped by the diachronic development of a given genre or register. The divergences separating print from manuscript, where orthographic features often end up showing a binary set of norms, provides a typical example illustrating the importance of focusing on comparable genres and registers in the study of regional and social diffusion. The same individuals responsible for authoring printed books following a specific orthographic standard often used a completely different one in handwritten material.

First, regional diffusion. Detecting orthographic diffusion across geographical areas requires extensive primary sources representative of the regions under analysis, of similar or different genres, depending on the research question, and distributing across whatever timespan one seeks to investigate. The empirical focus can be either synchronic, which may allow one to pursue the analysis of relative proportions of variants at a given period of time, or diachronic, which makes the process of orthographic diffusion even more evident. Using printed material, for example, Rössler (2005) studied geographical diffusion in a collection of texts from Bavaria and Austria. The two main genres represented in the collection were those of religious and secular titles from the early modern era. During this time, religious linguistic identity was in a constant state of flux. On the one hand, standardisation was spreading, accompanied by metalinguistic parallels, while on the other hand, localised orthographic norms still retained their important status. The regions represented in the corpus studied were those of different cities across Germany and Austria. Rössler suggested that several people were responsible for producing the texts in addition to the authors, including those working in printing shops. In fact, those who were in charge for the spellings of the final titles were greater in number than that of the authors. Rössler also suggested that printers had a greater impact on the orthography and grammar of a text than the authors, until authors became recognised more officially as influential figures from the late modern era. The primary resource material used in the study made a fairly large, reasonably representative collection.

The corpus was used to track down the decreasing amount of variation during the historical period under analysis. The results are interesting – the quantity of equivalent options decreased, together with the amount of geographically bound traditions. An important element in the study of such chronologically different writing traditions is the objective system on the basis of which the orthographic developments were studied, namely the historical-phonological framework. Drawing on historical sound correspondences, Rössler marked a separation across different layers of empirical work. The first level was that of the actual *variants* found in the primary material. Texts are frequently highly heterogeneous, and feature many variants for the same sound. All of the orthographic options, collected together, make up the *Schreibvarietät*, the text's extent of orthographic variation. The collection of several identifiable writing varieties, as a whole, make up the *Schreibvarietät eines Raums*, the writing variety of an area, namely the *localised writing traditions* behind a given text or collection.

As evidenced by the examples given so far, the concept of regional diffusion in historical writing is typical of research on a time immediately preceding modern standardisation. However, recent research in historical Dutch has demonstrated that handwritten material closer to our present day also show a degree of regional diffusion. Vosters et al. (2012) and Vosters and Rutten (2015), for instance, discussed the way in which Flemish administrative material from the early 1800s feature a remarkable orthographic development in the early nineteenth century during the lifetime of the nationalisation policy in the United Kingdom of the Netherlands (1814–30). The earliest texts featured about 42 per cent of orthographic variants normally identifiable as Flemish. Subsequently, the degree of orthographic variation lowered to 24 per cent, while the typically Dutch variants had continued to spread among southern authors.

A frequently occurring phenomenon in regional diffusion is that of the importation of letters and letter-sound correspondences from outside a given region into the region in question. The consequences of these developments are, in many cases, an increased mismatch between sounds and orthography (see also Chapter 7). Rutten and van der Wal (2014: 19–74) discussed the connection between sound and writing in a collection of seventeenth- and eighteenth-century Dutch letters. An example may be found in the rendition of originally distinct *e*-sounds: one region, that is to say, Zeeland, retained the historical distinction between the sharplong *e*, inherited from Germanic diphthongs, and the softlong *e*, caused by vowel lengthening; a different area, Holland, instead, featured a mix between sharplong and softlong *e*. Different regional orthographic conventions existed concurrently during the centuries under scrutiny, including a southern strand, which followed the principles adopted in Zeeland, and a number of northern strands which followed the principles used in Holland (Rutten & Vosters, 2013). The southern strand was eventually elevated to the official status of a 'standard' national variety in the early nineteenth century. Up until then, however, a number of authors from Zeeland had actually begun to informally use the blended spelling systems typical of Holland. Clearly, the power of regional diffusion was stronger than any language policy, regardless of whether the adopted conventions were more distant from the way in which writers from Zeeland spoke than the new standard form would have been for them.

9.4.2   Social and Genre Diffusion

While studies in regional diffusion are usually aided by the fact that the origins of most primary sources are often identifiable with a fair degree of precision, the matter is not as easy with social diffusion. For this aspect to be investigated in a meaningful way, one needs to be relatively certain about the identity of the author(s), collecting details that can help to determine the writer's profile. Examples include his/her role in a given social group, his/her instruction, the extent to which he/she contributed to the available corpus of written evidence, his/her gender, age, religion, family connections and the like. Clearly, finding out so much information about a historical person can be challenging at best. In this case, a focus on written material 'from below' might be a useful solution in order to include a breadth of social features in one's corpus. This approach entails preferring popular and often simpler texts, like, for example, private letters and personal notes. More traditional material, like literary simpler, are frequently explicitly connected to specific social circles, which gives one little metadata to work with.

More humble texts, however, because of their status, are more perishable, and not many collections exist for them, which can hinder the study of writing in these resources. Rössler (2005), in his work mentioned earlier on, sought an alternative to the lack of authorial details by zooming in on the printing location, used as a parameter to assess the impact of devotional conventions on textual orthographic features. His study showed a slow process of reduction of Upper German conventions from his collection of Upper German material. These findings were interpreted as evidence for a process of standardisation in German spelling, one which, however, froze almost completely during the seventeenth century, with the Catholic Counter-Reformation. During this time, Upper German writing conventions temporarily became a symbol of Catholic orientation, but later on, this association faded out and made room for nationalistic standardisation.

With enough details about who created the texts, researchers can investigate the correlation between social factors and spelling diffusion, focusing on the micro-scale perspective of single writers. Moving along these lines, Elspaß (2005) focused on a collection of German private letters sent from and to North America during the 1800s as a result of migration to America from Germany. The researcher managed to identify the educational profile of a few authors of the letters, distinguishing groups of writers with only primary education, and groups with primary and secondary instruction levels. These two groups, Elspaß argued, were each characterised by their own orthographic profile. Forms like *wier, mier* and *dier* for *wir, mir, dir*, for example, were hardly ever used in the letters written by those with secondary education, whereas they were present in the letters written by those who had only completed their primary education. Following similar lines of inquiry, Rutten and van der Wal (2014) also focused on private letters, this time from seventeenth- and eighteenth-century Dutch, focusing on gender and social class. Their corpus contained a large quantity of letters authored by women, representing four different social classes in Dutch society of the time. The authors borrowed a model of social stratification from social history, in order to identify the lower, lower-middle, upper-middle and upper social layers, on the basis of the authors' schooling and jobs: the writers included, among others, ill-educated sailors and their partners, and highly regarded captains and their partners.

An interesting characteristic of the corpus was the fact that punctuation remained of little relevance, for two reasons. A large number of letters did not feature any punctuation, and those that did frequently did so intermittently in each letter. Results drawn from the said collection suggested that punctuation in handwritten material gradually appeared more frequently as a social development from above. Only about 30 per cent of the seventeenth-century letters featured some use of punctuation, and c. 40 per cent in the following century. Interestingly, upper- and upper-middle-class men appeared to be at the forefront of the innovative use of punctuation, with almost two-thirds of the letters showing some kind of punctuation from the seventeenth century. Upper-class women came next, as their punctuation rose from c. 15 per cent in the seventeenth century to over 60 per cent in the following century. For everyone else, punctuation remained almost completely absent in the time span analysed. For Rutten and van der Wal (2014: 269), the social boundaries of class and gender were effects of the same social factor, writing skillfulness, understood as the extent to which people took part in the culture of writing.

Now for the last topic of this section – diffusion across genre. In research that seeks to investigate the regional and social diffusion of orthography, genre can become a useful parameter for understanding authorial profiles. In synchronic studies especially, these types of analysis provide interesting insights into the distribution of orthography. Many of the factors distinguishing genres and text-types are in fact dependent on the socio-historical framework in which the primary texts were produced. In her study, Stenroos (2004) focused on the development of the <th> form in Middle English, drawing on fourteenth- and fifteenth-century material from the *Linguistics Atlas of Late Mediaeval English* (2013–ongoing). Just as in present-day English, Middle English <th> indicated dental fricatives, both voiced and unvoiced, word-initially, word-medially and word-finally (compare the examples *thought, wither, cloth*). During the Middle Ages, these sound features were also sometimes covered by the letter thorn, <þ> and, occasionally, <y>. Among the different dialectal systems available in the English northern and southern regions, the three spellings were sometimes mixed in function, while at other times they were used in complementary distribution. In those systems where a principled distribution existed, <th> was found in voiceless positions first, and only subsequently in voiced elements.

Stenroos's findings testify to the presence of great localised variation, where text type and genre were a major factor in determining which variant letter was used. Among the groups of documents and literary material available, southern texts appeared more innovative in the use of <th> by the middle of the fifteenth century, but its appearance was, of course, still quite limited in literary sources. In the north of England, <th> appeared more often in voiceless functions, in both documents and literary sources, and only rarely was it used for voiced scenarios. The author also suggested that the diffusion in the north and the south, which was divergent in terms of speed, was in any case linked with genre. The <th> spelling spread from legal texts from the London/Westminster region to legal texts from other regions as a result of the power that Westminster had for legal studies. The work on the Flemish administrative material from the early nineteenth century mentioned earlier (Vosters et al., 2012; Vosters & Rutten, 2015; see also Vosters, 2011) account for variation on two different levels, both of which are connected to genre and context (the latter also affecting genre). First of all, the three main categories of texts in the corpus, police reports, interrogation reports and indictments, showed different spelling choices. The typically southern/Flemish spellings were c. 30 per cent in the police and interrogation reports, but it fell to below 20 per cent in the indictments. Another interesting level of variation in the texts related to the place where they were made. In the results collected, locally and regionally produced texts featured c. 30 per cent of southern/Flemish forms, while supraregional texts had only about 20 per cent.

Let us now take stock. All of the examples discussed so far show instances of orthographic diffusion at different degrees and junctures. Localised, emerging regional writing conventions diffuse regionally in a process that engulfs and supersedes other writing traditions. This process is called supralocalisation, and it is a stage that gives some fundamental energy for the process of standardisation. Supralocalisation is not univocal, but rather it develops in symbiosis with the formation of regional and national boundaries; the combination of these elements is of course complex and may lead to a scenario where different bursts of standardisation arise, from which conventions spread out, and give birth to different but connected orthographic rules locally or nationally. This situation is especially relevant to pluricentric languages, when they take the role of official languages across different nations, and where the pluricentricity has created some differences in the standardised form (Ammon et al., 2016: xxxix).

Overall, pluricentricity can help us to avoid viewing orthographic standardisation as "a single-minded march" towards regularity (Lass, 1976: xi, also mentioned in Chapter 8). Historical sociolinguistics has been especially keen to emphasise the pluricentricity aspect, alerting future researchers to avoid falling in the trap of a 'tunnel-vision' perspective of the overall process of standardisation (see Rutten, 2016). The alternative proposed by the sociolinguistic model of language change is an understanding of standardisation as a more complex, multilayered process, where orthographic variation is not just some background noise from which to make out the boundaries of fixity. Rather, variation is seen as a fundamental part of the overall standardisation 'DNA', an element which can provide information that we otherwise would not be aware of if we viewed standardisation as a single-minded march towards regularity. It is by studying regional writing traditions that one can trace the formation of a standard not as an exclusive national form, but rather as a pluricentric scenario. This statement applies to the standardisation of virtually every European vernacular: in the development of many European pluricentric orthographies, not least German and French, some writing traditions eventually became part of the overall profile of the regional influence through diffusion, while still not becoming a uniform fixed set of shibboleths for the whole geographical area. Developments like these eventually created a pluricentric scenario made of several regional and national conventions.

Further Reading

Jaffe, A., J. Androutsopoulos, M. Sebba & S. Johnson (eds.). 2012. *Orthography as Social Action: Scripts, Spelling, Identity and Power.* Berlin: Walter De Gruyter.
Labov, W. 2007. 'Transmission and diffusion'. *Language*, 83, pp. 344–87.

Rutkowska, H. & P. Rössler. 2012. 'Orthographic variables'. In J. M. Hernández-Campoy & J. C. Conde-Silvestre (eds.), *The Handbook of Historical Sociolinguistics*. Chichester: John Wiley & Sons, pp. 213–36.

Sebba, M. 2007. *Spelling and Society: The Culture and Politics of Orthography around the World*. Cambridge: Cambridge University Press.

Villa, L. & R. Vosters (eds.). 2015. *The Historical Sociolinguistics of Spelling* (Special issue of *Written Language & Literacy* 18, 2). Amsterdam; Philadelphia: John Benjamins.

10   Conclusion

10.1   Looking Ahead

In the history of modern linguistics, orthography has been among the most controversial, and perhaps least studied, aspect of historical linguistics. Yet, as it will hopefully have become apparent in this book, orthographic topics bear an undeniably important role for anyone interested in any aspect of the historical development of language. This book has attempted to provide an overview of some of the main concepts inherent to historical orthography – a burgeoning field of academic knowledge and empirical inquiry. The discussion has covered a range of methodological, theoretical, practical and even philosophical questions related to the field. An effort has been made to ensure that most of the topics are presented in a way that can be easily digested by the non-specialist reader. It is hoped that the present book-length introduction will provide a starting point for those interested in orthography and its analysis as a means to explore and discuss its potential place in historical linguistics. While this is very much a pioneering endeavour, the volume has summarised and elaborated on some extensive knowledge about orthography and its historical linguistic components, developments and causes, that have already been discussed in historical linguistics. The book has also made productive links between cognate lines of research across different scholarly areas, including, besides linguistics, general history, palaeography and bibliography. This does not mean, of course, that the book has attempted to do many things at the same time, but rather that readers familiar with these interrelated fields may find the subjects discussed in this volume relevant and, hopefully, interesting.

The book has aimed to be as comprehensive as possible, and it has done so by favouring breadth over depth. Inevitably, this has resulted in a lot of details being sacrificed for the sake of simplicity and accessibility, but considerable efforts have been made to ensure that the process of selecting information would not end up distorting the potential view that the reader might get of historical orthography as a whole, and of individual areas of knowledge and discussion within the field. Because of the inevitable deficiencies, however, readers are encouraged to use other books for wider reading, especially those mentioned at the end of each chapter, in order to explore any areas that may have been excluded or only lightly touched upon. The references, however, are not only a way of integrating information, but also, along with the book itself, a means of identifying possible avenues for future study. Promising pathways for future empirical research include the correlation between traditional, philological approaches and a range of sociolinguistic and sociopragmatic methods. The potential use of corpora and facsimiles offers further scope as a second tantalising area of future research, especially with regard to how we can access ever larger collections of primary data in a more philological fashion, and how we can coordinate this with the use of innovative empirical approaches. The fact that researchers are making increasing use of digitised material indicates that most future developments in corpus linguistics are likely to be relevant in historical orthography. The technology-oriented approach to studying orthography also inevitably raises questions about how we can, at the same time, preserve the good parts of our traditional outlook on historical orthography. Some of the topics outlined above naturally have a high potential for leading to uncharted areas of orthographic discussion.

The overview of historical orthography given in this book has been tailored to answer some of the most practical questions about orthography from a historical perspective, often making the most of whatever relevant knowledge exists from synchronic linguistics. The limitations that the present project has inevitably faced pose the question of whether future efforts in historical orthography would benefit from more theoretical planning. Abstract, theory-driven discussions are, of course, tricky, not least because of the youth of historical orthography, but also because of the number and complexity of the topics to be encompassed. These would include, for instance, relations between historical writing and other levels of language, such as phonology, morphology, syntax and semantics to mention only a few. A discussion of each of these linguistic levels of analysis would be further complicated by language-specific differences across individual writing systems. Relevant differences fall across a number of areas, including orthographic depth, the type of phonography and the amount of morphography within each writing system. Inevitably, the complexities existing from the theoretical point of view may push future discussions in historical orthography towards a more pragmatic route.

These and many other potential topics are doubtlessly interesting, and while most of the potential questions to be answered in the future are not new, the comparative approach that historical orthography aims to take on historical orthography systems definitely *is* new. Not all that is new is automatically worth exploring. Why, therefore, should we want a comparative perspective at all? While much of the potential advantage of a comparative perspective on historical writing systems is yet to be uncovered, historical orthography has an important role to play as a comparative 'container' of linguistic information. It is through the comparative focus that a scholar can gain a useful amount of distance from their objects of study, which has an obvious advantage for some research questions. A more distanced perspective affords researchers the ability to look at the objects of analysis without having to account for small differences in detail, and focusing instead on the macroscopic scale, fundamental similarities that become evident. Thus, comparability encourages new perspectives of exploration, which may not necessarily be obvious to those working exclusively on the orthography of an individual historical language. The comparative historical approach carries with it a specific epistemological value: since a comparison often enables one to spot differences between the compared objects, their possible causes also become relevant issues upon which to reflect. By undertaking an investigation of the differences existing across the objects of comparison, one is inevitably encouraged to try to explain orthographic change. If the same conditions have led to different orthographic features, there have to be different properties inherent to each individual writing system responsible for the differences. The epistemological value of the comparative approach in historical orthography is thus its ability to act as a pathway to explain change, and the way in which it allows researchers to identify correlations that can be interpreted as causes.

An additional advantage of the comparative perspective inherent in historical orthography may be found in the possibility of establishing whether language-internal or language-external factors were more relevant in shaping historical writing systems. In particular, a more language-internal oriented approach may afford greater depth and precision; a more language-external perspective may grant researchers the ability to make more contextualised claims and suggestions about their findings; a mixed approach, which would encompass the two, may favour breadth of information while allowing for interesting levels of detail, but may also result in unbearable practical complexities. If taken individually, language-internal and language-external factors can both act as impulses or as limiting elements. Endogenous factors can stop, weaken, slow down or, conversely, reinforce, speed up or even help uncover the effects of exogenous factors. So far, there are clearly many reasons why the comparative approach that has been the main driver of the rise of historical orthography as a field of academic inquiry promises to be useful to future researchers. The potential advantages of a comparative approach, however, do not automatically sweep away the potential difficulties deriving from it.

Those who wish to take a comparative stance on the development of historical writing systems will have to be made aware of the fact that there are potentially unsolvable clashes and contradictions resulting from cultural, nationalistic, chronological and geographical limitations. To make matters worse, there are also a range of questions in historical orthography that it will probably not be possible to answer anytime soon. To begin with, there is the problem of the object of analysis: how do we know which elements of orthography are most suitable for common discussion? A large number of researchers in western orthographies focus on spelling, and their rationale for their decision is based, albeit often implicitly, on the idea that spelling is indeed the central component of many writing systems. Focusing on spelling, therefore, has the advantage of linking an individual study of a single writing system to the wider umbrella of western languages. However, it inevitably excludes other potentially interesting historical writing systems which, as we have seen in the present book, may not necessarily work as we expect from our cultural context. As well as inevitably creating 'A-class' and 'B-class' categories of historical writing systems, this majority-wins approach might lead, in the long run, to the neglect of highly interesting areas of discussion in historical orthography, for example those of punctuation and capitalisation – which we should protect from being labelled as elitist and niche.

If, however, we focus too much on areas in historical orthography that might presently be considered more neglected than others, we might risk the perils of creating too specialised a subcategory of knowledge within historical orthography – which would, in turn, undermine the idea of unity and comparability that is sought in the present book. That said, it is not clear whether a harmonious, well-balanced coverage of all aspects of orthography as a system necessarily entails progress in finding a more universal approach to studying the subject from a comparative perspective. In addition to the conceptual challenges explained above, then, there are also the more practical organisational aspects that future discussion of historical orthography should reflect upon, for example with reference to how scholars of orthography can interact with cognate families of researchers. The purpose of historical orthography is, of course, not to create a category of scholars detached from other linguistic fields which are very much in vogue in recent times, like historical sociolinguistics, but rather to encourage interconnection emanating from a more confident self-awareness and sense of identity. It is difficult to say, however, what these hopes might entail in a pragmatic sense, and what would be the effects of comparing our approaches with those of cognate communities of research.

Providing responses to all of the questions outlined above is clearly beyond the remit of any short introduction to historical orthography. Nevertheless, all of these unresolved issues constitute interesting material for future discussion among those interested in historical orthography, regardless of age, level of competency and area of academic interest. Finding answers to some of the queries above might help not only those working in historical orthography to better understand the role and relevance of their scholarly efforts, but also the wider community of linguists working in cognate areas of knowledge. The positive outcomes of comparative approaches are evident in many other subfields of historical linguistics, such as phonology and syntax, so there is promise in taking the same approach with orthography. For this reason, we should not be discouraged by the complexities presented by the ambitious goal of identifying, defining and, more generally, contributing to historical orthography, as not everything is beyond our reach. In the midst of the many undeniable difficulties, there are some easier steps for future writers and researchers to take, with a view to contributing to the field. For instance, from a theoretical and methodological perspective, more work could be done to establish generally accepted definitions for basic elements of linguistic and extra-linguistic knowledge. To date, the description of orthography is still undergoing development, and so far there appears to be no one established system of definition available for researchers to use beyond the simplified fundamentals presented in this and similar volumes. It is hoped that the present volume will provide a basis to inspire future scholars to achieve some of the goals outlined above.

Bibliography

Agha, A. 2003. 'The social life of cultural value'. *Language and Communication*, 23, pp. 231–73.

Agha, A. 2006. *Language and Social Relations*. Cambridge: Cambridge University Press.

Allen, J. D., D. Anderson, J. Becker, R. Cook, M. Davis, P. Edberg, M. Everson, A. Freytag, J. H. Jenkins, R. McGowan, L. Moore, E. Muller, A. Phillips, M. Suignard & K. Whistler (eds.) 2012. *The Unicode Standard. Version 6.2 – Core Specification*. Mountain View: Unicode Consortium, https://unicode.org/versions/Unicode6.2.0/ [accessed 2 August 2021].

Ambrosiani, P. 2020. 'Graphematic features in Glagolitic and Cyrillic orthographies: a contribution to the typological model of biscriptality'. In M. Condorelli (ed.), *Advances in Historical Orthography, c. 1500–1800*. Cambridge: Cambridge University Press, pp. 46–66.

Ammon, U., H. Bickel & A. N. Lenz. 2016. *Variantenwörterbuch des Deutschen. Die Standardsprache in Österreich, der Schweiz, Deutschland, Liechtenstein, Luxemburg, Ostbelgien und Südtirol sowie Rumänien, Namibia und Mennonitensiedlungen*. Berlin: De Gruyter Mouton.

Ayres-Bennett, W. 1994. 'Elaboration and codification: standardization and attitudes towards the French language in the sixteenth and seventeenth centuries'. In M. M. Parry, W. V. Davis & R. A. M. Temple (eds.), *The Changing Voices of Europe: Social and Political Changes and Their Linguistic Repercussions*. Temple: University of Wales Press, pp. 53–73.

Baddeley, S. 1993. *L'Orthographe française au temps de la réforme*. Geneva: Droz.

Baddeley, S. 2012. 'French orthography in the 16th century'. In S. Baddeley & A. Voeste (eds.), *Orthographies in Early Modern Europe*. Berlin; Boston: De Gruyter, pp. 97–125.

Baddeley, S. & A. Voeste. 2012a. 'Introduction. Orthographies in Early Modern Europe: a comparative view'. In S. Baddeley & A. Voeste (eds.), *Orthographies in Early Modern Europe*. Berlin: De Gruyter Mouton, pp. 1–13.

Baddeley, S. & A. Voeste (eds.). 2012b. *Orthographies in Early Modern Europe*. Berlin; Boston: De Gruyter Mouton.

Baines, J., J. Bennet & S. Houston (eds.). 2008. *The Disappearance of Writing Systems: Perspectives on Literacy and Communication*. London: Equinox Publishing.

Baker, P. 1997. 'Developing ways of writing vernaculars: problems and solutions in a historical perspective'. In A. Tabouret-Keller, R. B. Le Page, P. Gardner-Chloros & G. Varro (eds.), *Vernacular Literacy: A Re-evaluation*. Oxford: Clarendon Press, pp. 93–141.

Bakhtin, M. M. 1981. *The Dialogic Imagination*, ed. M. Holquist; trans. C. Emerson & M. Holquist. Austin: University of Texas Press.

Barteld, F., S. Hartmann & R. Szczepaniak. 2016. 'The usage and spread of sentence-internal capitalization in Early New High German: a multifactorial approach'. *Folia Linguistica*, 50(2), pp. 385–412.

Basbanes, N. A. 2013. *On Paper: The Everything of Its Two-Thousand-Year History*. New York: Alfred A. Knopf.

Basu, A. 2016. '"Ill shapen sounds, and false orthography": a computational approach to Early English orthographic variation'. In L. Estill, D. K. Jackaki & M. Ullyot (eds.), *Early Modern Studies after the Digital Turn*. Tempe: Iter Press and ACMRS (Arizona Center for Medieval and Renaissance Studies), pp. 167–200.

Bell, A. 2007. 'Style and the linguistic repertoire'. In C. Llamas, L. Mullany & P. Stockwell (eds.), *The Routledge Companion to Sociolinguistics*. London: Routledge, pp. 95–100.

Benskin, M. 2004. 'Chancery standard'. In C. Kay, C. Hough & I. Wotherspoon (eds.), *New Perspectives on English Historical Linguistics*, vol. II. Amsterdam: John Benjamins, pp. 1–40.

Berg, K. 2019. *Die Graphematik der Morpheme im Deutschen und Englischen*. Berlin; Boston: Walter de Gruyter.

Berg, K. & M. Aronoff. 2017. 'Self-organization in the spelling of English suffixes: the emergence of culture out of anarchy'. *Language*, 93(1), pp. 37–64.

Berg, K., B. Primus & L. Wagner. 2016. 'Buchstabenmerkmal, Buchstabe, Graphem'. In B. Primus & U. Domahs (eds.), *Laut – Gebärde – Buchstabe*. Berlin; New York: Walter de Gruyter, pp. 337–55.

Bergmann, R. & D. Nerius. 1998. *Die Entwicklung der Großschreibung im Deutschen von 1500 bis 1710*. Heidelberg: Winter.

Berkenbusch, E. 1997. *Übungsbuch der chinesischen Schriftzeichen für praktisches Chinesisch*, vol. I. Beijing: Kommerzieller Verlag.

Berlanda, E. 2006. 'New perspectives on digraphia: a framework for the sociolinguistics of writing systems'. Major research paper, York University, Toronto.

Bickham, G. 1733–41. *The Universal Penman*. London: H. Overton.

Bishop, H. G. 1895. *The Practical Printer: A Book of Instruction for Beginners; a Book of Reference for the More Advanced*, 3rd edn. Oneonta: H. G. Bishop.

Bland, M. 2005. 'Further information: Drummond's *Democritie, A Labyrinth of Delight* and his "Certain Informations and Manners of Ben Jonson"'. *TEXT*, 17, pp. 145–86.

Bland, M. 2010. *A Guide to Early Printed Books and Manuscripts*. London: Wiley-Blackwell.

Blank, P. 1996. *Broken English: Dialects and the Politics of Language in Renaissance Writings*. London: Routledge.

Bloomfield, L. 1933. *Language*. New York: Holt, Rinehart and Winston. Bodleian Library, Oxford, Rawlinson Poetry MS 31.

de Boer, B. 2011. 'Self-organization and language evolution'. In K. R. Gibson & M. Tallerman (eds.), *The Oxford Handbook of Language Evolution*. Oxford: Oxford University Press, pp. 612–20.

Bredel, U. 2005. 'Zur Geschichte der Interpunktionskonventionen des Deutschen – dargestellt an der Kodifizierung des Punktes'. *Zeitschrift für Germanistische Linguistik*, 33, pp. 179–211.

Bredel, U. 2008. *Die Interpunktion des Deutschen: Ein kompositionelles System zur Online-Steuerung des Lesens.* Tübingen: Max Niemeyer Verlag.

Bredel, U. 2009. 'Das Interpunktionssystem des Deutschen'. In A. Linke & H. Feilke (eds.), *Oberfläche und Performanz: Untersuchungen zur Sprache als dynamischer Gestalt.* Tübingen: Max Niemeyer Verlag, pp. 117–35.

Brengelman, F. H. 1980. 'Orthoepists, printers, and the rationalization of English spelling'. *Journal of English and Germanic Philology,* 79, pp. 332–54.

Brooksbank, J. 1651. *An English Monosyllabary* [. . .]. London: Printed for Edward Brewster.

Bullokar, W. [1580] 1968. *The Amendment of Orthographie for English Speech,* repr. Amsterdam: Theatrum Orbis Terrarum.

Bunčić, D. 2012. 'The standardization of Polish orthography in the 16th century'. In S. Baddeley & A. Voeste (eds.), *Orthographies in Early Modern Europe.* Berlin; Boston: De Gruyter, pp. 219–54.

Bunčić, D., S. L. Lippert and A. Rabus. 2016. *Biscriptality: A Sociolinguistic Typology.* Heidelberg: Winter.

Burkhard, C. 2002. 'Zur Ungleichzeitigkeit in der Weltgesellschaft. Erkenntnistheoretische Kommentare zur Kriegsursachenforschung, Arbeitspapier 1/2002'. Universität Hamburg – IPW, Forschungsstelle Kriege, Rüstung und Entwicklung, www.wiso.uni-hamburg.de/fileadmin/sowi/akuf/Text_2010/Weltgesellschaft-Conrad-2002.pdf [accessed 27 February 2021].

Butler, C. 1633. *The English Grammar* [. . .]. Oxford: William Turner.

Calle-Martín, J. 2009. 'Line-final word division in late Middle English *Fachprosa*'. In J. Díaz Vera & R. Caballero (eds.), *Textual Healing: Studies in Medieval English Medical, Scientific and Technical Texts.* Frankfurt: Peter Lang, pp. 35–53.

Calle-Martín, J. 2011. 'Line-final word division in early English handwriting'. In J. Thaisen & H. Rutkowska (eds.), *Scribes, Printers, and the Accidentals in Their Texts.* Frankfurt: Peter Lang, pp. 15–29.

Campbell, L. 2021. *Historical Linguistics: An Introduction,* 4th edn. Edinburgh: Edinburgh University Press.

Cappelli, A. 1899. *Lexicon Abbreviaturarum Dizionario di Abbreviature Latine ed Italiane.* Milan: Ulrico Hoepli.

Carney, E. 1994. *A Survey of English Spelling.* London: Routledge.

Catach, N. 1978. *L'orthographe.* Paris: Presses Universitaires de France.

Cawdrey, R. 1604. *A Table Alphabeticall* [. . .]. London: I. R. for Edmund Weaver.

Chassant. A. A. L. 1846. *Dictionnaire des abréviations latines et francaises usitées dans les inscriptions lapidaires et métalliques, les manuscrits et les chartes du Moyen Âge.* Evreux: Cornemillot.

Cheshire, J., P. Kerswill, S. Fox & E. Torgersen. 2011. 'Contact, the feature pool and the speech community: The emergence of Multicultural London English'. *Journal of Sociolinguistics,* 15, pp. 151–96.

Christin, A.-M. (ed.). 2002. *A History of Writing: From Hieroglyph to Multimedia.* Paris: Flammarion.

Claridge, C. & M. Kytö (eds.). 2020. *Punctuation in Context: Past and Present Perspectives.* Bern: Peter Lang.

Clement, F. 1587. *The Petie Schole with an English Orthographie* [. . .]. London: Thomas Vautrollier.

Conde-Silvestre, J. C. 2019. 'Spelling focusing and proto-standardisation in a fifteenth-century English community of practice'. *Studia Neophilologica*, 91, pp. 11–30.

Condorelli, M. 2020a. 'From the early modern era to an international research area'. In M. Condorelli (ed.), *Advances in Historical Orthography, c. 1500–1800*. Cambridge: Cambridge University Press, pp. 1–15, https://doi.org/10.1017/9781108674171.001 [accessed 1 March 2021].

Condorelli, M. 2020b. 'Positional spelling redistribution: word-initial <u>/<v> and <i>/ <j> in Early Modern English (1500–1700)', *English Language and Linguistics*, https://doi.org/10.1017/S1360674320000349 [accessed 1 March 2021].

Condorelli, M. 2020c. 'The standardisation of *i* and *y* in Early Modern English (1500–1700)'. *English Studies*, printed in 2021 in 102(1), pp. 101–23, https://doi.org/10.1080/0013838X.2020.1785169 [accessed 1 March 2021].

Condorelli, M. (ed.). 2020d. *Advances in Historical Orthography, c. 1500–1800*. Cambridge: Cambridge University Press.

Condorelli, M. 2022. *Standardising English Spelling: The Role of Printing on Sixteenth and Seventeenth-Century Graphemic Developments*. Studies in English Language. Cambridge: Cambridge University Press.

Condorelli, M. Forthcoming. 'The standardisation of vowel diacritic spelling in Early Modern English (1500–1700)'. *Journal of Historical Sociolinguistics*.

Condorelli, M. & H. Rutkowska (eds.). Forthcoming. *The Cambridge Handbook of Historical Orthography*. Cambridge University Press.

Condorelli, M. & A. Voeste. 2020. 'Synergic dialogue in historical orthography: national philologies, comparability and questions for the future'. In M. Condorelli (ed.), *Advances in Historical Orthography, c. 1500–1800*. Cambridge: Cambridge University Press, pp. 238–49.

Coote, E. 1596. *Englishe Scholemaister* [. . .]. London: Widow Orwin for Icksten and Robert Dexter.

Corrie, M. 2006. 'Middle English – dialects and diversity'. In L. Mugglestone (ed.), *The Oxford History of English*. Oxford: Oxford University Press, pp. 86–119.

Coulmas, F. 1996. *The Blackwell Encyclopedia of Writing Systems*. Cambridge: Blackwell.

Coulmas, F. 2003. *Writing Systems: An Introduction to Their Linguistic Analysis*. Cambridge: Cambridge University Press.

Coulmas, F. 2012. *Writing Systems: An Introduction to Their Linguistic Analysis*. Cambridge: Cambridge University Press.

Cresci, G. F. 1560. *Essemplare di più Sorti Lettere* [. . .]. Rome: per Antonio Blado ad instanza del autore.

Crystal, D. 2012. *Spell It Out: The Story of English Spelling*. London: St Martin's Press.

Crystal, D. 2015. *Making a Point: The Pernickety Story of English Punctuation*. London: Profile Books.

Dale, I. 1980. 'Digraphia'. *International Journal of the Sociology of Language*, 26, pp. 5–13.

Daniels, P. 2018. *An Exploration of Writing*. Sheffield; Bristol: Equinox.

Daniels, P. 2001. 'Writing systems'. In M. Aronoff & J. Rees-Miller (eds.), *The Handbook of Linguistics*. Oxford: Blackwell, pp. 43–80.

De Vinne, T. L. 1901. *The Practice of Typography* [. . .]. New York: Century Co.

Denholm-Young, N. 1954. *Handwriting in England and Wales*. Cardiff: University of Wales Press.

Deumert, A. & W. Vandenbussche 2003. 'Standard languages: taxonomies and histories'. In A. Deumert & W. Vandenbussche (eds.), *Germanic Standardizations: Past to Present*. Amsterdam; Philadelphia: John Benjamins, pp. 1–14.

Dobson, E. J. 1957. *English Pronunciation 1500–1700*, vols. I–II. Oxford: Clarendon Press.

Dumville, D. 1993. *English Caroline Script and Monastic History: Studies in Benedictinism A.D. 950–1030*. Woodbridge: The Boydell Press.

Dürscheid, C. [2002] 2016. *Einführung in die Schriftlinguistik*, 5th edn. Göttingen: Vandenhoeck & Ruprecht.

Early English Books Online (Text Creation Partnership). 2015–. www.textcreationpartner ship.org/tcp-eebo/ [accessed 15 May 2021].

Einhard. 811 [1880]. *Vita Karoli Magni* (Österreichische Nationalbibliothek) Cod. 529.

Elmentaler, M. 2003. *Struktur und Wandel vormoderner Schreibsprachen*. Berlin; New York: De Gruyter.

Elmentaler, M. 2018. *Historische Graphematik des Deutschen*. Tübingen: De Gruyter.

Elspaß, S. 2005. *Sprachgeschichte von unten: Untersuchungen zum geschriebenen Alltagsdeutsch im 19. Jahrhundert*. Tübingen: Max Niemeyer Verlag.

Elspaß, S. 2012. 'The use of private letters and diaries in sociolinguistic investigation'. In J. M. Hernández-Campoy & J. C. Conde-Silvestre (eds.), *The Handbook of Historical Sociolinguistics*. Chichester: Wiley-Blackwell, pp. 156–69.

Evans, J. 1621. *The Palace of Profitable Pleasure* [. . .]. London: W. Stansby.

Evans, M. 2013. *The Language of Queen Elizabeth I: A Sociolinguistic Perspective on Royal Style and Identity*. Oxford: Wiley Blackwell.

Feldherr, A. & G. Hardy (eds.). 2011. *The Oxford History of Historical Writing: Beginnings to AD 600*. Oxford: Oxford University Press.

Feldman, L. B. & D. Barac-Cikoja. 1996. 'Serbo-Croatian: a biscriptal language'. In P. Daniels & W. Bright (eds.), *The World's Writing Systems*. New York: Oxford University Press, pp. 769–72.

Van der Feest Viðarsson, H. 2017. 'The syntax of others: "un-Icelandic" verb placement in 19th- and early 20th-century Icelandic'. In I. Tieken-Boon van Ostade & C. Percy (eds.), *Prescription and Tradition in Language: Establishing Standards Across Time and Space*. Bristol: Multilingual Matters, pp. 152–67.

Firth, J. R. 1935. 'The technique of semantics'. *Transactions of the Philological Society*, pp. 36–72.

Fischer, S. R. 2003. *A History of Writing*. London: Reaktion Books.

Fisher, J. H. 1996. *The Emergence of Standard English*. Lexington: University Press of Kentucky.

Fleischer, W. 1966. *Strukturelle Untersuchungen zur Geschichte des Neuhochdeutschen*. Berlin: Akademie-Verlag.

Franklin, S. 2019. *The Russian Graphoshere, 1450–1850*. Cambridge: Cambridge University Press.

Fuhrhop, N., F. Buchmann & K. Berg. 2011. 'The length hierarchy and the graphematic syllable: evidence from German and English'. *Written Language & Literacy*, 14(2), pp. 275–92.

Gallmann, P. 1985. *Graphische Elemente der geschriebenen Sprache. Grundlagen für eine Reform der Orthographie* (= Reihe Germanistische Linguistik 60). Tübingen: Max Niemeyer Verlag.

Gaskell, P. 1972. *A New Introduction to Bibliography*. Oxford: Oxford University Press.

Gnanadesikan, A. E. 2009. *The Writing Revolution: Cuneiform to the Internet*. Malden: Wiley-Blackwell.

Goebl, H. 1970. *Die Normandische Urkundensprache: Ein Beitrag zur Kenntnis der nordfranzösischen Urkundensprachen des Mittelalters*, Sitzungsberichte der Österreichischen Akademie der Wissenschaften, phil.-hist. Klasse, Band 269.

Goebl, H. 1995. 'Französische Skriptaformen III. Normandie. Les scriptae françaises III. Normandie'. *Lexicon der Romanistischen Linguistik*, 2(2), pp. 314–37.

Goody, J. 1986. *The Logic of Writing and the Organization of Society*. Cambridge: Cambridge University Press.

Görlach, M. 1990. 'The development of standard Englishes'. In M. Görlach (ed.), *Studies in the History of the English Language*. Heidelberg: Winter, pp. 9–64. English version of M. Görlach. 1988. 'Sprachliche Standardisierungsprozesse im englischprachigen Bereich'. In U. Ammon, K. J. Mattheier & P. H. Nelde (eds.), *Sociolinguistica: Internationales Jahrbuch für Europäische Soziolinguistik 2*. Tübingen: Max Niemeyer Verlag.

Grimm, C. 1991. *Zum Mythos Individualstil: mikrostilistische Untersuchungen zu Thomas Mann*. Würzburg: Königshausen & Neumann.

Haas, W. 1970. *Phono-Graphic Translation*. Manchester: Manchester University Press.

Harpel, O. (1870) *Harpel's Typograph, or Book of Specimens Containing Useful Information, Suggestions and a Collection of Examples of Letterpress Job Printing Arranged for the Assistance of Master Printers, Amateurs, Apprentices, and Others*. Cincinnati: Oscar H. Harpel.

Hart, J. [1569] 1955. *An Orthographie*. In B. Danielsson, *John Hart's Works on English Orthography and Pronunciation* [1551. 1569. 1576], 2 vols. Stockholm: Almqvist & Wiksell, pp. 165–228.

Haugen, E. 1966. 'Dialect, language, nation'. *American Anthropologist*, 68, pp. 922–35.

Haugen, E. 1987. 'Language planning'. In U. Ammon, N. Dittmar, K. J. Mattheier & P. Trudgill (eds.), *Sociolinguistics*, vol. I. Berlin; New York: De Gruyter, pp. 626–37.

Hector, L. C. 1958. *The Handwriting of English Documents*. London: Edward Arnold.

Heikkonen, K. 1996. 'Regional variation in standardization: a case study of Henry V's Signet Office'. In T. Nevalainen & H. Raumolin-Brunberg (eds.), *Sociolinguistics and Language History: Studies Based on the Corpus of Early English Correspondence*. Amsterdam: Rodopi, pp. 111–27.

Hellinga, L. 2014. *Texts in Transit: Manuscript to Proof and Print in the Fifteenth Century*. Leiden: Brill.

Hernández-Campoy, J. M. 2015. *Sociolinguistic Styles (Language in Society)*. Maiden: Wiley-Blackwell.

Hernández-Campoy, J. M. & J. C. Conde-Silvestre (eds.). 2012. *The Handbook of Historical Sociolinguistics*. Malden; Chichester: Wiley-Blackwell.

Hladký, J. 1985. 'Notes on the history of word division in English'. *Brno Studies in English*, 16, pp. 73–83.

Hodges, R. 1644. *A Special Help to Orthographie* [...]. London: Richard Cotes.

Hodges, R. 1649. *The Plainest Directions for the True-Writing of English* [...]. London: William Dugard for Thomas Euster.

Hodges, R. 1653. *Most Plain Directions for True-Writing* [...]. London: William Dugard.

Hope, J. 2000. 'Rats, bats, sparrows and dogs: biology, linguistics and the nature of Standard English'. In L. Wright (ed.), *The Development of Standard English 1300–1800*. Cambridge: Cambridge University Press, pp. 49–56.

Horobin, S. 2013. *Does Spelling Matter?* Oxford: Oxford University Press.

Householder, F. W. 1969. '*Language and its Structure: Some Fundamental Linguistic Concepts* by Ronald W. Langacker'. *Language*, 45(4), pp. 886–97.

Howard-Hill, T. 2006. 'Early modern printers and the standardization of English spelling'. *The Modern Language Review*, 101, pp. 16–29.

Huloet, R. 1552. *Abcedarium anglico latinum* [. . .]. London: William Riddel.

Huloet, R. & J. Higgins. 1572. *Huloets Dictionarie* [. . .]. London: Thomas Marsh.

Hume, A. 1617. *Of the Orthographie and Congruitie of the Britan Tongue* [. . .]. London: Truebner & Co.

Jacobi, C. T. 1890. *Printing*. London: C. Whittingham.

Jacobi, C. T. 1892. *Some Notes on Books and Printing; a Guide for Authors, Publishers, & Others*. London: C. Whittingham.

Jacobs, A. & A. Jucker. 1995. 'The historical perspective in pragmatics'. In A. Jucker (ed.), *Historical Pragmatics: Pragmatic Developments in the History of English*. Amsterdam: John Benjamins, pp. 3–33.

Jaffe, A., J. Androutsopoulos, M. Sebba & S. Johnson (eds.). 2012. *Orthography as Social Action: Scripts, Spelling, Identity and Power*. Berlin: Walter De Gruyter.

Janečková, M. 2009. *K jazyku českého baroka. Hláskosloví, pravopis a tisk, označování kvantity*. Prague: Arsci.

Jones, R. F. 1953. *The Triumph of the English Language: A Survey of Opinions Concerning the Vernacular from the Introduction of Printing to the Restoration*. Oxford: Oxford University Press.

Joshi, R. M. & P. G. Aaron (eds.). 2014. *Handbook of Orthography and Literacy*. London; New York: Routledge.

Kaverina, V.V. 2010. Stanovlenie russko orfografii XVII–XIX vv.: pravopisny uzus i kodifikacii a. Dissertation summary, Moscow State University.

Keszler, B. 2003. 'A magyar írásjelhasználat és Európa'. *Magyar Nyelvőr*, 127, pp. 24–36.

Keszler, B. 2004. *Írásjeltan: az írásjelhasználat szabályai, problémái és történet*. Budapest: National Textbook Publisher.

Kirchhoff, F. &. B. Primus. 2016. 'Punctuation'. In V. Cook & D. Ryan (eds.), *The Routledge Handbook of the English Writing System*. London; New York: Routledge, pp. 114–31.

Klinkenberg, J-M. & S. Polis. 2018. 'On scripturology'. *Signata. Annals of Semiotics 9/ Signatures. Sémiotique de l'écriture*, 9, pp. 57–102.

Krogull, A. 2018. Policy versus practice: language variation and change in eighteenth- and nineteenth-century Dutch. Dissertation, Netherlands Graduate School of Linguistics (LOT), Utrecht.

Labov, W. 1994. *Principles of Linguistic Change*, vol. I: *Internal Factors*. Oxford; Cambridge: Blackwell.

Labov, W. 2007. 'Transmission and diffusion'. *Language*, 83, pp. 344–87.

Lass, R. 1976. *English Phonology and Phonological Theory*. Cambridge: Cambridge University Press.

Lass, R. 2004. 'Ut custodiant litteras: editions, corpora and witnesshood'. In M. Dossena & R. Lass (eds.), *Methods and Data in English Historical Dialectology*. Bern: Peter Lang, pp. 21–48.

Leith, D. 1983. *A Social History of English*. London: Routledge & Kegan Paul.

Lepschy, A. L. & Lepschy, G. 2008. 'Punteggiatura e linguaggio'. In B. Mortara Garavelli (ed.), *Storia della punteggiatura in Europa*. Rome-Bari: Laterza, pp. 3–24.

Liuzza, R. M. 1996. 'Orthography and historical linguistics'. *Journal of English Linguistics*, 24(1), pp. 25–44.

Llamas Pombo. 2020. 'Punctuation in sixteenth- and seventeenth-century French and Spanish: a model of diachronic and comparative graphematics'. In M. Condorelli (ed.), *Advances in Historical Orthography, 1500–1800*. Cambridge: Cambridge University Press, pp. 93–123.

Locher, M. A. & J. Strässler. 2008. 'Introduction: standards and norms'. In M. A. Locher & J. Strässler (eds.), *Standards and Norms in the English Language*. Berlin: Mouton de Gruyter, pp. 1–20.

Lutz, A. 1986. 'The syllabic basis of word division in Old English manuscripts'. *English Studies*, 67(3), pp. 193–210.

Maas, U. 2007. 'Die Grammatikalisierung der satzinternen Großschreibung: Zur schriftkulturellen Dimension der Orthographieentwicklung'. In A. Redder (ed.), *Diskurse und Texte: Festschrift für Konrad Ehlich*. Tübingen: Stauffenburg, pp. 385–99.

MacKellar, T. 1866. *The American Printer: A Manual of Typography, Containing Complete Instructions for Beginners, as Well as Practical Directions for Managing Every Department of a Printing Office*. Philadelphia: MacKellar Smiths & Jordan.

Malone, E. A. 2006. 'Learned correctors as technical editors: specialization and collaboration in early modern European printing houses'. *Journal of Business and Technical Communication*, 20(4), pp. 389–424.

Martin, G. (trans.). New Testament: 1582. *The Nevv Testament* [...]. Reims: John Fogny; Old Testament: 1609–1610. *The Holie Bible* [...]. Douai: Laurence Kellam.

Martineau, F. 2013. 'Written documents: what they tell us about linguistic usage'. In M. J. van der Wal & G. Rutten (eds.), *Touching the Past: Studies in the Historical Sociolinguistics of Ego-documents*. Amsterdam; Philadelphia: John Benjamins, pp. 129–47.

McEnery, T. & A. Hardie. 2012. *Corpus Linguistics: Method, Theory and Practice*. Cambridge: Cambridge University Press.

McKenzie, D. F. 2002. 'Printing and publishing 1557–1700: constraints on the London book trades'. In J. Barnard & D. F. McKenzie (eds.), *The Cambridge History of the Book in Britain*, vol. IV: *1557–1695*. Cambridge: Cambridge University Press, pp. 553–67.

McKitterick, D. 1992. *A History of Cambridge University Press*, vol. I: *Printing and the Book Trade in Cambridge 1534–1698*. Cambridge: Cambridge University Press.

McLelland, N. 2014. 'Language description, prescription and usage in seventeenth-century German'. In G. Rutten, R. Vosters & W. Vandenbussche (eds.), *Norms and Usage in Language History, 1600–1700: A Sociolinguistic and Comparative Perspective*. Amsterdam; Philadelphia: John Benjamins, pp. 251–76.

Meisenburg, T. 1990. 'Die großen Buchstaben und was sie bewirken können: Zur Geschichte der Majuskel im Französischen und Deutschen'. In W. Raible (ed.), *Erscheinungsformen kultureller Prozesse: Jahrbuch 1988 des Sonderforschungsbereichs 'Übergänge und Spannungsfelder zwischen Mündlichkeit und Schriftlichkeit'*. Tübingen: Narr, pp. 281–315.

Meletis, D. 2019. 'The grapheme as a universal basic unit of writing'. *Writing Systems Research*, 11(1), pp. 26–49.

Meletis, D. 2020. *The Nature of Writing: A Theory of Grapholinguistics*. Brest: Fluxus Editions.

Mihm, A. 2007. *Sprachwandel im Spiegel der Schriftlichkeit: Studien zum Zeugniswert der historischen Schreibsprachen des 11. bis 17. Jahrhunderts*. Frankfurt am Main: Peter Lang.

Milroy, J. 1992a. *Linguistic Variation and Change*. Oxford; Cambridge: Blackwell.

Milroy, J. 1992b. 'Middle English dialectology'. In N. Blake (ed.), *The Cambridge History of the English Language,* vol. II: *1066–1476*. Cambridge: Cambridge University Press, pp. 156–206.

Milroy, J. 1994. 'The notion of "standard language" and its applicability to the study of Early Modern English pronunciation'. In D. Stein & I. Tieken–Boon van Ostade (eds.), *Towards a Standard English 1600–1800*. Berlin; New York: Mouton de Gruyter, pp. 19–29.

Milroy, J. 2000. 'Historical description and the ideology of the standard language'. In L. Wright (ed.), *The Development of Standard English, 1300–1800: Theories, Descriptions, Conflicts* (Studies in English Language). Cambridge; New York: Cambridge University Press, pp. 11–28.

Milroy, J. 2001. 'Language ideologies and the consequences of standardization'. *Journal of Sociolinguistics*, 5(4), pp. 530–55.

Milroy, L. 2007. 'Off the shelf or under the counter? On the social dynamics of sound changes'. In C. M. Cain & G. Russom (eds.), *Studies in the History of the English Language III. Managing Chaos: Strategies for Identifying Change in English*. Berlin: Mouton de Gruyter, pp. 149–72.

Milroy, J. & J. Milroy. 1985a. *Authority in Language: Investigating Language Prescription and Standardisation*. London: Routledge & Kegan Paul.

Milroy, J. & L. Milroy. 1985b. 'Linguistic change, social network and speaker innovation'. *Journal of Linguistics*, 21, pp. 339–84.

Milroy, J. & L. Milroy. 1999. *Authority in Language: Investigating Language Prescription and Standardisation*, 3rd edn. London: Routledge & Kegan Paul.

Mortara Garavelli, B. 2008. *Storia della Punteggiatura in Europa*. Rome; Bari: Laterza.

Mountford, J. 1989. 'Language and writing-systems'. In N. E. Collinge (ed.), *An Encyclopedia of Language*. London: Routledge, pp. 701–39.

Moxon, J. 1683. *Mechanick Exercises: or the Doctrine of Handy-Works* [...], vol. I. London: J. Moxon at the sign of the Atlas on Ludgate Hill.

Mulcaster, R. 1582. *The First Part of the Elementarie* [...]. London: Tomas Vautroullier.

Neef, M., S. Sahel & R. Weingarten (eds.). 2012. 'Schriftlinguistik/Grapholinguistic'. In *Wörterbücher zur Sprach- und Kommunikationswissenschaft/Dictionaries of Linguistics and Communication Science* 5. Berlin; Boston: De Gruyter, www.degruyter.com/view/db/wsk [accessed 28 June 2021].

Nevalainen, T. 2012. 'Variable focusing in English spelling between 1400 and 1600'. In S. Baddeley & A. Voeste (eds.), *Orthographies in Early Modern Europe*. Berlin; Boston: De Gruyter Mouton, pp. 127–65.

Nevalainen, T. 2015. 'What are historical sociolinguistics?'. *Journal of Historical Sociolinguistics*, 1(2), 243–69.

Nevalainen, T. & H. Raumolin-Brunberg. 2003. *Historical Sociolinguistics: Language Change in Tudor and Stuart England* (Longman Linguistics Library). London: Longman.

Nevalainen, T. & H. Raumolin-Brunberg. 2005. 'Sociolinguistics and the history of English: a survey'. *International Journal of English Studies*, 5(1), pp. 33–58.

Nevalainen, T. & H. Raumolin-Brunberg. 2012. 'Historical sociolinguistics: origins, motivations, and paradigm'. In J. M. Hernández-Campoy & J. C. Conde Silvestre (eds.), *The Handbook of Historical Sociolinguistics*. Oxford: Wiley Blackwell, pp. 22–40.

Nevalainen, T. & H. Raumolin-Brunberg. 2016. *Historical Sociolinguistics: Language Change in Tudor and Stuart England*, 2nd edn. London: Routledge.

Nevalainen T. & I. Tieken-Boon van Ostade. 2006. 'Standardisation'. In R. Hogg & D. Denison (eds.), *A History of the English Language*. Cambridge: Cambridge University Press, pp. 271–311.

Nichols, S. G. 1990. 'Introduction: philology in a manuscript culture'. *Speculum*, 65(1), pp. 1–10.

Nowak, J. 2019. 'Satzinterne Großschreibung diachron-kontrastiv: Englisch – Niederländisch – Deutsch'. In R. Szczepaniak, S. Hartmann & L. Dücker (eds.), *Historische Korpuslinguistik* (Jahrbuch für Germanistische Sprachgeschichte 10). Berlin; Boston: De Gruyter, pp. 96–118.

Osipov, B. I. 1992. *История русской орфографии и пунктуации*. Novosibirsk: University Publishing House.

Oxford English Dictionary. 2021. Oxford University Press, http://dictionary.oed.com/ [accessed 3 May 2021].

Parkes, M. B. 1976. 'The influence of the concepts of *ordinatio* and *compilatio* on the development of the book'. In J. J. G. Alexander & M. T. Gibson (eds.), *Medieval Learning and Literature: Essays Presented to Richard William Hunt*. Oxford: Clarendon Press, pp. 115–41, and IX–XVI.

Peikola, M., A. Mäkilähde, M.-L. Varila, H. Salmi & J. Skaffari (eds.). 2017. *Verbal and Visual Communication in Early English Texts*. Turnhout: Brepols.

Percy, C. 2012. 'Standardization: codifiers'. In A. Bergs & L. J. Brinton (eds.), *English Historical Linguistics: An International Handbook*. Berlin; Boston: De Gruyter Mouton, pp. 1006–20.

Peter, R. (in collaboration with C. Fischer and N. Nagel). 2017. *Atlas spätmittelalterlicher Schreibsprachen des niederdeutschen Altlandes und angrenzender Gebiete (ASnA)*. Berlin; Boston: De Gruyter.

Petti, A. G. 1977. *English Literary Hands from Chaucer to Dryden*. Cambridge, MA: Harvard University Press.

Powell, B. B. 2009. *Writing: Theory and History of the Technology of Civilization*. Oxford: Blackwell.

Puttenham, G. [1589] 1968. *The Arte of English Poesie*. Menston: Scholar Press.

Richardson, M. 1980. 'Henry V, the English Chancery, and Chancery English'. *Speculum*, 55(4), pp. 726–50.

Rissanen, M., M. Kytö, L. Kahlas-Tarkka, M. Kilpiö, S. Nevanlinna, I. Taavitsainen, T. Nevalainen & H. Raumolin-Brunberg. 1991. *Helsinki Corpus of English Texts*. Helsinki: Department of Modern Languages, University of Helsinki.

Robinson, A. 1999. *The Story of Writing*, 2nd edn. London: Thames & Hudson.

Robinson, A. 2009. *Writing and Script: A Very Short Introduction*. Oxford: Oxford University Press.

Rocha, L. M. 1998. 'Selected self-organization and the semiotics of evolutionary systems'. In G. Van de Vijver, S. N. Salthe & M. Delpos (eds.), *Evolutionary Systems: Biological and Epistemological Perspectives on Selection and Self-Organization*. Dordrecht: Kluwer Academic Publishers, pp. 341–58.

Roe, G. E. 1996. *Writing Instruments: A Technical History and How They Work*. Stockport: G. E. Roe.

Rogers, H. 2005. *Writing Systems: A Linguistic Approach*. Malden; Oxford: Blackwell Publishing.

Rogos, J. 2013. 'Crafting text language: spelling systems in manuscripts of the "Man of Law's Tale" as a means of constructing scribal community of practice'. In J. Kopaczyk & A. H. Jucker (eds.), *Communities of Practice in the History of English*. Amsterdam: John Benjamins, pp. 105–21.

Romaine, S. 1998. 'Introduction'. In S. Romaine (ed.), *The Cambridge History of the English Language*, vol. IV: *1776–1997*. Cambridge: Cambridge University Press, pp. 1–56.

Rössler, P. 2005. *Schreibvariation, Sprachregion, Konfession: Graphematik und Morphologie in österreichischen und bayerischen Drucken vom 16. bis ins 18. Jahrhundert*. Frankfurt am Main: Peter Lang.

Rössler, P., P. Besl & A. Saller (eds.). 2021. *Vergleichende Interpunktion – Comparative Punctuation* (Linguistik – Impulse & Tendenzen). Berlin; Boston: De Gruyter.

Ruszkiewicz, P. 1976. *Modern Approaches to Graphophonemic Investigations in English*. Katowice: Uniwersytet Śląski.

Rutkowska, H. 2012. 'Linguistic levels: orthography'. In A. Bergs & L. J. Brinton (eds.), *English Historical Linguistics: An International Handbook*, vol. I. Berlin; Boston: De Gruyter, pp. 224–37.

Rutkowska, H. 2013a. *Orthographic Systems in Thirteen Editions of the 'Kalender of Shepherdes' (1506–1656)* (Polish Studies in English Language and Literature). Frankfurt am Main: Peter Lang.

Rutkowska, H. 2013b. 'Typographical and graphomorphemic features of five editions of the *Kalender of Shepherdes* as elements of the early printers' community of practice'. In J. Kopaczyk & A. H. Jucker (eds.), *Communities of Practice in the History of English*. Amsterdam; Philadelphia: John Benjamins, pp. 123–49.

Rutkowska, H. 2016. 'Orthographic regularization in Early Modern English printed books: grapheme distribution and vowel length indication'. In C. Russi (ed.), *Current Trends in Historical Sociolinguistics*. Warsaw; Berlin: De Gruyter, pp. 165–93.

Rutkowska, H. & P. Rössler. 2012. 'Orthographic variables'. In J. M. Hernández-Campoy & J. Camilo Conde-Silvestre (eds.), *The Handbook of Historical Sociolinguistics*. Chichester: John Wiley & Sons, pp. 213–36.

Rutten, G. 2016. 'Diaglossia, individual variation and the limits of standardization: Evidence from Dutch'. In C. Russi (ed.), *Current Trends in Historical Sociolinguistics*. Berlin: De Gruyter, pp. 194–218.

Rutten, G. 2019. *Language Planning as Nation Building: Ideology, Policy and Implementation in the Netherlands, 1750–1850*. Amsterdam; Philadelphia: John Benjamins.

Rutten, G. & R. Vosters. 2013. 'Une tradition néerlandaise? Du bon usage aux Pays-Bas (1686–1830)'. In W. Ayres-Bennett & M. Seijido (eds.), *Bon usage et variation sociolinguistique: perspectives diachroniques et traditions nationales*. Lyon: Editions de l'Ecole Normale Supérieure (ENS), pp. 233–43.

Rutten, G. & M. J. van der Wal. 2014. *Letters as Loot: A Sociolinguistic Approach to Seventeenth- and Eighteenth-Century Dutch*. Amsterdam; Philadelphia: John Benjamins.

Ruus, H. 2005. 'The development of Danish from the mid-16th century to 1800'. In O. Bandle, K. Braunmüller, E. H. Jahr, A. Karker, H-P. Naumann & U. Teleman (eds.), *The Nordic Languages: An International Handbook of the History of the North Germanic Languages*. Berlin: De Gruyter, pp. 1282–91.

Ryan, D. 2016. 'Linguists' descriptions of the English writing system'. In V. Cook & D. Ryan (eds.), *The Routledge Handbook of the English Writing System*. London; New York: Routledge, pp. 41–64.

Saggs, H. 1989. *Civilization Before Greece and Rome*. New Haven: Yale University Press.

Sairio, A. 2009. *Language and Letters of the Bluestocking Network: Sociolinguistic Issues in Eighteenth-century Epistolary English* (Mémoires de La Société Néophilologique de Helsinki 75). Helsinki: Société Néophilologique.

Salesbury, W. 1547. *A Dictionary in Englyshe and Welshe*. London: John Waley.

Salmon, V. 1999. 'Orthography and punctuation'. In R. Lass (ed.), *The Cambridge History of the English Language*, vol. III: *1476–1776*. Cambridge: Cambridge University Press, pp. 13–55.

Sampson, G. 1985. *Writing Systems: A Linguistic Introduction*. Stanford: Stanford University Press.

Samuels, M. L. 1969 [1963]. 'Some applications of Middle English dialectology'. In R. Lass (ed.), *Approaches to English Historical Linguistics*. New York: Holt, Rinehart & Winston, pp. 404–18 [Repr. from *English Studies*, 44, pp. 81–94].

Samuels, M. L. 1972. *Linguistic Evolution, with Special Reference to English*. Cambridge: Cambridge University Press.

Samuels, M. L. 1981. 'Spelling and dialect in the late and post-Middle English periods'. In M. Benskin & M. L. Samuels (eds.), *So Meny People Longages and Tonges: Philological Essays in Scots and Mediaeval English Presented to Angus McIntosh*. Edinburgh: Middle English Dialect Project, pp. 43–54.

Sapir, E. [1921] 1949. *Language: An Introduction to the Study of Speech*. New York: Harcourt, Brace and World.

Saussure, F. de. [1915] 1993. *Troisième cours de linguistique generale (1910–1911): d'après les cahiers d'Emile Constantin*, ed. E. Komatsu & R. Harris. Oxford: Pergamon Press.

Schaeken, J. 2019. *Voices on Birchbark: Everyday Communication in Medieval Russia*. Leiden; Boston: Brill.

Schlögl, R. 2013. *Alter Glaube und moderne Welt*. Frankfurt am Main: S. Fischer Verlag.

Scholfield, P. 2016. 'Modernization and standardization since the seventeenth century'. In V. Cook & D. Ryan (eds.), *The Routledge Handbook of the English Writing System*. London; New York: Routledge, pp. 143–61.

Scragg, D. G. 1974. *A History of English Spelling*. Manchester: Manchester University Press.

Sebba, M. 2007. *Spelling and Society: The Culture and Politics of Orthography around the World*. Cambridge: Cambridge University Press.

Severus, S. 2nd quarter of the ninth century. *Vita Martini*. Paris, BnF, lat. 10848.

Sgall, P. 1987. 'Towards a theory of phonemic orthography'. In P. A. Luelsdorff (ed.), *Orthography and Phonology*. Amsterdam; Philadelphia: John Benjamins, pp. 1–30.

Schoemaker, B. & G. Rutten. 2019. 'One nation, one spelling, one school: writing education and the nationalisation of orthography in the Netherlands (1750–1850)'. *Paedagogica Historica*, 55, pp. 754–71.

Shute, R. 2017. 'Pressed for space: the effects of justification and the printing process on fifteenth-century orthography'. *English Studies*, 98(3), pp. 262–82.

Simpson, P. 1935. *Proof-reading in the Sixteenth, Seventeenth, and Eighteenth Centuries*. Oxford: Oxford University Press.

Smith, J. 1996. *An Historical Study of English: Function, Form and Change*. London; New York: Routledge.

Smith, J. J. 2012. 'From Middle English to Early Modern English'. In L. Mugglestone (ed.), *The Oxford History of English*, updated edn. Oxford: Oxford University Press, pp. 147–79.

Snijders, T. 2015. *Manuscript Communication: Visual and Textual Mechanics of Communication in Hagiographical Texts from the Southern Low Countries, 900–1200*. Turnhout: Brepols.

Sperry, K. 1998. *Reading Early American Handwriting*. Baltimore: Genealogical Pub. Co.

Sproat, R. 2000. *A Computational Theory of Writing Systems*. Cambridge: Cambridge University Press.

Stanford, J. & L. Kenny. 2013. 'Revisiting transmission and diffusion: an agent-based model of vowel chain shifts across large communities'. *Language Variation and Change*, 25, pp. 119–53.

Stenroos, M. 2004. 'Regional dialects and spelling conventions in late Middle English. Searches for (th) in LALME data'. In M. Dossena & R. Lass (eds.), *Methods and Data in English Historical Dialectology*. Bern: Peter Lang, pp. 257–85.

Šinkūnas, M. 2014. 'Mažosios Lietuvos raštų ortografijos reforma XVII amžiuje: I. Pučiamųjų priebalsių ir afrikatų žymėjimas'. *Archivum Lithuanicum*, 16, pp. 9–58.

Taavitsainen, I. & S. Fitzmaurice. 2007. 'Historical pragmatics: what it is and how to do it'. In Susan Fitzmaurice & I. Taavitsainen (eds.), *Methods in Historical Pragmatics*. Berlin; New York: Mouton de Gruyter, pp. 11–36.

Taavitsainen, I., P. Pahta, T. Hiltunen, M. Mäkinen, V. Marttila, M. Ratia, C. Suhr & J. Tyrkkö (compilers). 2010. *Early Modern English Medical Texts*. CD-ROM. Amsterdam: John Benjamins.

Tagliamonte, S. & D. Denis. 2014. 'Expanding the transmission/diffusion dichotomy. Evidence from Canada'. *Language*, 90, pp. 90–136.

Tamošiūnaitė, A. 2015. 'Defining "Lithuanian": orthographic debates at the end of the nineteenth century'. *Written Language & Literacy*, 18(2), pp. 309–26.

Tesnière, M-H. 2020. 'The *mise-en-page* in Western manuscripts'. In F. Coulson & R. Babcock (eds.), *The Oxford Handbook of Latin Palaeography*. Oxford: Oxford University Press, pp. 619–32.

The Holy Bible [. . .]. 1611. London: Robert Barker.

Traxel, O. M. 2004. *Language Change, Writing and Textual Interference in Post-Conquest Old English Manuscripts: The Evidence of Cambridge University Library, Ii. l. 33*. Frankfurt am Main: Peter Lang.

Trice Martin, C. 1892. *The Record Interpreter: A Collection of Abbreviations, Latin Words and Names Used in English Historical Manuscripts and Records*. London: Reeves and Turner.

Trudgill, P. 1986. *Dialects in Contact*. Oxford: Blackwell.

Trudgill, P. 2001. *Sociolinguistic Variation and Change*. Edinburgh: Edinburgh University Press

Twain, M. 1874. *Life on the Mississippi*. New York: Harper and Row.

Tyrkkö, J. 2013. 'Printing houses as communities of practice: orthography in early modern medical books'. In J. Kopaczyk & A. H. Jucker (eds.), *Communities of Practice in the History of English*. Amsterdam: John Benjamins, pp. 151–75.

Upward, C. & G. Davidson. 2011. *The History of English Spelling*. Chichester; Malden: Wiley-Blackwell.

Vandenbussche, W. 2002. 'The standardization of Dutch orthography in lower, middle and upper class documents in 19th century Flanders'. In A. Linn & N. McLelland (eds.), *Standardization: Studies from the Germanic Languages* (Current Issues in Linguistic Theory 235). Amsterdam: John Benjamins, pp. 27–42.

Videsott, P. 2009. *Padania scrittologica. Analisi scrittologiche e scrittometriche di testi in italiano settentrionale antico dalle origini al 1525*. Tübingen: De Gruyter.

Villa, L. & R. Vosters (eds.). 2015. *The Historical Sociolinguistics of Spelling* (Special issue of *Written Language & Literacy* 18(2)). Amsterdam; Philadelphia: John Benjamins.

Voeste, A. 2007. 'Traveling through the Lexicon: "self-organized" spelling changes'. *Written Language & Literacy*, 10(2), pp. 89–102.

Voeste, A. 2008. *Orthographie und Innovation: Die Segmentierung des Wortes im 16. Jahrhundert*. Hildesheim: Olms.

Voeste, A. 2012. 'The emergence of suprasegmental spellings in German'. In S. Baddeley & A. Voeste (eds.), *Orthographies in Early Modern Europe*. Berlin: De Gruyter Mouton, pp. 167–91.

Voeste, A. 2015. 'Proficiency and efficiency: why German spelling changed in early modern times'. *Written Language & Literacy*, 18(2), 248–59. (Special issue ed. L. Villa & R. Vosters.)

Voeste, A. 2020. 'Investigating methods: intra-textual, inter-textual and cross-textual variable analyses'. In M. Condorelli (ed.), *Advances in Historical Orthography, c. 1500–1800*. Cambridge: Cambridge University Press, pp. 141–53.

Vosters, R 2011. Taalgebruik, taalnormen en taalbeschouwing in Vlaanderen tijdens het Verenigd Koninkrijk der Nederlanden Een historisch-sociolinguïstische verkenning van vroeg-negentiende-eeuws Zuidelijk Nederlands. Doctoral dissertation, Vrije Universiteit Brussel.

Vosters, R. & G. Rutten. 2015. 'Three Southern shibboleths: spelling features as conflicting identity markers in the Low Countries'. *Written Language & Literacy*, 18, pp. 160–74.

Vosters, R., G. Rutten & W. Vandenbussche. 2012. 'The sociolinguistics of spelling: a corpus-based case study of orthographical variation in nineteenth-century Dutch in Flanders'. In A. van Kemenade & N. de Haas (eds.), *Historical Linguistics 2009: Selected Papers from the 19th International Conference on Historical Linguistics*. Amsterdam; Philadelphia: John Benjamins, pp. 253–74.

Völker, H. 2003. *Skripta und Variation: Untersuchungen zur Negation und zur Substantivflexion in altfranzösischen Urkunden der Grafschaft Luxemburg (1237–1281)*. Tübingen: de Gruyter.

Watts, R. J. 2015. 'Setting the scene: letters, standards and historical sociolinguistics'. In A. Auer, D. Schreier & R. J. Watts (eds.), *Letter Writing and Language Change*. Cambridge: Cambridge University Press, pp. 1–13.

Wharton, J. 1654. *The English-Grammar* [. . .]. London: William Du-Gard.

Wright, L. 1994. 'On the writing of the history of Standard English'. In F. Fernandez, M. Fuster Márquez & J. J. Calvo (eds.), *English Historical Linguistics 1992* (Current Issues in Linguistic Theory 113). Amsterdam: John Benjamins, pp. 105–15.

Wright, L. (ed.) 2020. *The Multilingual Origins of Standard English*. Berlin; Boston: Mouton de Gruyter.

Žagar, M. 2019. *Introduction to Glagolitic Paleography*. Heidelberg: Verlag.

Index

CPSIA information can be obtained
at www.ICGtesting.com
Printed in the USA
BVHW031808140922
647054BV00007B/33